THE BRITISH ROYAL FAMILY AND ITS RELATIONSHIPS WITH THE R[OYAL] FAMILIES OF EUROPE 1738-1981

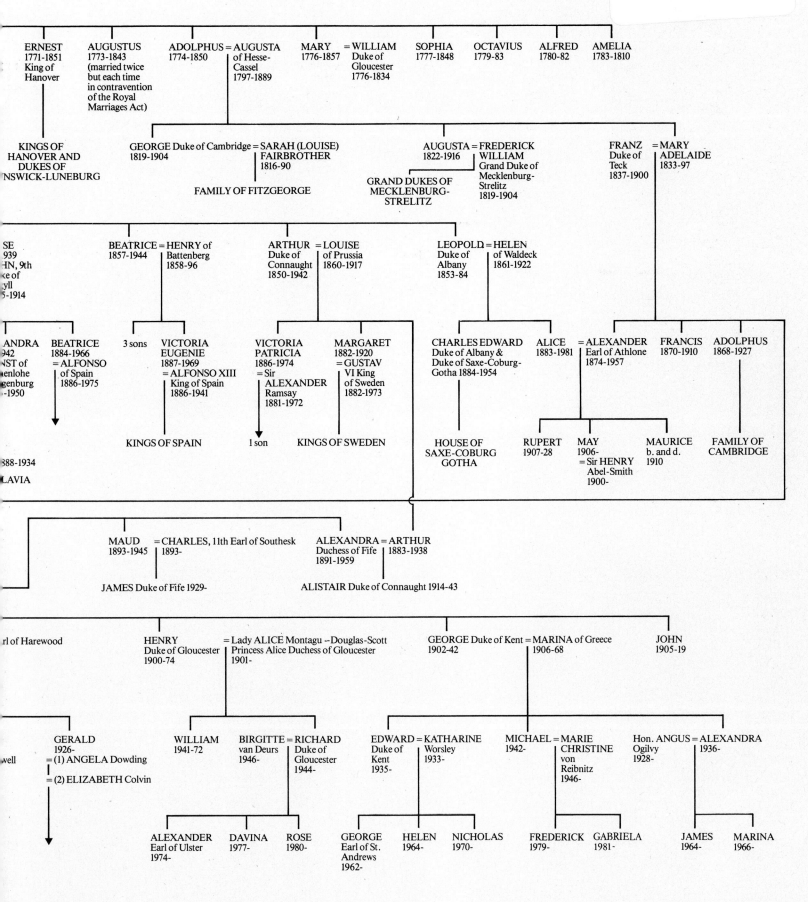

ERNEST 1771-1851 King of Hanover

AUGUSTUS 1773-1843 (married twice but each time in contravention of the Royal Marriages Act)

ADOLPHUS 1774-1850 = AUGUSTA of Hesse-Cassel 1797-1889

MARY 1776-1857 = WILLIAM Duke of Gloucester 1776-1834

SOPHIA 1777-1848

OCTAVIUS 1779-83

ALFRED 1780-82

AMELIA 1783-1810

KINGS OF HANOVER AND DUKES OF [BRU]NSWICK-LUNEBURG

GEORGE Duke of Cambridge = SARAH (LOUISE) FAIRBROTHER 1819-1904 | 1816-90

FAMILY OF FITZGEORGE

AUGUSTA = FREDERICK WILLIAM 1822-1916 | Grand Duke of Mecklenburg-Strelitz 1819-1904

GRAND DUKES OF MECKLENBURG-STRELITZ

FRANZ Duke of Teck 1837-1900 = MARY ADELAIDE 1833-97

[LOUI]SE [18]39 [JOH]N, 9th [Du]ke of [Arg]yll [183]5-1914

BEATRICE 1857-1944 = HENRY of Battenberg 1858-96

ARTHUR Duke of Connaught 1850-1942 = LOUISE of Prussia 1860-1917

LEOPOLD Duke of Albany 1853-84 = HELEN of Waldeck 1861-1922

[ALEX]ANDRA [E]NST of [Hoh]enlohe [Lan]genburg [?]-1950

BEATRICE 1884-1966 = ALFONSO of Spain 1886-1975

3 sons

VICTORIA EUGENIE 1887-1969 = ALFONSO XIII King of Spain 1886-1941

VICTORIA PATRICIA 1886-1974 = Sir ALEXANDER Ramsay 1881-1972

MARGARET 1882-1920 = GUSTAV VI King of Sweden 1882-1973

CHARLES EDWARD Duke of Albany & Duke of Saxe-Coburg-Gotha 1884-1954

ALICE 1883-1981 = ALEXANDER Earl of Athlone 1874-1957

FRANCIS 1870-1910

ADOLPHUS 1868-1927

[18]88-1934 [YUGOS]LAVIA

KINGS OF SPAIN

1 son

KINGS OF SWEDEN

HOUSE OF SAXE-COBURG GOTHA

RUPERT 1907-28

MAY 1906- = Sir HENRY Abel-Smith 1900-

MAURICE b. and d. 1910

FAMILY OF CAMBRIDGE

MAUD 1893-1945 = CHARLES, 11th Earl of Southesk 1893-

ALEXANDRA Duchess of Fife 1891-1959 = ARTHUR 1883-1938

JAMES Duke of Fife 1929-

ALISTAIR Duke of Connaught 1914-43

[Ea]rl of Harewood

HENRY Duke of Gloucester 1900-74 = Lady ALICE Montagu--Douglas-Scott Princess Alice Duchess of Gloucester 1901-

GEORGE Duke of Kent = MARINA of Greece 1902-42 | 1906-68

JOHN 1905-19

GERALD 1926- = (1) ANGELA Dowding = (2) ELIZABETH Colvin

[Las]well

WILLIAM 1941-72

BIRGITTE van Deurs 1946- = RICHARD Duke of Gloucester 1944-

EDWARD Duke of Kent 1935- = KATHARINE Worsley 1933-

MICHAEL 1942- = MARIE CHRISTINE von Reibnitz 1946-

Hon. ANGUS Ogilvy 1928- = ALEXANDRA 1936-

ALEXANDER Earl of Ulster 1974-

DAVINA 1977-

ROSE 1980-

GEORGE Earl of St. Andrews 1962-

HELEN 1964-

NICHOLAS 1970-

FREDERICK 1979-

GABRIELA 1981-

JAMES 1964-

MARINA 1966-

THE
Golden Age of Royalty
Photography from 1858~1930

Trevor Hall

Designed by
Philip Clucas MSIAD

Produced by
Ted Smart and David Gibbon

COOMBE BOOKS

First published in Great Britain 1981 by
Colour Library International Ltd.
© 1981 Illustrations and text:
Colour Library International Ltd.,
New Malden, Surrey, England.
Colour separations by
FerCrom, Barcelona, Spain.
Filmsetting by The Printed Word,
London, England.
Printed by Jisa-Rieusset, bound
by Eurobinder-Barcelona-Spain
ISBN 0 906558 73 5

COOMBE BOOKS

D.L.B.-18.527/81

CONTENTS

Introduction *9*

Great Britain: The Royal Houses of
Saxe-Coburg-Gotha and Windsor *11*

The House of Battenberg (Mountbatten) *98*

The Family of Teck (Athlone) *102*

Greece: The Royal House of Oldenburg *104*

Russia: The Imperial House of Romanov *108*

Germany: The Imperial House of Hohenzollern *112*

Denmark: The Royal House of Oldenburg *116*

Norway: The Royal House of Oldenburg *118*

Sweden: The Royal House of Bernadotte *120*

Belgium: The Royal House of Saxe-Coburg-Gotha *122*

Luxemburg: The Grand Ducal House of Orange Nassau *124*

The Grand Ducal House of Baden *125*

Portugal: The Royal House of Braganza *126*

Spain: The Royal House of Bourbon-Anjou *128*

Italy: The Royal House of Savoy *130*

France: The Royal House of Bourbon
and the Imperial House of Bonaparte *132*

Austria: The Imperial House of Hapsburg *134*

Brunswick-Luneburg: The Royal House of Guelf *136*

Bulgaria: The Imperial House of Wettin *137*

Roumania: The Royal House of Hohenzollern *138*

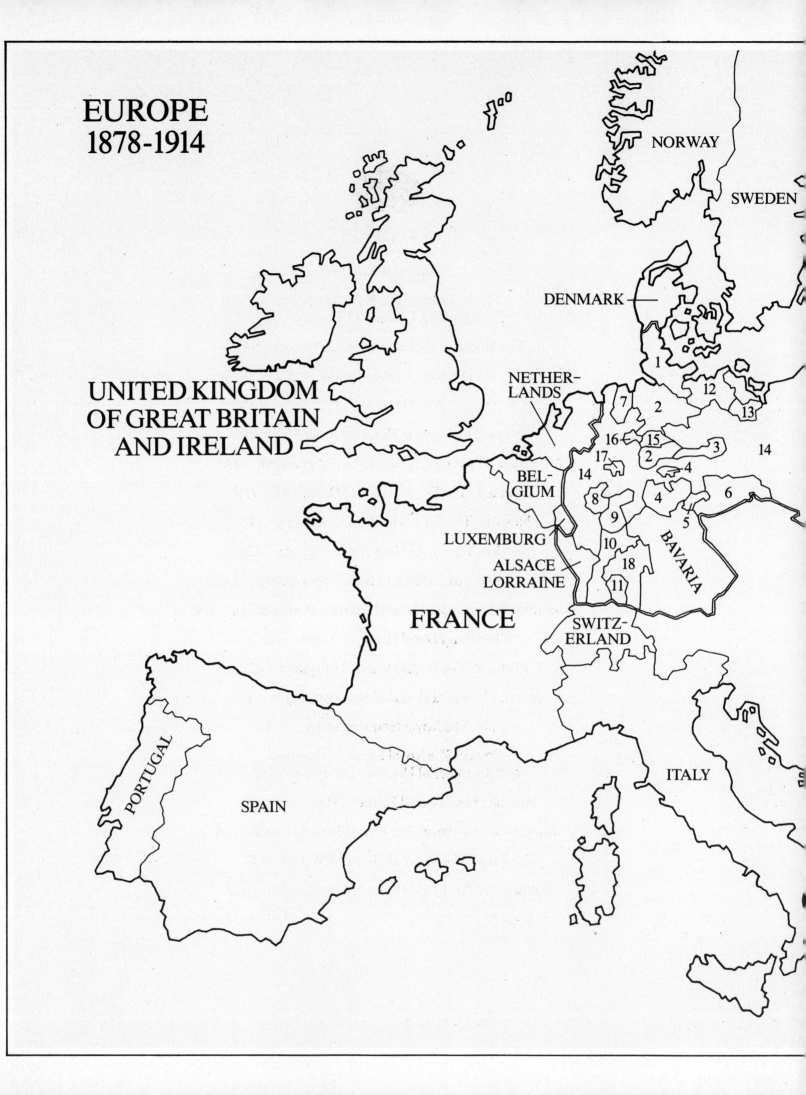

EUROPE
1878-1914

NORWAY

SWEDEN

DENMARK

UNITED KINGDOM
OF GREAT BRITAIN
AND IRELAND

NETHER-
LANDS

1

12

7

2

13

16   15

3

17

2

14

BEL-
GIUM

14

4

6

8

4

5

9

LUXEMBURG

10

BAVARIA

ALSACE
LORRAINE

18

FRANCE

11

SWITZ-
ERLAND

PORTUGAL

ITALY

SPAIN

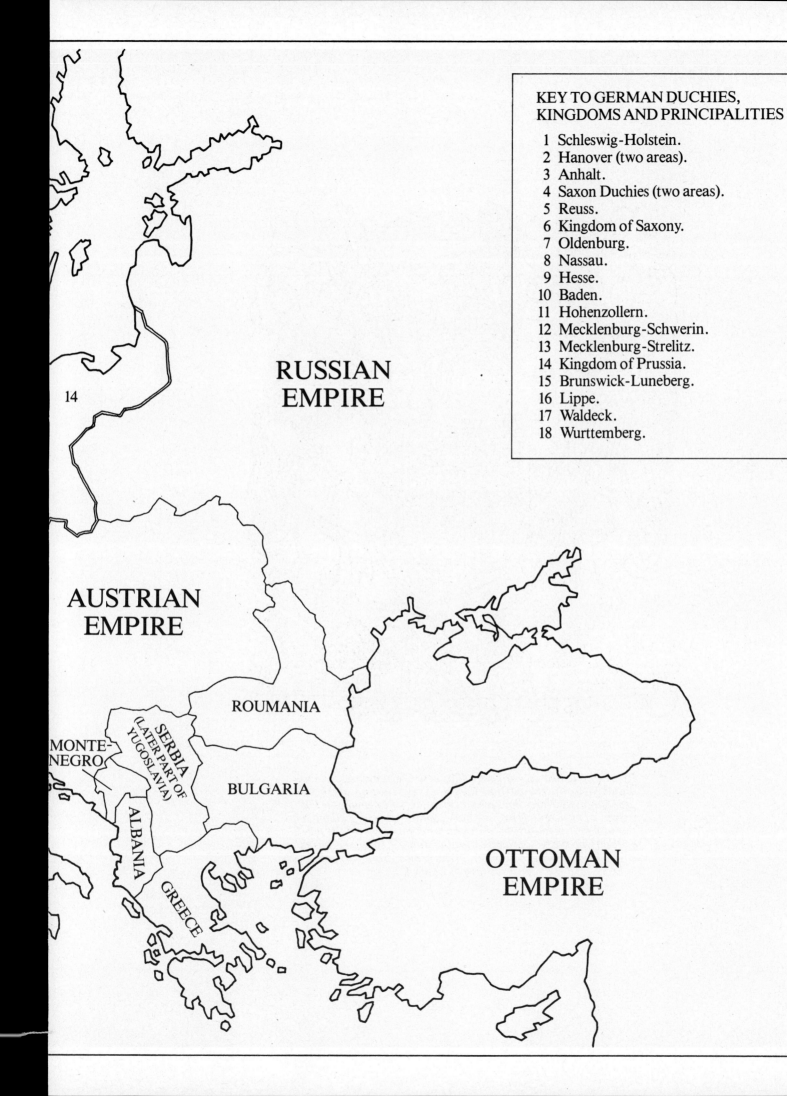

KEY TO GERMAN DUCHIES,
KINGDOMS AND PRINCIPALITIES

1 Schleswig-Holstein.
2 Hanover (two areas).
3 Anhalt.
4 Saxon Duchies (two areas).
5 Reuss.
6 Kingdom of Saxony.
7 Oldenburg.
8 Nassau.
9 Hesse.
10 Baden.
11 Hohenzollern.
12 Mecklenburg-Schwerin.
13 Mecklenburg-Strelitz.
14 Kingdom of Prussia.
15 Brunswick-Luneberg.
16 Lippe.
17 Waldeck.
18 Wurttemberg.

RUSSIAN
EMPIRE

14

AUSTRIAN
EMPIRE

ROUMANIA

MONTE-
NEGRO

SERBIA
(LATER PART OF
YUGOSLAVIA)

BULGARIA

ALBANIA

OTTOMAN
EMPIRE

GREECE

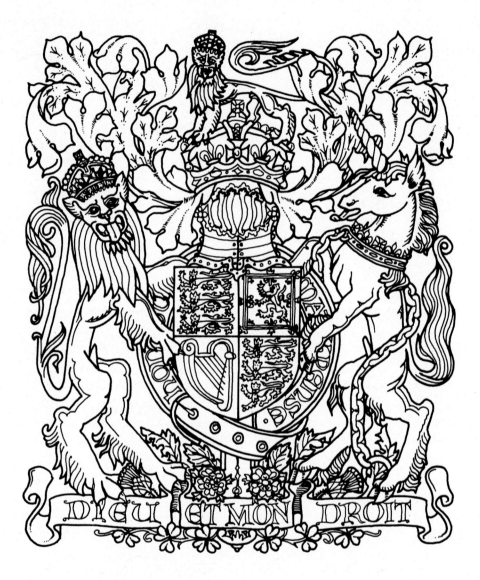

The Armorial Bearings of Queen Elizabeth II express with symbols displayed in ordered and time-honoured ways, historic and noble aspirations: the three lions passant guardant of England, the lion rampant within a double tressure flory counter-flory of Scotland, and the harp or stringed argent of Ireland are components of the shield encircled with the blue garter bearing the words, "Honi soit qui mal y pense". The famous Royal motto, "Dieu et mon droit" has been used since the time of Henry V.

National and international peace and stability have always been notoriously elusive, but if European civilisation could claim ever to have enjoyed them to any noticeable degree, it would justify that claim by reference to the period between 1848 and 1914. In that three quarters of a century Europe stretched her confines eastward, welcomed new sovereign states into her midst and, having despatched most of the contentions involving her ruling nations, settled down to enjoy and consolidate the fruits of tranquillity, enterprise and the unprecedented wealth of increasing industrialisation. International peace had been achieved by the Congress of Vienna in 1815 which, by determining territorial claims arising after the downfall of Napoleon, laid the foundations of a century free from major cataclysm and disturbed only by the Crimean War of 1854-6, the Franco-Prussian War fifteen years later, and the grumbling Balkan troubles of the mid 1870s. The internal restlessness of nations took longer to overcome, but after the multiple national revolutions of 1830 and 1848 came a long period of calm – except in France, where the tide of the 1789 Revolution took the best part of a century to smooth into a mere ripple.

This almost universal and enduring stability was characterised, if not in some way perpetuated, by the symbol and statement of kingship as the only viable means of presiding over national affairs. Of course, kings, emperors and sovereign princes had ruled over their respective patches since time out of mind, but power had been their companion and their raison d'être: they were either kings because they were powerful or powerful because they were kings. By the early nineteenth century this was not always so, and the link with power declined as the century wore on, vanishing almost entirely after the Great War. Britain had already developed a form of constitutional monarchy which proved itself readily adaptable to gradual but inevitable change; France endured both liberalism and autocracy before emerging as an embryo democracy in 1871; the old Empires of Spain and Austria depended less on the power of the head of state than on the power of those around him, whilst the experimental constitutions of the newly-born nations effectively reduced their elected sovereigns to little more than comparative figureheads.

Nonetheless the concept of royalty, whether as a powerhouse or as a symbol of power residing elsewhere, flourished and became respectable in this period. Revolution rarely overthrew one sovereign without replacing him with another – thus in the 1848 revolutions it was not the Austrian, Sardinian and Bavarian thrones which toppled, but their occupants who were succeeded by their close heirs in the fulfilment of the concept of 'legitimate' rule. The emergence, whether by revolt or by treaty, of new states preceded a general search for members of existing royal families willing to fill the new presidential thrones – thus Prince Leopold of Saxe-Coburg-Gotha to Belgium in 1832, Prince Otto of Bavaria to Greece in 1832 (and when he fell in 1862, Prince William of Denmark took his place a year later), Prince Alexander of Battenberg to Bulgaria in 1879 (to be succeeded on his downfall by Prince Ferdinand of Saxe-Coburg-Gotha in 1886), Prince Charles of Denmark to Norway in 1905, and Prince William of Wied to Albania in 1913.

Meanwhile the old established monarchies, however liberal or autocratic, continued pretty well unchanged, except for the compromises and adaptations occasioned by the unification of Germany under the Prussian House of Hohenzollern, and of Italy under the House of Savoy. But however long or recently established each royal house was, the common aim of all its members served to be – as one might well expect – the perpetuation of royalty by interbreeding. The latter half of the nineteenth century saw this process surge forward with a vigour and sense of purpose never before witnessed. History records that marriages and the furtherance of dynasties had always been carefully arranged amongst royal families in order to preserve power, independence or territories: the failure of a union or the death of its only child could and did wreak terrible consequences, as witness the incessant political machinations of the reigns of Henry VIII and his children in England, and the

Introduction

ferocious wars of succession in seventeenth and eighteenth century Europe. By 1850, however, royal marriages, though no less arranged than before, occurred for prestige of a more social nature and for the continued existence of a species whose role in life had already begun to slide into decline. This circumstance, coupled with the general increase in the size of families, made the ensuing decades the golden age of royalty indeed.

The British royal house affords an excellent example of domestic horizons widened by marriages into different foreign dynasties. The foreign marriages (mostly German orientated) of George III's many children had almost entirely petered out in divorce or childlessness, leaving the popular vision of the royal family as small, parochial and utterly domestic. Queen Victoria's children – or, more accurately, Queen Victoria herself – fundamentally changed this image: with her eldest daughter married to the heir to the throne of ascendant Prussia, another into the prolific grand dukedom of Hesse, and a third to its comparatively influential offshoot Battenberg, she began to wield the sort of social power and sway that befitted the sovereign of the greatest nation of the time. She nurtured renewed links with Denmark – which itself was shortly to emerge from political obscurity into dynastic prestige – by engineering the marriage of the Prince of Wales to King Christian's eldest daughter. King Christian IX's attitude mirrored and complemented that of Queen Victoria: through the marriage of his other daughters he became father-in-law to the Tsar of Russia and the erstwhile Crown Prince of Hanover; while his second son became King of Greece and founded the line from which Princess Marina of Kent and the present Duke of Edinburgh married back into the British royal family. Without a doubt, however, the most meteoric rise to power as well as mere prestige belonged to the House of Saxe-Coburg-Gotha. This tiny German duchy, which had assumed its permanent territories only in 1826, produced in only two generations the founder of the present Belgian dynasty, a reigning King of Portugal, a wily and resilient Tsar of Bulgaria, and the energetic Prince Consort of Great Britain. Alongside this duchy came the grand duchy of Hesse-Darmstadt which produced the Battenbergs with their Swedish, Greek and Spanish connections, as well as the unfortunate females who married into the Russian Imperial family and met brutal deaths in 1918.

The dynastic connections of many royalties were, however, maintained at a more local level. The Scandinavian monarchies provided spouses for each other in considerable number, and tended to look no further than Britain and northern Germany for partners. The mighty and highly-nationalistic Prussian monarchy preferred German marriages almost exclusively: of all the children of Frederick III and Wilhelm II combined, only one – Princess Sophie who married King Constantine I of Greece – married outside the old German Confederation. Naturally the Roman Catholic monarchies opted for Roman Catholic marriages, so that the enormous Bourbon, Hapsburg and Wittelsbach families of Spain, France, Sicily, Austria and Bavaria were confined to maintaining continuously close links with one another. Similarly the Balkan states, comparatively newly emerged, and with traditions and ancestries far less sophisticated than those of western Europe, found little opportunity to break out of their enforced enclave – thus the royal families of Greece, Yugoslavia, Romania and Montenegro were considerably intermarried.

This monumental profusion of royal marriages and the subtle, or at times not so subtle, political influences they carried with them, came to an abrupt end in 1914. Almost a fitting comment on what had gone before, it was the assassination of a member of a royal family – Archduke Franz-Ferdinand of Austria – which unleashed decades of pent up nationalism and envy in the fury of European war. It was wholly ironic that the entire cousinhood of royal heads of state found themselves powerless or reluctant to prevent strife against each other. By the time the holocaust was accomplished almost a dozen reigning monarchies, together with a host of ruling duchies and principalities, had disappeared.

Naturally it was less easy – and somehow less purposeful – to prolong, by the same method, the concept of royalty in the breezy, new, liberated, post-war world dominated by the great republic across the Atlantic. Nevertheless it still happened: among a surprisingly large number of royal dynastic marriages since 1918, the most notable were those celebrated between Crown Prince Leopold of Belgium and Princess Astrid of Sweden in 1926; Crown Prince Olav of Norway and Princess Martha of Sweden in 1929; Crown Prince Umberto of Italy and Princess Maria-José of Belgium in 1930; Crown Prince Frederick of Denmark and Princess Ingrid of Sweden in 1935; King Peter of Yugoslavia and Princess Alexandra of Greece in 1944; Princess Elizabeth of Great Britain and Prince Philip of Greece in 1947; Prince Juan Carlos of Spain and Princess Sophie of Greece in 1962, and King Constantine II of Greece and Princess Anne-Marie of Denmark in 1964. At the same time it is a sobering thought that out of the seven reigning sovereigns in today's Europe, only two are married to consorts of royal descent: a far cry from the not so distant days when European sovereigns did little more than scan the pages of the Almanach de Gotha – that 'who's who' of Europe's royalty – before deciding the matrimonial fate of their children.

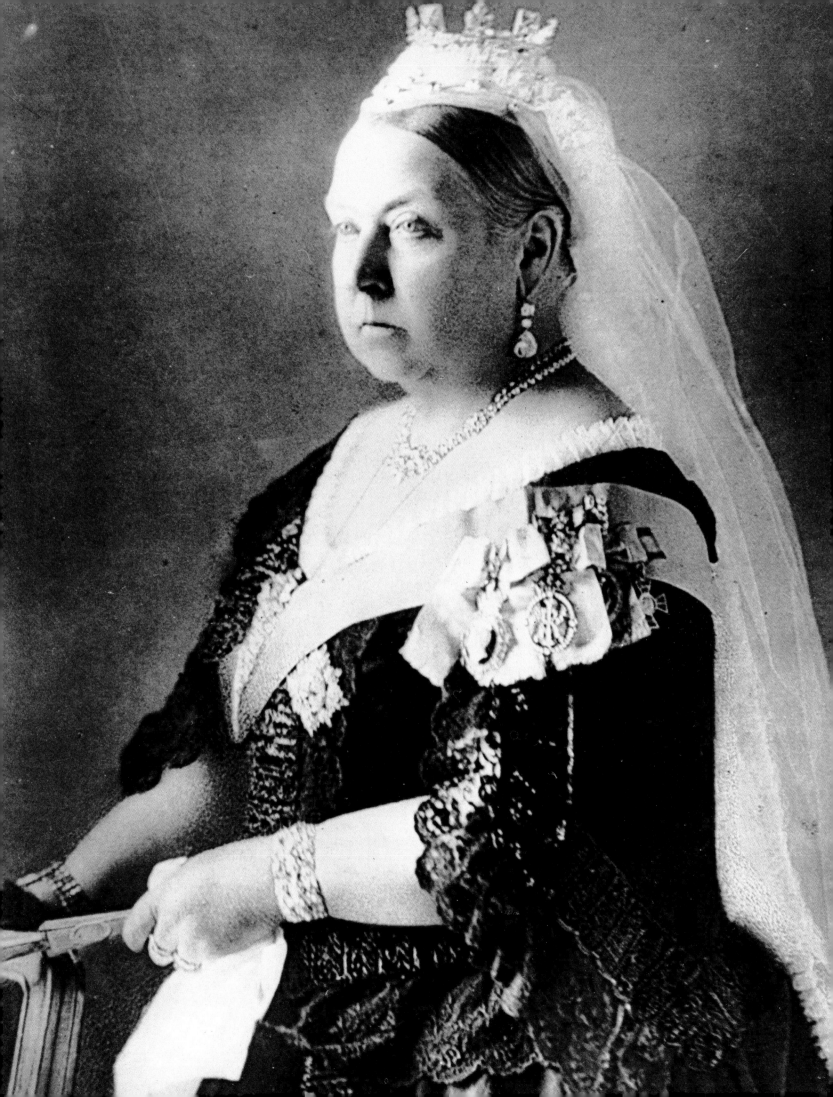

Great Britain

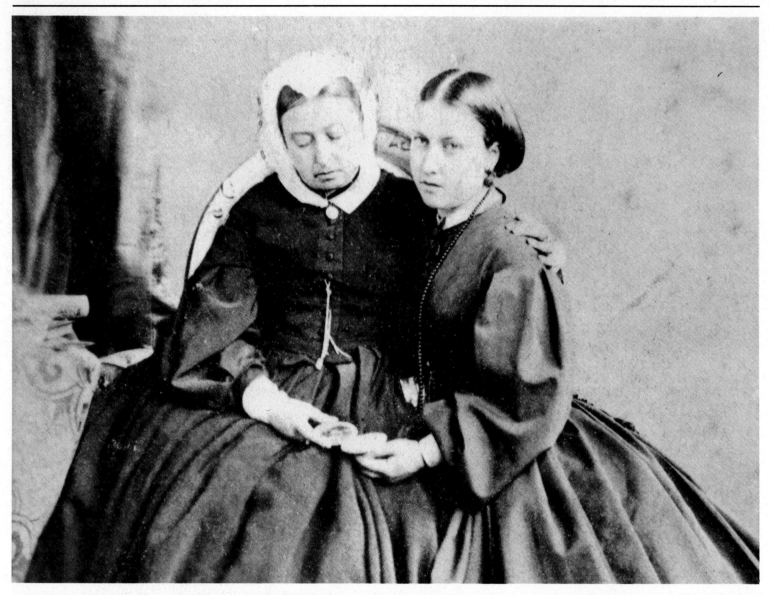

Queen Victoria, *previous page,* and *opposite page, right,* was born Princess Alexandrina Victoria of Kent in 1819. Her father, Prince Edward, Duke of Kent (1767-1820) was the fourth son of the reigning King, George III: her mother, formerly Princess Victoria of Saxe-Coburg-Gotha (1786-1861), was a sister of the reigning Duke Ernst I of Saxe-Coburg-Gotha (1786-1844) and of King Leopold I of the Belgians (1790-1865), and the widow of Emich, reigning Prince of Leiningen (1763-1814).

Princess Alexandrina Victoria came to the throne of England in 1837 following the successive deaths between 1820 and 1837 of King George III and his first four sons without other living issue. In 1840 she married her first cousin, Prince Albert of Saxe-Coburg-Gotha (1819-1861), the younger son of Duke Ernst I. The couple had nine children, of whom the eldest, Princess Victoria (1840-1901) married Crown Prince Frederick William of Prussia, later Emperor Frederick III of Germany (1831-1888) and became mother of Kaiser Wilhelm II (1859-1941). Of the remainder, Prince Albert Edward (1841-1910) became Edward VII and married Princess Alexandra (1844-1925) of the prolific and well-connected Danish Royal house. Princess Alice (1843-1878) became consort to the reigning Grand Duke Ludwig IV of Hesse-Darmstadt, and mother to the Empress Alexandra of Russia (1872-1918). Prince Alfred (1844-1900) lived to inherit the Dukedom of Saxe-Coburg-Gotha and was the father of Queen Marie of Roumania (1875-1938). And Princess Beatrice (1857-1944) married Prince Henry of Battenberg and her only daughter became Queen Victoria-Eugenie of Spain (1887-1969).

Widowed in 1861, and created Empress of India in 1877, Queen Victoria died in 1901, the oldest and longest reigning sovereign in British history.

The photograph, *above,* – the locket contains the late Prince Consort's portrait – was taken by the Belgian partnership of Ghémar Frères in about 1863, and depicts Queen Victoria with Princess Helena, her fifth child, born in 1846. In 1866 Helena married Prince Christian of Schleswig-Holstein-Sonderburg-Augustenburg, a Danish province which was about to be annexed by Prussia, and of which his father was Duke. They had six children, but no grandchildren: two sons died in infancy, another two died unmarried (one of them, Prince Christian Victor (1867-1900) died at Pretoria whilst fighting on the British side against the Boers), and of their two daughters, Princess Helena Victoria (1870-1948) died unmarried, and the marriage in 1891 of Princess Marie Louise (1872-1956) to Prince Aribert of Anhalt-Dessau was dissolved, childless, in 1900. Princess Helena died in 1923, outliving her husband who died aged 86 in 1917.

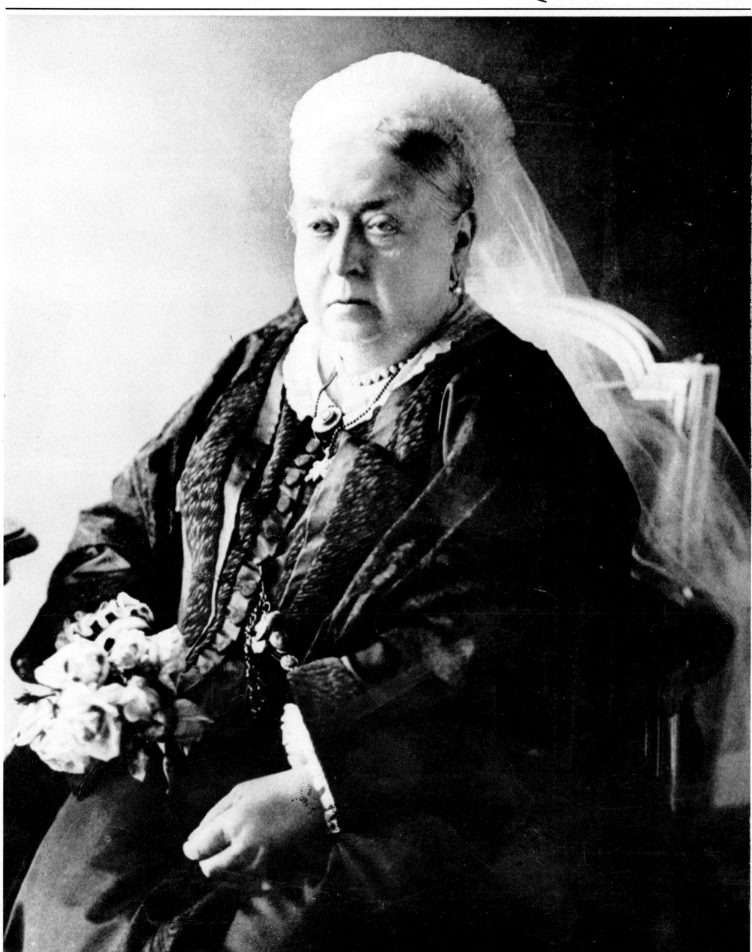

Great Britain

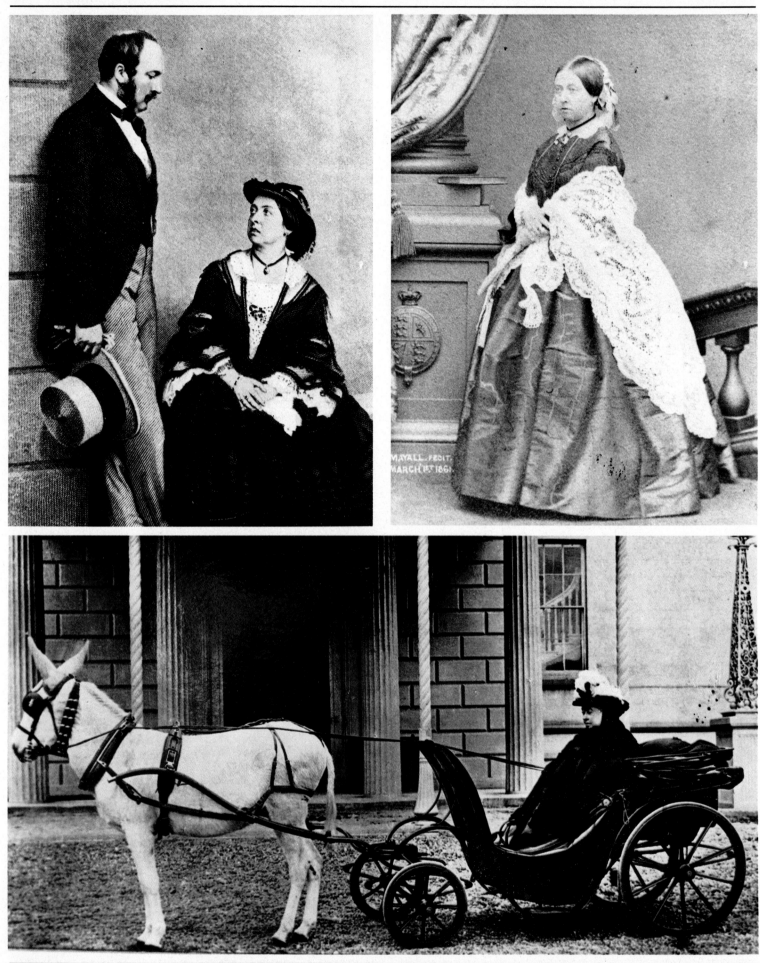

Prince Albert, The Prince Consort

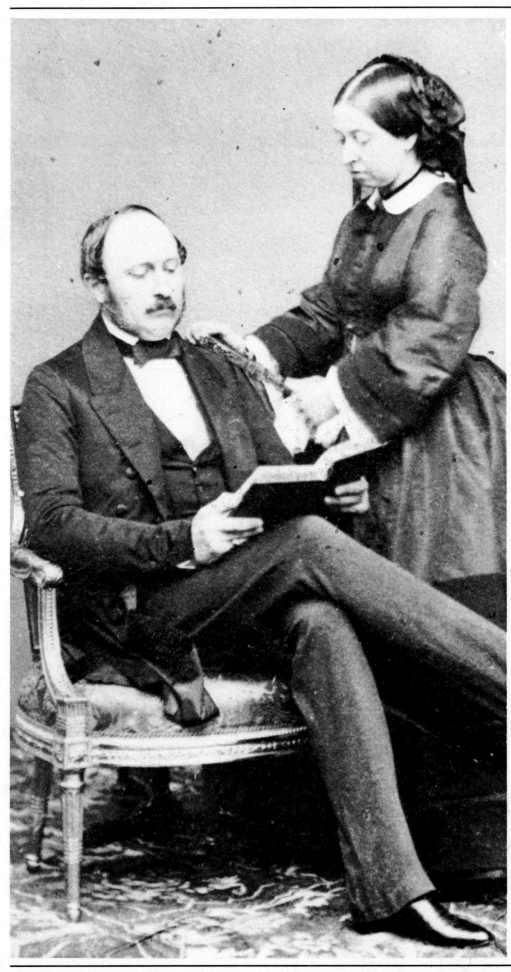

Prince Albert (1819-1861) was the younger son of Duke Ernst I of Saxe-Coburg-Gotha (1784-1844) and of his first wife Princess Dorothea Louise (1800-1831) of Saxe-Altenburg. He was thus a nephew of Queen Victoria's mother and therefore cousin to Queen Victoria herself. The photograph, *left,* is one of a group taken at Buckingham Palace by J E Mayall on 15th May, 1860. The photograph, *opposite page, top left,* was taken during the previous summer at Osborne House.

Prince Albert was created Prince Consort in 1857, four years before his death from pneumonia and typhoid at the age of 42.

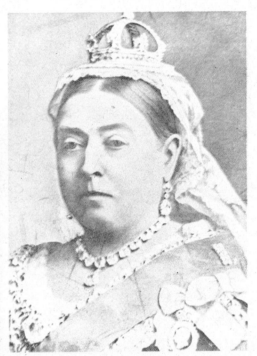

Opposite page, top right. A photograph of Queen Victoria taken by J E Mayall of Regent Street, at Buckingham Palace on 1st March, 1861.

Above. A photograph published in celebration of Queen Victoria's Golden Jubilee in June 1887. It is part of a larger picture in which she is seated between her eldest son and heir, Albert Edward, Prince of Wales, and her daughter-in-law Princess Alexandra. The photographer was Bassano of London.

Opposite page. This photograph was taken as Queen Victoria took one of her customary rides in her pony cart: this particular occasion was in April 1900 outside the Governor's residence in Dublin, during her last visit to Ireland – less than ten months before her death – at the age of 80.

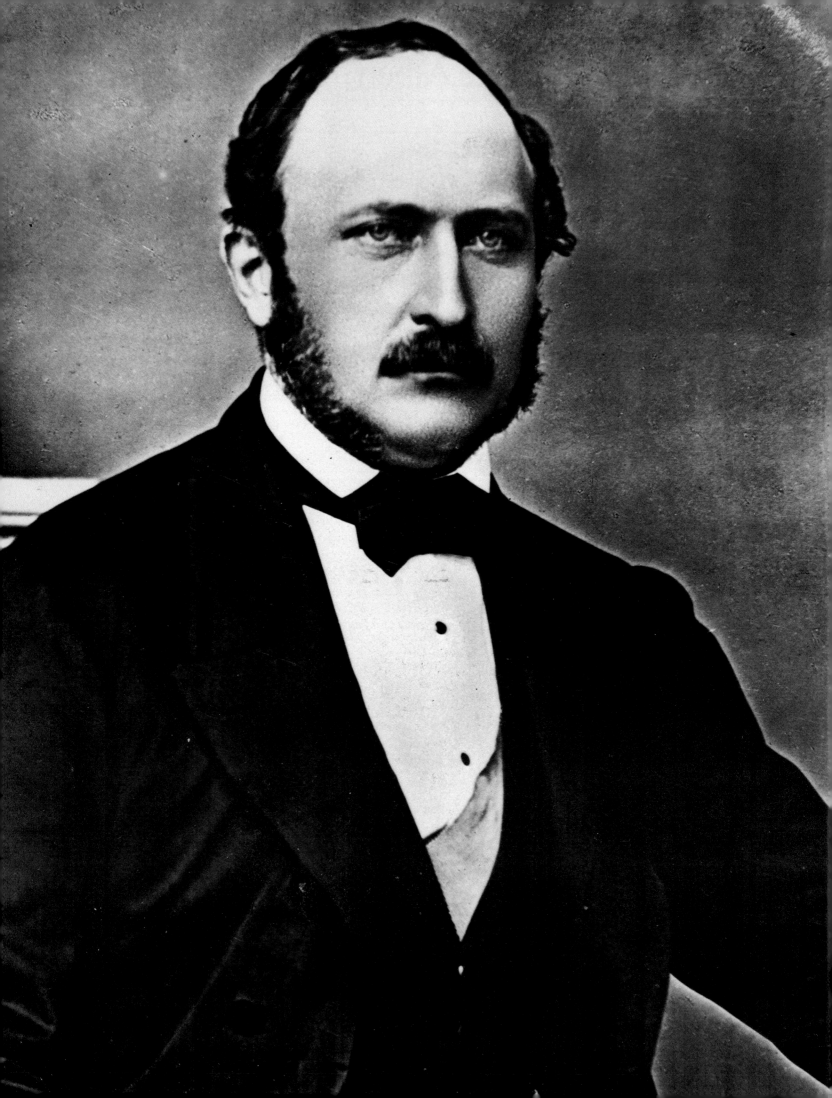

Prince Albert, The Prince Consort

Prince Albert, *opposite page, left, and below*, proved to be extremely well connected to many European dynasties. His uncle (Duke Ernst's brother) was elected the first King of the newly independent Belgium in 1832 as Leopold I and founded the line now represented by the present King Baudouin. Another uncle, Prince Ferdinand, was the father of Ferdinand, King Consort of Portugal (1816-1885), and grandfather to Tsar Ferdinand, the first of two Kings of Bulgaria.

Prince Albert's marriage to Queen Victoria in 1840 produced nine children through whom their already prestigious dynastic connections were further extended. Through the marriages of their children they became related to the ruling branches of the royal houses of Denmark, Prussia, Hesse and Russia, and the marriages of their grandchildren made them direct ascendants of the eventual monarchs of Norway, Sweden, Spain, Roumania, Yugoslavia, Germany and Greece.

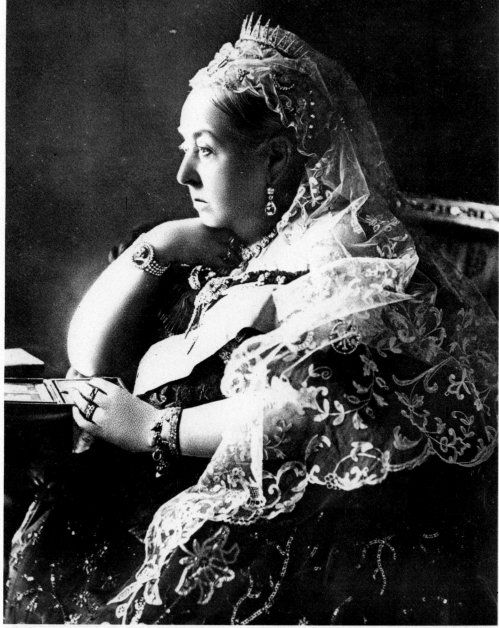

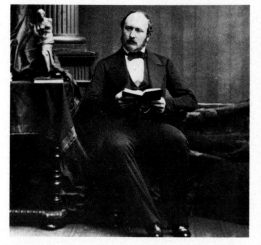

Above right. One of the official Diamond Jubilee portraits of Queen Victoria by Gunn and Stewart – issued in the Spring of 1897.

Right. This photograph was taken during a camera call at Coburg on 21st April, 1894, two days after Queen Victoria and her eldest daughter Empress Frederick of Germany – along with many members of English and European Royal Families – had attended the wedding at Coburg of Princess Victoria Melita (1876-1936), daughter of Queen Victoria's second son Prince Alfred, to the Grand Duke Ernst Ludwig of Hesse (1868-1937), son of Queen Victoria's second daughter Princess Alice.

Far right. A photograph taken in about 1866 of the future Emperor Frederick III of Germany; husband of Queen Victoria's eldest child.

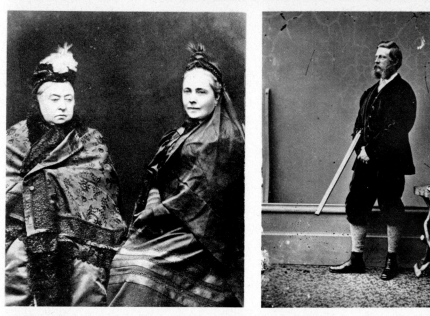

Great Britain

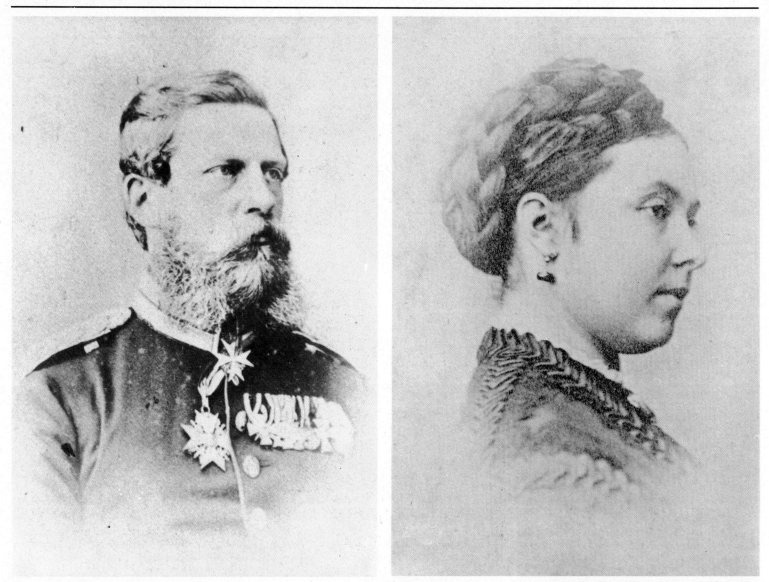

Princess Victoria, *above right,* was born in 1840, the eldest of the nine children of Queen Victoria and Prince Albert, the Prince Consort. Being the eldest daughter of a reigning sovereign, she was created Princess Royal in the year of her birth. She was one of five sisters of King Edward VII.

She was engaged at the age of only 14 to Crown Prince Frederick William of Prussia (1831-1888), *above, left,* the elder child and only son of King Wilhelm I of Prussia (1797-1888) and of his wife, Princess Marie Augusta (1811-1890) formerly of Saxe-Weimar-Eisenach. The marriage took place in 1858; of the seven children of the union, the eldest became Kaiser Wilhelm II, whilst the third daughter, Princess Sophie, married Prince Constantine of Greece (1868-1923) and became Queen Consort of Greece on his accession in 1913.

Princess Victoria became Empress of Germany in 1888, when Crown Prince Frederick William succeeded his father as King of Prussia and Emperor of Germany under the style of Frederick III. He was already the victim of throat cancer, and died after a reign of less than four months. He was succeeded by Kaiser Wilhelm II.

Princess Victoria, known throughout her widowhood as the Empress Frederick, died – also of cancer – and 1901, only six months after the death of her mother, Queen Victoria.

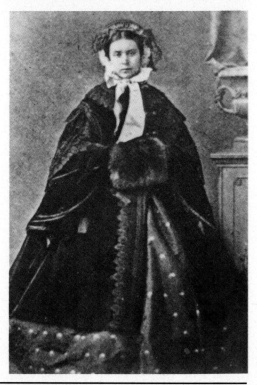

Right. A photograph taken at the time of Princess Victoria's engagement in September 1855.

Opposite page, right. A photograph of Princess Victoria; taken by the Paris firm of Levitsky in about 1868.

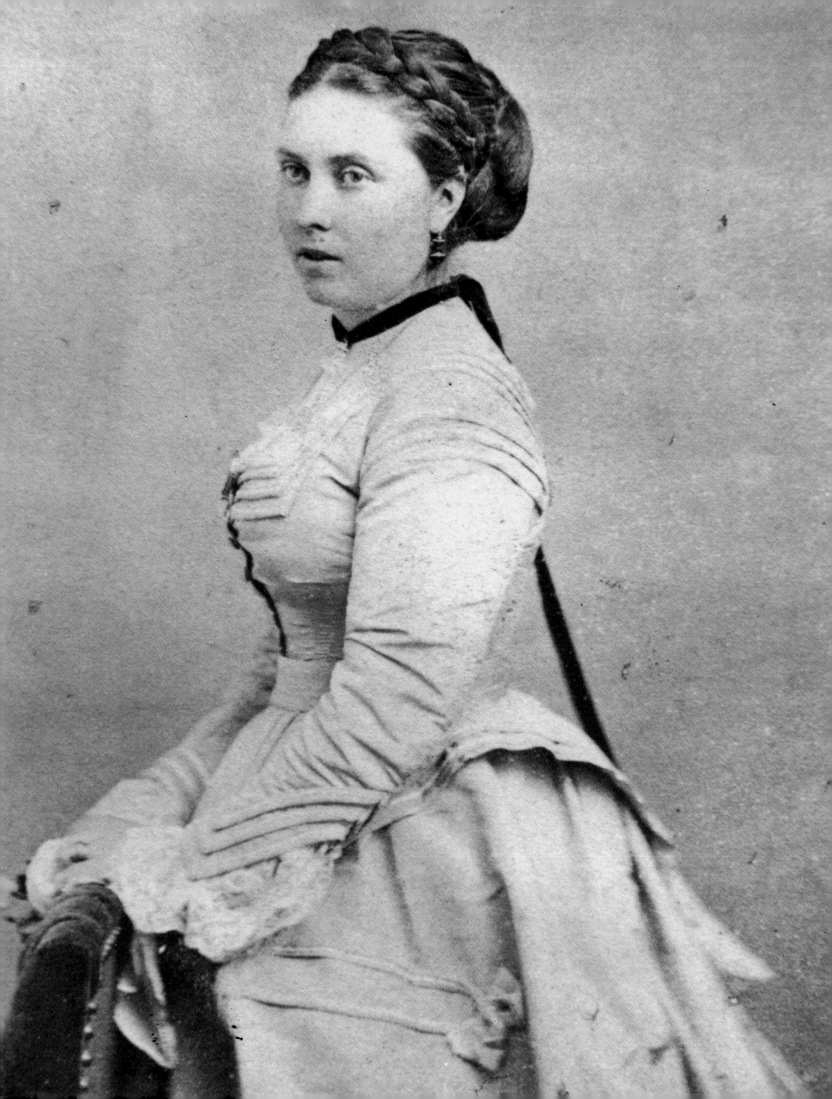

Great Britain

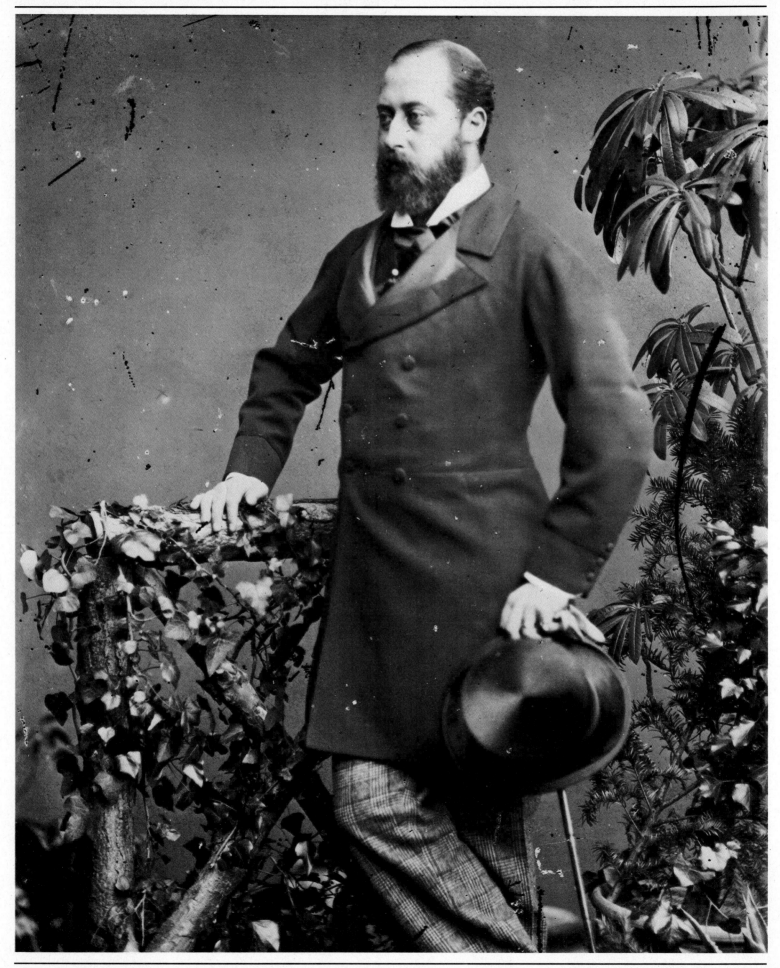

King Edward VII, (portrait *opposite page, left,* whilst Prince of Wales) was born Prince Albert Edward in 1841, the second child and eldest of four sons of Queen Victoria and Prince Albert, the Prince Consort. He was created Prince of Wales in December 1841, and bore this title until ultimately, on the death of his mother, he became King in 1901. He reigned for just over nine years, and died in 1910.

In 1863 he married Princess Alexandra (1844-1925), eldest daughter of Prince Christian (later King Christian IX) of Denmark (1818-1906) and Queen Louise (1817-1898), formerly Princess of Hesse-Cassel. Through this marriage, King Edward VII became linked in time to the royal families of Russia, Greece, Norway and Hanover.

Of King Edward VII's six children, three died unmarried: these were Prince Albert Victor, Duke of Clarence (1864-1892), the eldest son and heir until his early death from pneumonia; Princess Victoria (1868-1935) and Prince Alexander (who died less than 24 hours after his birth in April 1872). Of King Edward's remaining children, the second son succeeded him as King George V (1865-1936); the eldest daughter Princess Louise (1867-1931) married the 1st Duke of Fife in 1889; and the youngest daughter, Princess Maud (1869-1938) became Queen of Norway nine years after her marriage to Prince Carl of Denmark (1872-1957) who was elected to rule over the newly independent state of Norway in 1905 as King Haakon VII.

Prince Alfred, *right,* born in 1844, was the second son and fourth child of Queen Victoria and Prince Albert. He was thus brother to King Edward VII (1841-1910), the Empress Frederick of Germany and Grand Duchess Alice of Hesse-Darmstadt (1843-1878).

He was created Duke of Edinburgh in 1866. In 1874, he was married to the Grand Duchess Marie (1853-1920), the only daughter of Tsar Alexander II of Russia (1818-1881) and his first wife Princess Marie of Hesse-Darmstadt (1824-1880). They had five children.

Their eldest daughter, Princess Marie (1875-1938) married Crown Prince Ferdinand of Roumania in 1893, and became Queen of Roumania on his accession as King in 1914. The second daughter, Princess Victoria Melita (1876-1936) was twice married: first to her cousin Grand Duke Ernst Ludwig of Hesse-Darmstadt (1868-1937), the son of Grand Duchess Alice; and secondly to another cousin, Grand Duke Kyrill of Russia (1876-1938), a grandson of Tsar Alexander II. The third daughter, Princess Alexandra (1878-1942) married the 7th Prince of Hohenlohe-Langenburg – their son married Princess Margharita of Greece, the sister of Prince Philip, the present Duke of Edinburgh. The fourth daughter, Princess Beatrice (1884-1966) married a great-grandson of King Louis-Phillippe of France.

Prince Alfred had only one son – also named Alfred – who predeceased him: he lived from 1874 to 1899.

In 1893, Prince Alfred Duke of Edinburgh succeeded to the Dukedom of Saxe-Coburg-Gotha on the death of his uncle, Duke Ernst II (1818-1893) the only brother of the Prince Consort and consequent on the prior disclaimer of that title by the otherwise rightful heir the Prince of Wales (King Edward VII). Prince Alfred held this title until his death in 1900.

The photograph, *top right,* was taken in 1866; whilst the portrait, *bottom right,* shows Prince Albert aged about 13 in the uniform of a midshipman.

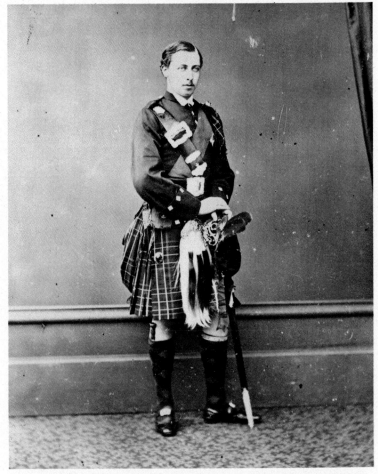

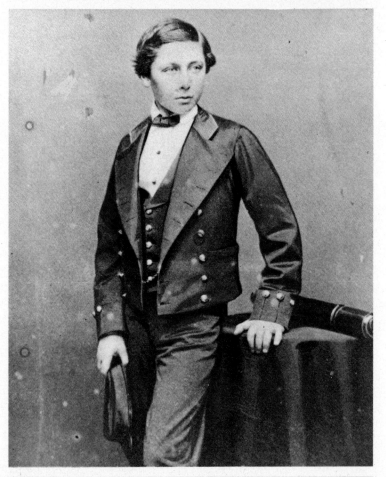

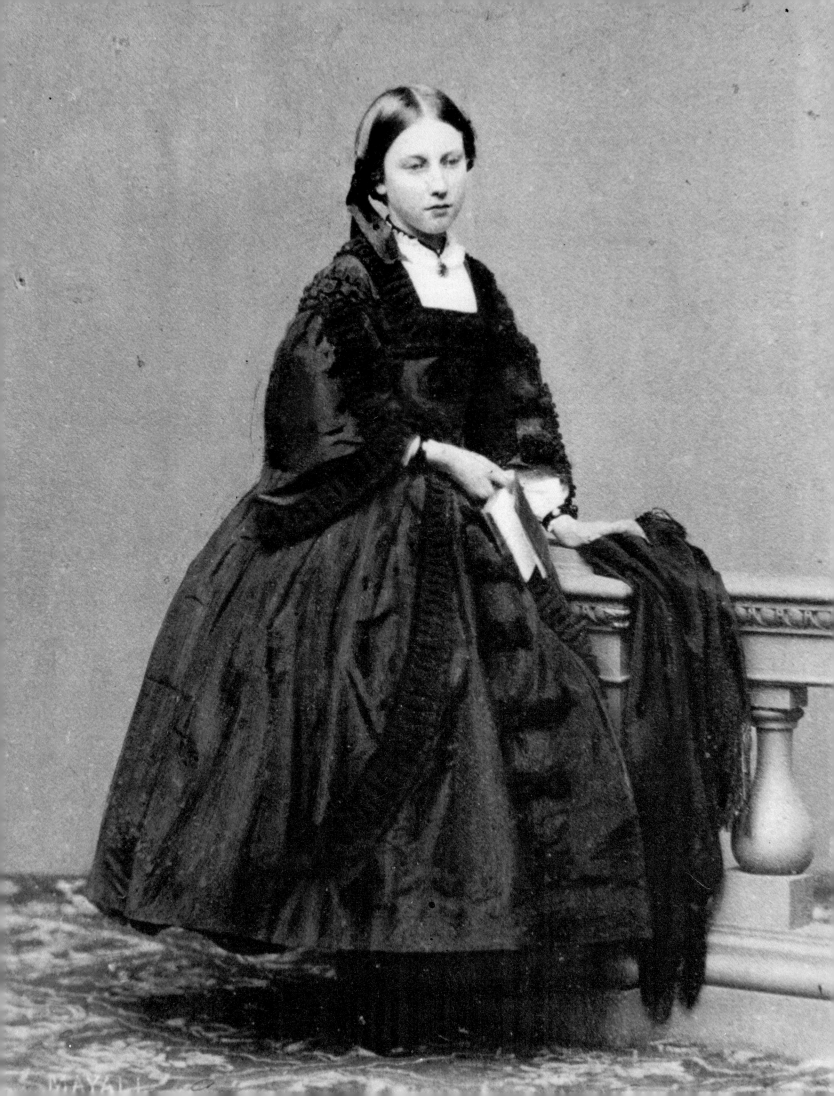

Princess Alice and Princess Helena

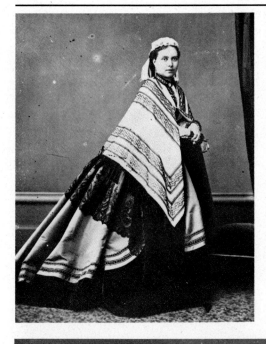

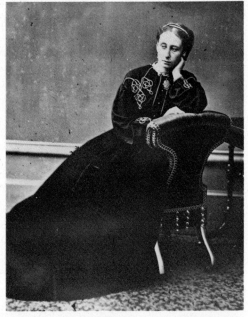

Princess Alice, *immediate left*, was born in 1843, the third of Queen Victoria's nine children. In 1862, she married Prince Ludwig (Louis) of Hesse-Darmstadt (1837-1892) who succeeded as reigning Grand Duke of Hesse under the style of Ludwig IV, on the death of his uncle Ludwig III in 1877.

Princess Alice had seven children. Her eldest son, Prince Ernst-Ludwig (1868-1937) married Princess Victoria Melita (1876-1936), a daughter of Princess Alice's brother Prince Alfred, Duke of Edinburgh, and later Duke of Saxe-Coburg-Gotha; this marriage ended in divorce in 1903. Of Princess Alice's remaining children, Princess Victoria (1863-1950) who married Admiral of the Fleet Prince Louis of Battenberg, became the mother of the late Earl Mountbatten of Burma (1900-1979) and of Queen Louise of Sweden (1889-1965), as well as grandmother of the present Duke of Edinburgh; Princess Irene (1866-1953) married Kaiser Wilhelm II's brother Prince Henry of Prussia (1862-1929); and Princess Alexandra (1872-1918) married Tsar Nicholas II of Russia (1868-1918) in 1894, and was executed along with her entire family during the Russian Revolution.

Two of Princess Alice's children died young: Prince Frederick (1870-1873) from haemophilia and Princess Marie (1874-1878) from black diphtheria. Princess Alice herself contracted diphtheria from her young daughter, and also died in 1878.

Princess Helena was Queen Victoria's fifth child. Born in 1846 she married, shortly after her 20th birthday, Prince Christian of Schleswig-Holstein-Sonderburg-Augustenburg, who was an uncle of the Empress Augusta Victoria of Germany (1858-1921), the wife of Kaiser Wilhelm II. The Duchy of Schleswig-Holstein was annexed by the Prussians in the year of Princess Helena's marriage.

Princess Helena is shown on the opposite page aged 14, and, *left*, with her fiancé at the time of their engagement.

Above left. The oldest sister of Princesses Alice and Helena – Princess Victoria, the Princess Royal – photographed at the time of Helena's engagement to Prince Christian.

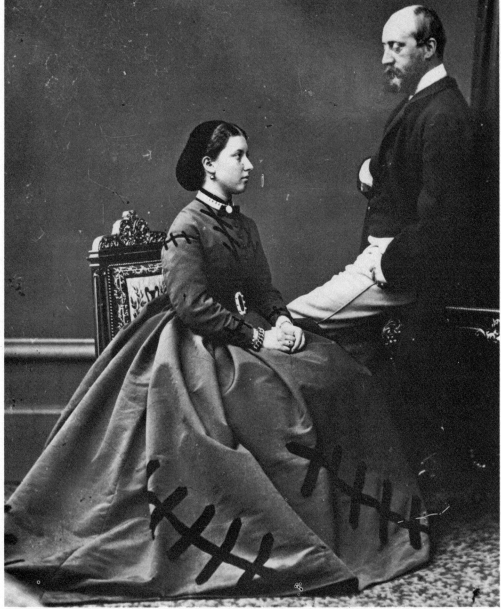

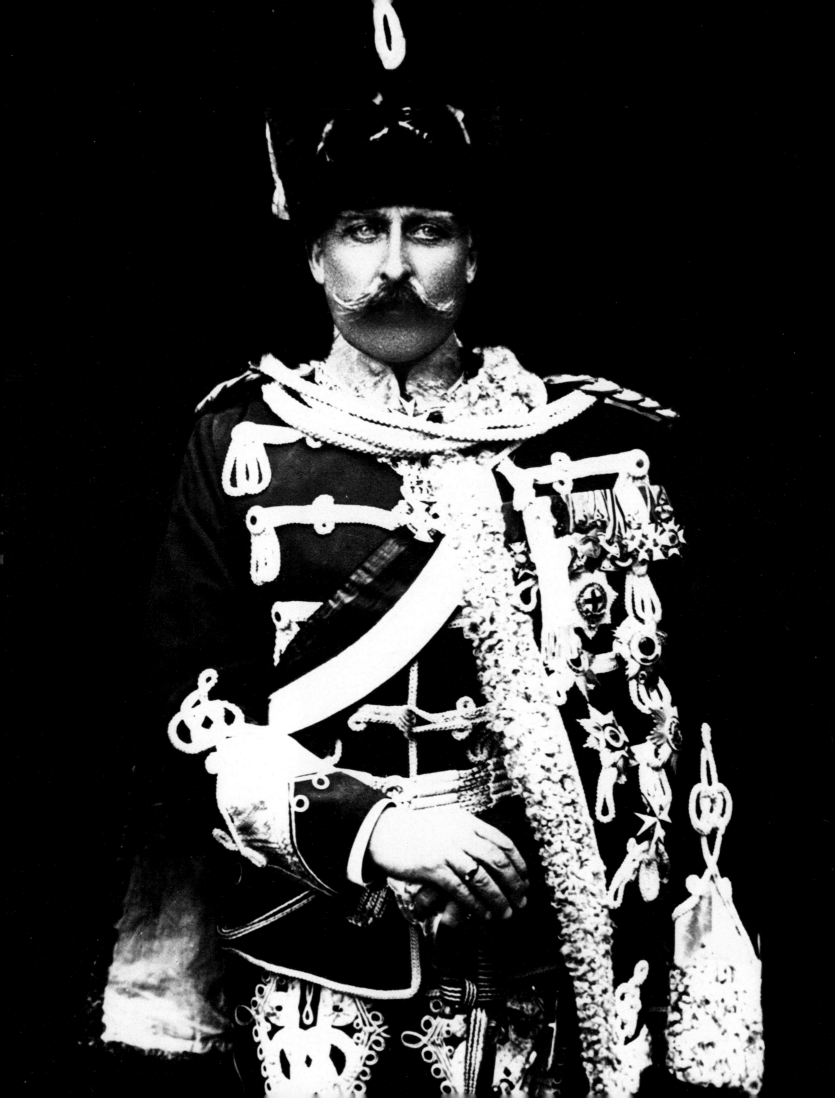

Prince Arthur, Duke of Connaught

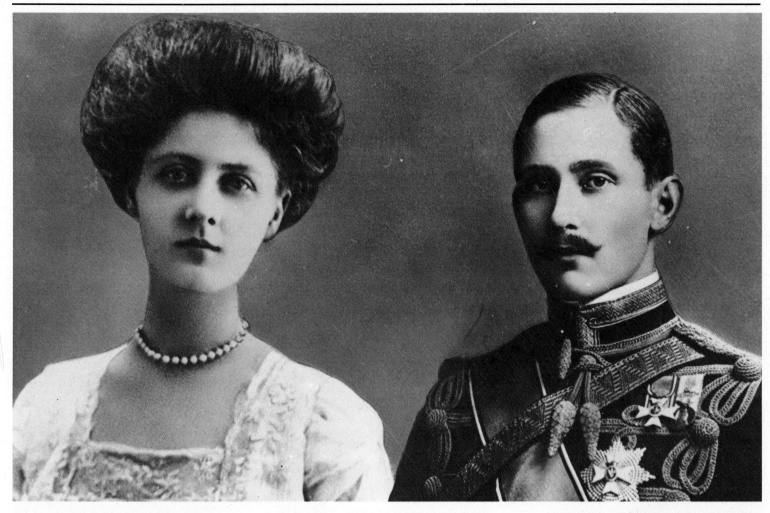

Prince Arthur, *opposite page, left,* in 1894, was the third son of Queen Victoria and Prince Albert, and was born in 1850. He was created Duke of Connaught and Strathearn in 1874.

In 1879 he married Princess Louise (1860-1917), the third daughter of Prince Frederick Charles of Prussia (1828-1885), second cousin of the Duke of Connaught's nephew, Kaiser Wilhelm II. By her, he had three children; Prince Arthur (1883-1938), who married his first cousin once removed, Princess Alexandra, Duchess of Fife (1891-1959), a granddaughter of King Edward VII; Princess Margaret (1882-1920) who married Crown Prince Gustav (later King Gustav VI) of Sweden (1882-1973); and Princess Victoria Patricia (1886-1974) who became Lady Patricia Ramsay on her marriage in 1919 to Sir Alexander Ramsay, a son of the 13th Earl of Dalhousie.

Above. Prince Arthur of Connaught and his fiancée photographed at the time of their engagement in 1913. She was formerly Princess Alexandra, Duchess of Fife, born in 1891. Her father was Alexander, 1st Duke of Fife (1849-1912) and her mother was Princess Louise (1867-1931), Princess Royal and eldest daughter of the Duke of Connaught's brother, King Edward VII.

Prince Arthur and Princess Alexandra were married in October 1913. In 1914 their only child was born: this was Alistair, Earl of Macduff, photograph *right,* taken in about 1920. Prince Arthur died in 1938, predeceasing his father, and thus not having inherited the title Duke of Connaught. The Earl of Macduff did inherit it on the death of the old Duke in 1942, but he died in 1943, unmarried and the title became extinct.

Princess Alexandra, who after her marriage was known as Princess Arthur of Connaught, reverted to the style of Princess Alexandra Duchess of Fife during her widowhood. She died in 1959.

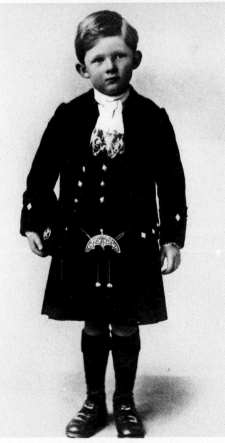

Great Britain

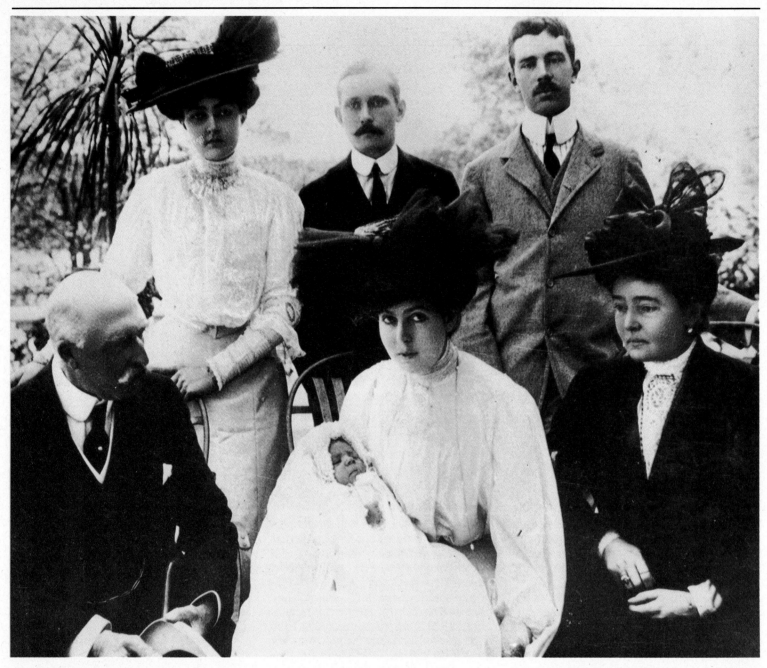

Above. This photograph shows Prince Arthur, Duke of Connaught sitting on the left, and his wife, the Duchess, sitting on the right.

Between them sits their eldest child, Princess Margaret, holding her first child, Prince Gustav of Sweden (1906-1947). The child's father, also known as Prince Gustav (later King Gustav VI) of Sweden, is standing on the right of the photograph: he married Princess Margaret in 1905.

Princess Margaret's sister is standing behind the Duke of Connaught – she was Lady Patricia Ramsay, formerly Princess Victoria Patricia of Connaught, and she married Sir Alexander Ramsay (1881-1972) in 1919.

Finally, in the centre at the back is Prince Arthur the Connaughts' only son who married Princess Alexandra of Fife, seven years after this photograph was taken.

Opposite page, right. The two daughters of the Duke of Connaught, in the robes they wore at the Coronation of King George V and Queen Mary on June 22nd 1911.

Princess Victoria Patricia, standing on the right, was the younger of the two. She renounced her royal titles and became Lady Patricia Ramsay on her marriage. Her only child, Alexander (b. 1919) who is married to the Hon. Flora Fraser has three children.

Crown Princess Margaret of Sweden married Prince (later Crown Prince) Gustav of Sweden, (1882-1973) who became King Gustav VI in 1950. The eldest of her children, Prince Gustav (1906-1947), died before he could inherit, but was the father of King Gustav VI's successor, King Carl XVI (b. 1946). Crown Princess Margaret's only daughter was Princess Ingrid (b. 1910) who, in 1935, married the future King Frederick IX of Denmark (1899-1972) and is the mother of the present Queen of Denmark, Margrethe II (b. 1940).

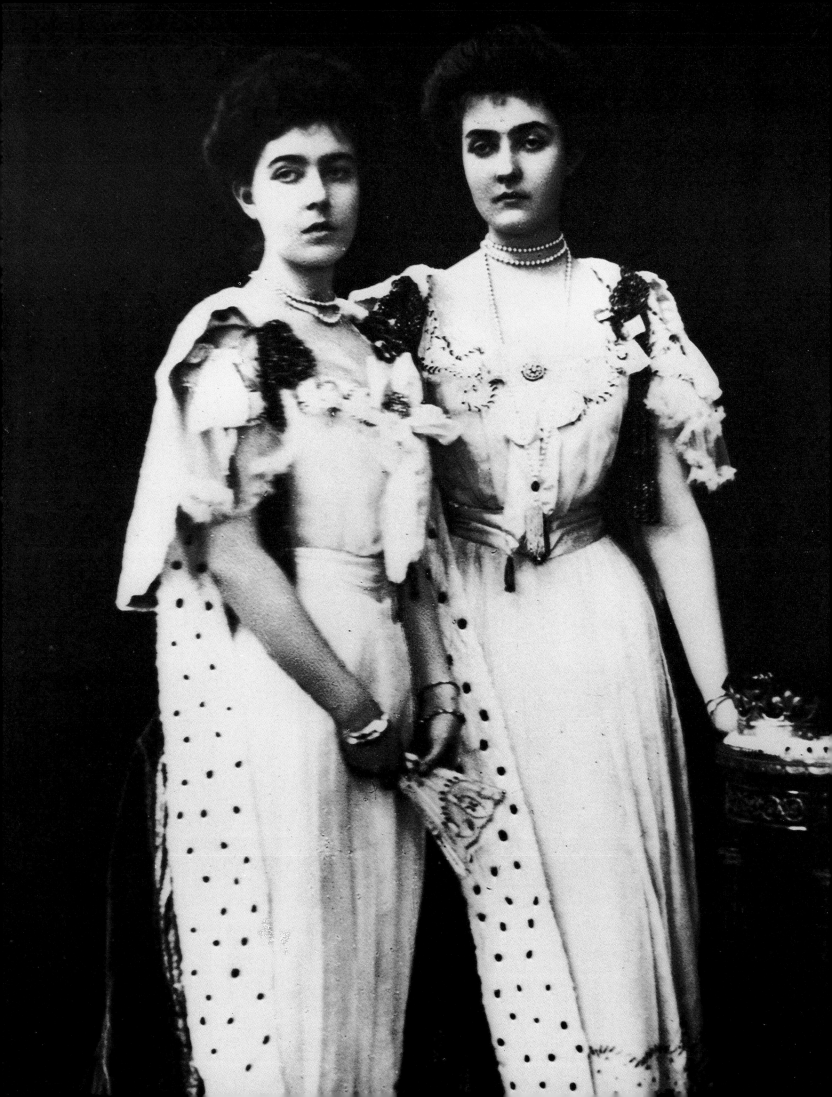

Great Britain

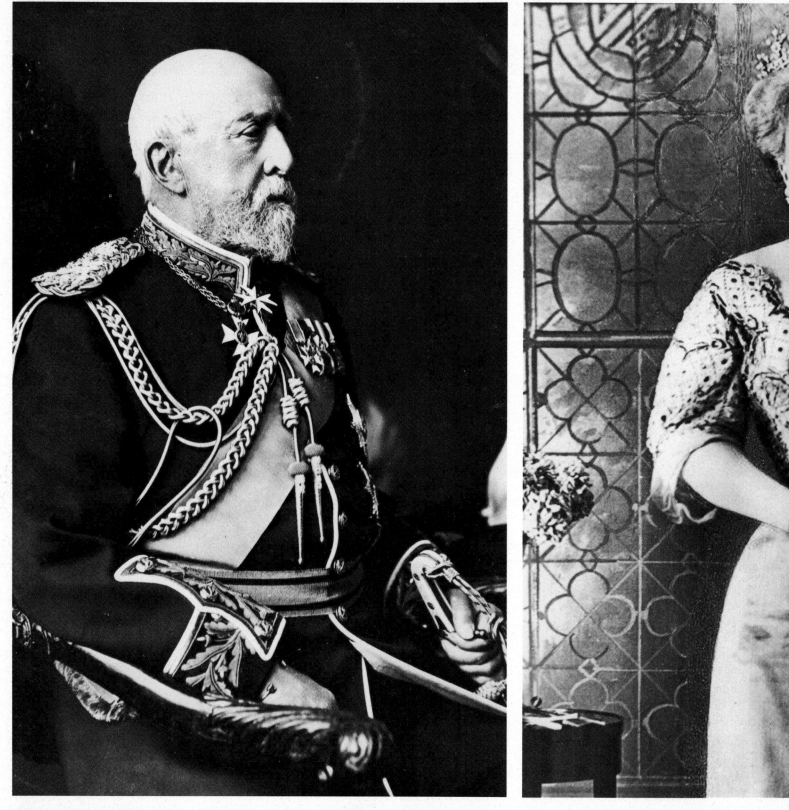

Prince Christian, *above left,* was born in 1831, the third son of Duke Christian I of the Danish duchy of Schleswig-Holstein-Sonderburg-Augustenburg. He was also brother to Duke Christian's successor to the Dukedom, Duke Frederick VIII (1829-1880) who married Princess Adelheid (1835-1900) of Hohenlohe-Langenburg, the second daughter of Queen Victoria's half-sister, Princess Feodora of Leiningen (1807-1872).

In 1866, Prince Christian married Queen Victoria's third daughter, Princess Helena, *above right*. They had six children (including a stillborn son in 1877) of whom only one, Princess Marie-Louise (1872-1956), married: her marriage to Prince Aribert of Anhalt-Dessau (1864-1933) was dissolved after nine years, in 1900, and there were no children. Of the remainder, the eldest, Prince Christian Victor (1867-1900) died at Pretoria whilst fighting in the Boer War; Prince Frederick Harald died aged three in 1876; Princess Helena Victoria (1870-1948) and Prince Albert (1869-1931) died unmarried. Prince Albert succeeded to the Dukedom

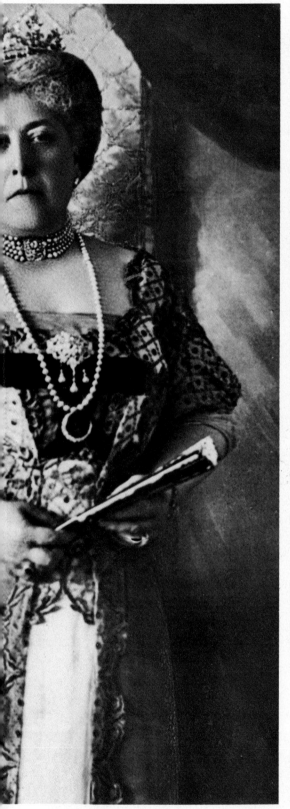

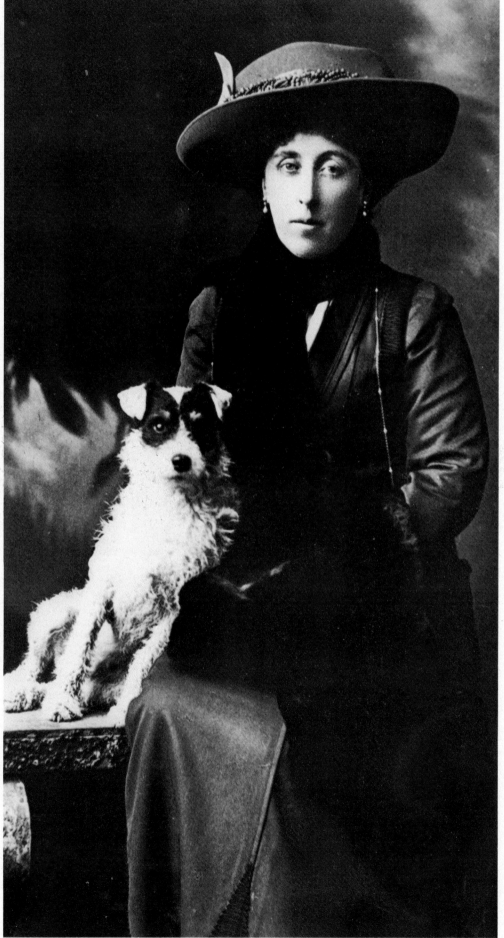

of Schleswig - Holstein - Sonderburg - Augustenburg in 1921, on the death without issue of Duke Frederick VIII's only surviving son, Duke Ernst Gunther.

Princess Helena Victoria of Schleswig-Holstein, the third of six children of Prince and Princess Christian photographed, *right,* in about 1916.

Great Britain

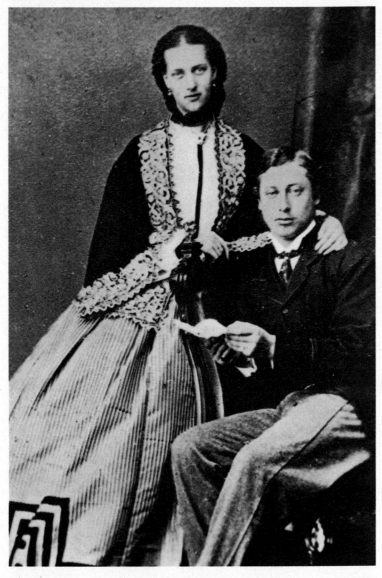

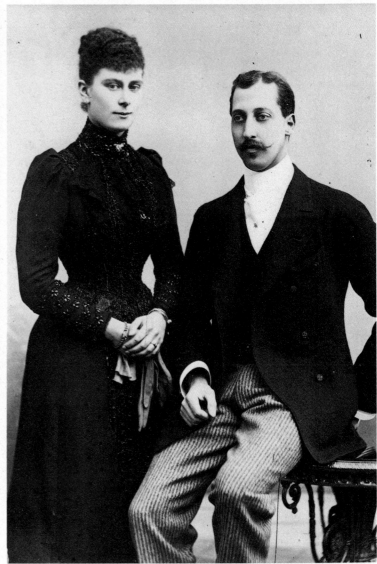

Queen Alexandra, *opposite page, right,* aged about 18, was born in 1844. Formerly Princess Alexandra of Denmark, she was the eldest daughter of Prince Christian of Schleswig-Holstein-Sonderburg-Glucksburg – later King Christian IX of Denmark (1818-1906) and of his wife, Queen Louise (1817-1898), formerly Princess of Hesse-Cassel. Princess Alexandra was sister to King George I of Greece (1845-1913), to Tsarina Marie of Russia (1847-1928) and to Princess Thyra (1853-1933) who became Duchess of Cumberland, Luneburg and Brunswick, and Princess of Hanover. In addition, Princess Alexandra became aunt to Prince Carl of Denmark (1872-1957) – the second son of her brother King Frederick VIII of Denmark – who was elected to the throne of Norway as King Haakon VII in 1905.

In 1863 she married Prince Albert Edward (1841-1910) the eldest son and heir of Queen Victoria of England, and later to become King Edward VII. The photograph, *above left,* shows the couple on 9th September, 1862, on the day when their engagement was conducted. By him she had six children of whom the eldest, Prince Albert Victor died unmarried, from pneumonia, leaving the second as eventual heir to the British throne as King George V. Of her daughters, only one married into foreign royalty – this was the youngest, Princess Maud (1869-1938) who married Prince Carl of Denmark in 1896, and

became Queen Maud of Norway, mother of the present King Olav V (b. 1903).

Princess Alexandra became Queen Consort on the accession of her husband in 1901, and Queen Mother on his death in 1910. She survived him by fifteen years until her death in November, 1925.

Prince Albert Victor, her eldest child was created Duke of Clarence and Avondale in 1890, and in the following year became engaged to Princess Victoria Mary of Teck. The photograph, *above right,* was taken in December 1891 to record their engagement. Within a month, however, he died of pneumonia at Sandringham, six days after his twenty-eighth birthday, on 14th January, 1892.

Princess Victoria Mary of Teck was born in 1867. Her father was Prince Franz, Duke of Teck – a minor branch of the former Kingdom of Wurttemberg – and her mother was Princess Mary Adelaide (1833-1897), a daughter of Prince Adolphus, Duke of Cambridge, the seventh son of King George III.

Princess Victoria Mary (also known popularly as Princess May), after her abortive engagement to Prince Albert Victor became engaged to and, in 1893 married, his only brother Prince George, Duke of York.

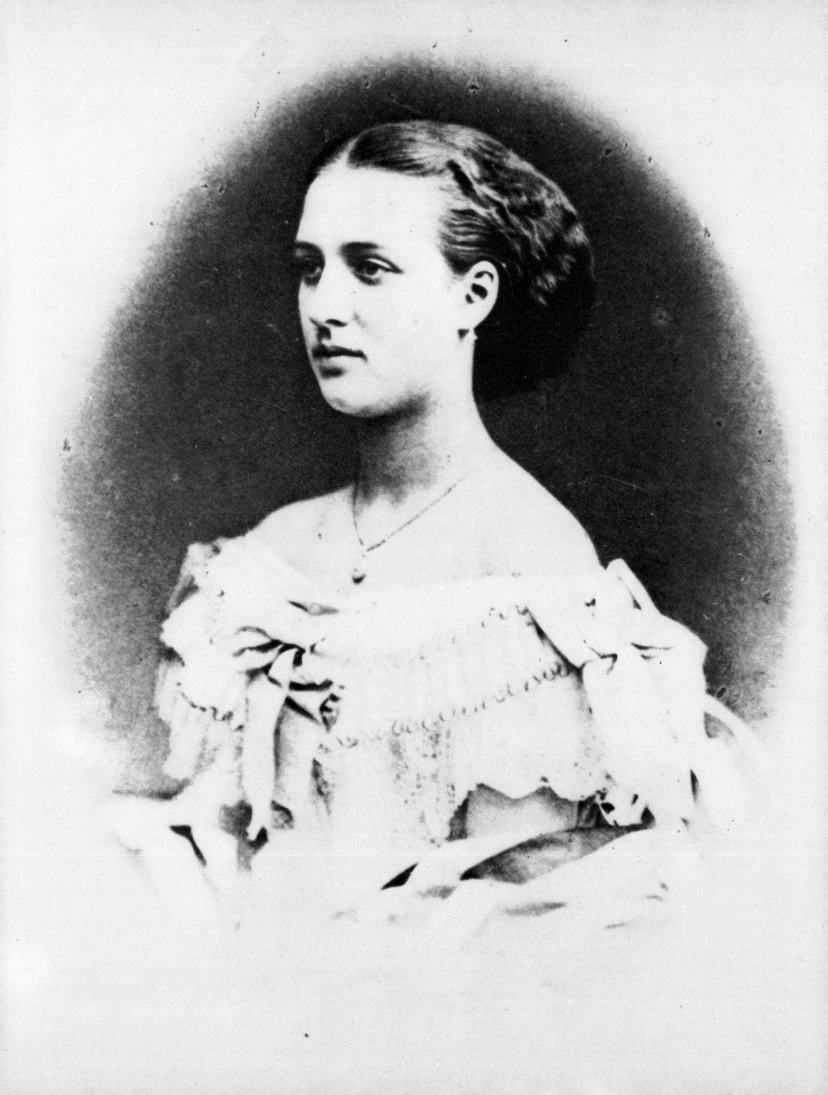

Great Britain

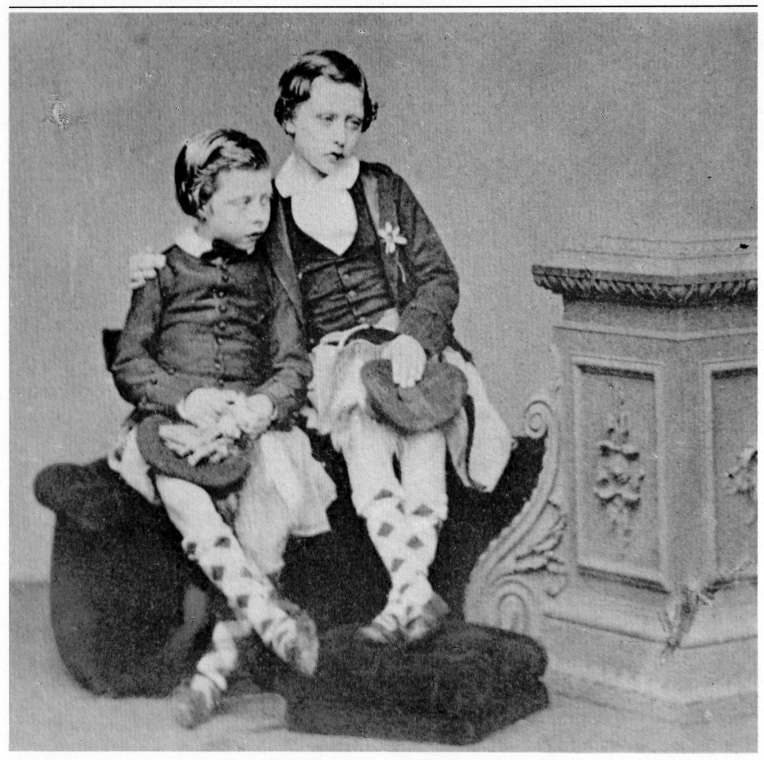

Prince Arthur and Prince Leopold, *above,* c 1858, were the two youngest sons of Queen Victoria and Prince Albert, the Prince Consort.

Prince Arthur, *opposite page, top left,* aged about 13, and *opposite page, top right,* aged about 19) was born in 1850. His godfather was the old hero of Waterloo, the Duke of Wellington, who died two years later. Prince Arthur was created Duke of Connaught and Strathearn in 1874.

Prince Leopold was born in 1853, and was created Duke of Albany in 1881, a year before his marriage to Princess Helena of Waldeck-Pyrmont (1861-1922), a sister of Queen Emma (1858-1934) of the Netherlands and thus great-aunt to the present

Princess Juliana. Prince Leopold had two children: Princess Alice (1883-1981) the last survivor of Queen Victoria's grandchildren; and Prince Charles Edward (1884-1954) who in 1900 succeeded to the Dukedom of Saxe-Coburg-Gotha on the death of his uncle, Prince Alfred, Duke of Edinburgh (1844-1900).

Opposite page, bottom left. Prince Alfred, Duke of Edinburgh, the second son of Queen Victoria and Prince Albert. The photograph was taken in 1866.

Opposite page, bottom right. The future King Edward VII, photographed in 1885 whilst he was Prince of Wales.

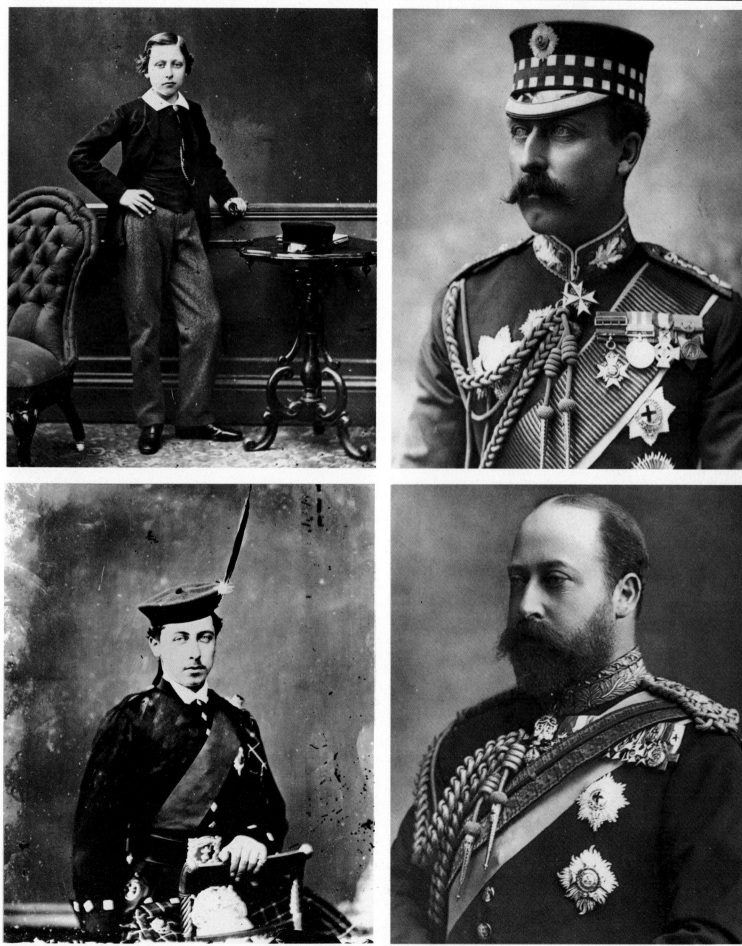

Great Britain

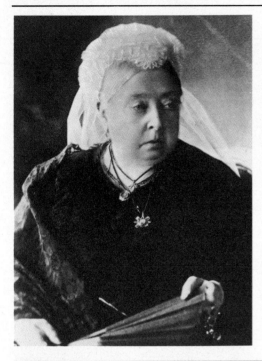

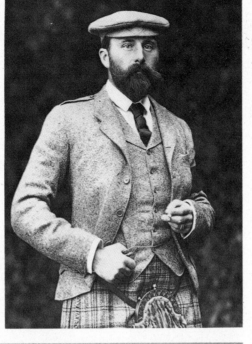

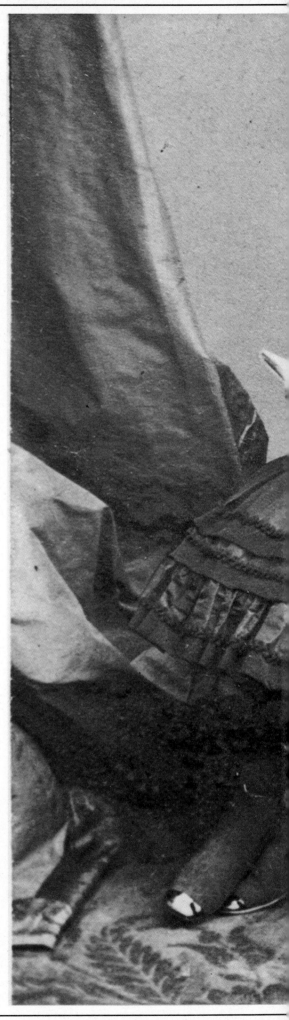

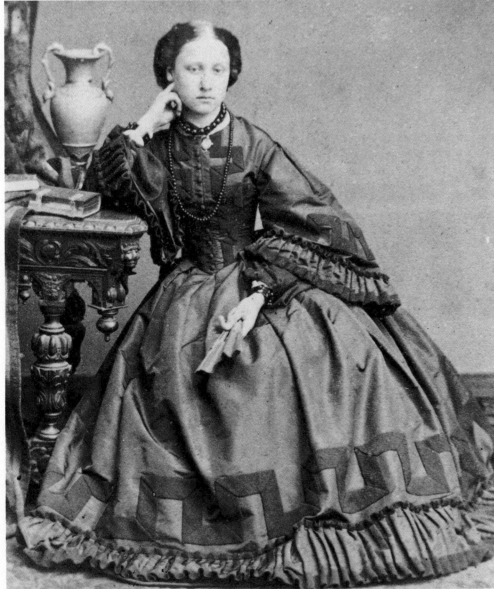

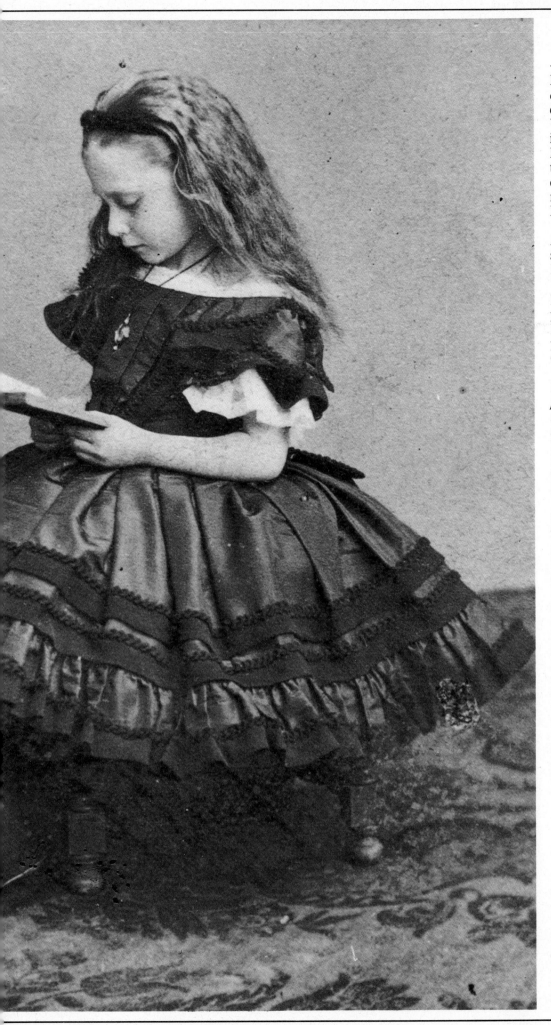

Princess Louise and Princess Beatrice

Princess Louise, Marchioness of Lorne, *opposite page, lower left,* was the fourth daughter and sixth child of Queen Victoria and Prince Albert. She was born in 1848 and in 1871 married John, Marquis of Lorne (1845-1914). She was thus the only one of Queen Victoria's nine children to marry otherwise than into royalty, and otherwise than into a European family.

Princess Louise became Duchess of Argyll in 1900 when her husband succeeded to the Dukedom as the 9th Duke, on the death of his father.

Princess Beatrice, *left,* aged 7, was the youngest child of Queen Victoria and Prince Albert. She was born in 1857, the year that her father was created Prince Consort.

In 1885 she was married to Prince Henry of Battenberg (1858-1896), *opposite page, top right,* the brother of sovereign Prince Alexander I of Bulgaria, and of the Earl Mountbatten's father, Prince Louis, 1st Marquis of Milford Haven. Prince Henry died of fever during the Ashanti Expedition to the Gold Coast in 1895-6.

Princess Beatrice had four children: her only daughter was Princess Victoria Eugenie (1887-1969) who married King Alfonso XIII of Spain (1886-1941) and became grandmother to the present King of Spain, Juan Carlos. Of Princess Beatrice's three sons, the eldest, Prince Alexander (1886-1960) was created Marquis of Carisbrooke (after the use of the surname Battenberg was discontinued in the Great War), and married Lady Irene Denison, whilst the other two died unmarried – Prince Leopold (1889-1922) and Prince Maurice (1891-1914); the latter was killed on active service in France in October 1914.

Opposite page, top left. One of a series of portraits of Queen Victoria taken at Osborne House by Hughes and Mullins in July 1897.

Overleaf. Two photographs that show the occupants of the first four places in the line of precedence and succession to the throne in 1894 *(right)* and 1899 *(left).* They are, Queen Victoria; her eldest son, Prince Albert Edward (the future King Edward VII); her grandson, Prince George (the future King George V); and her great grandson, who was to succeed to the Throne in 1936 as King Edward VIII.

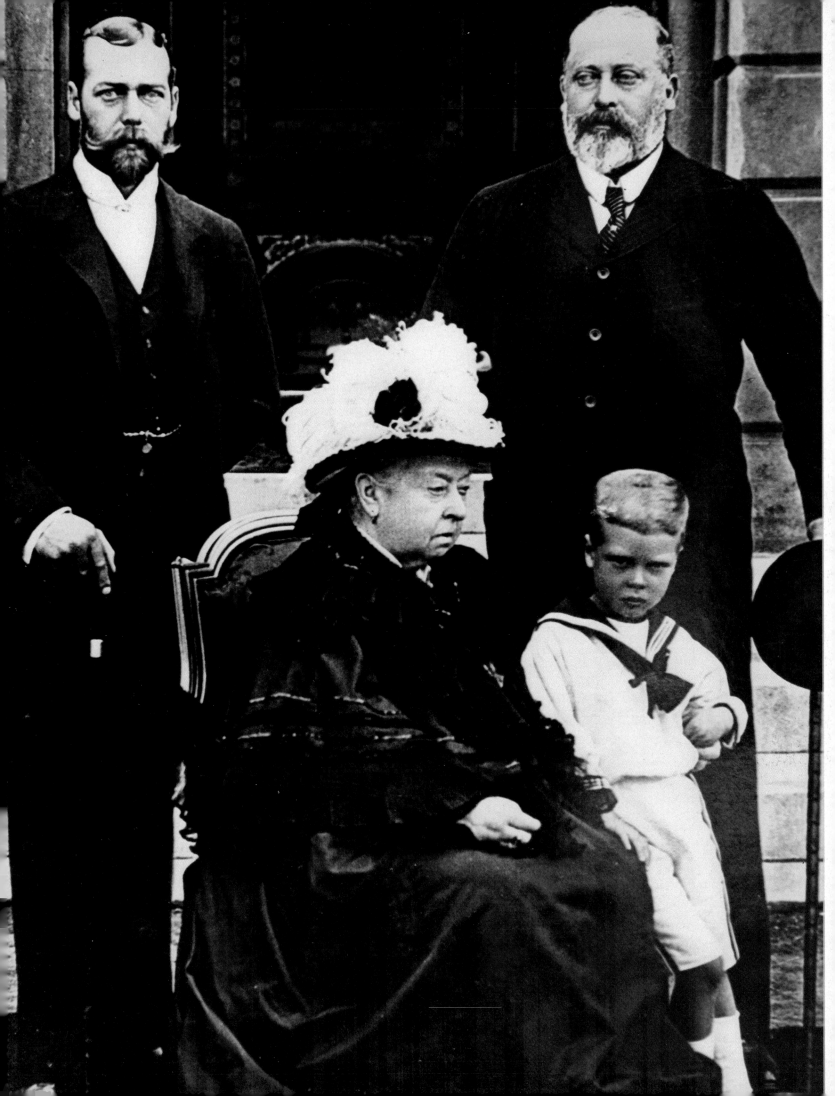

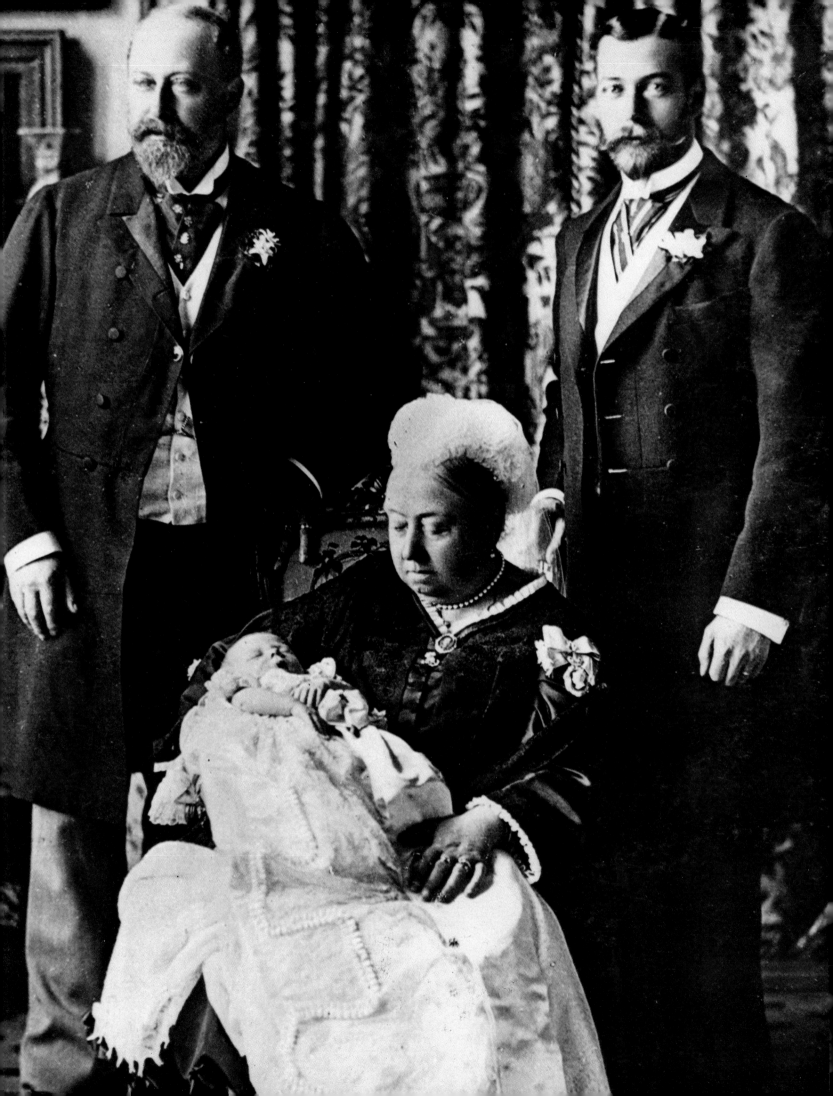

Great Britain

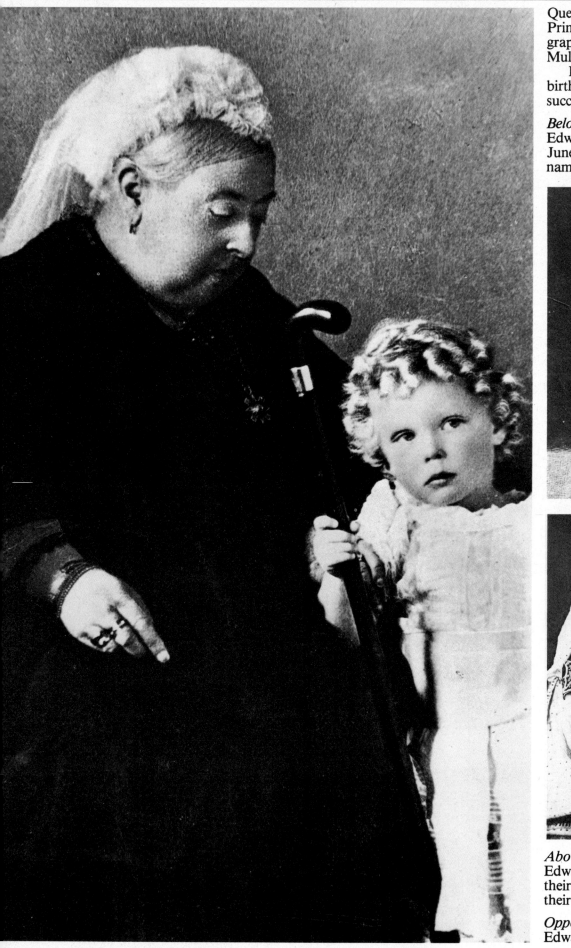

Queen Victoria with her great grandchild Prince Edward of York, *left* – a photograph taken by Messrs. Hughes and Mullins at Osborne House in July 1897.

Prince Edward was, at the time of his birth in 1894, third in direct line of succession to the throne.

Below. A photograph taken during King Edward's visit to friends at Crichel on 2nd June, 1909. The dog was the King's pet, named Caesar.

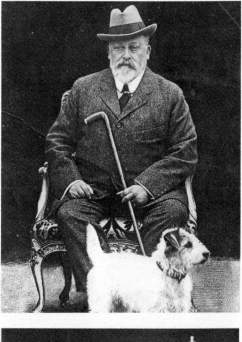

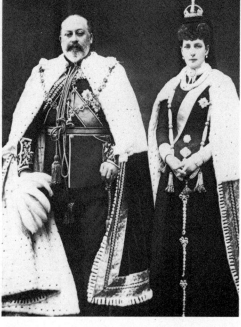

Above. A photograph showing King Edward VII and Queen Alexandra on their way to open the first parliament of their reign – on 14th February, 1901.

Opposite page, right. A portrait of King Edward VII taken in 1902.

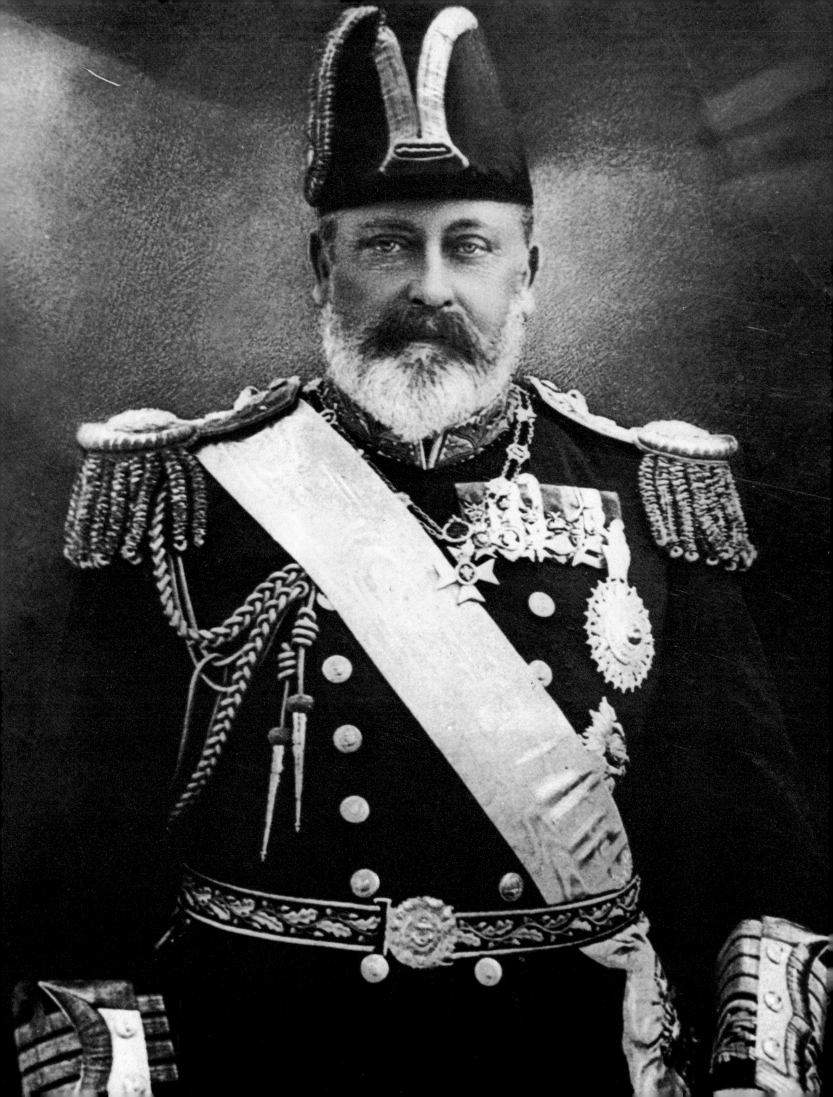

Great Britain

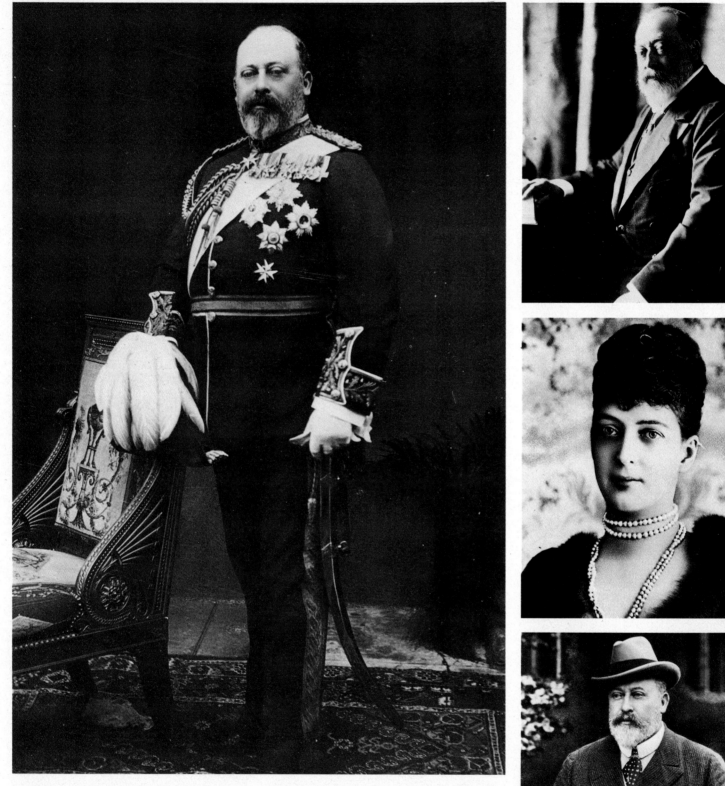

Above. An official portrait of King Edward VII by the photographers, Messrs. Gunn and Stewart. It was taken in 1895, when the King was Prince of Wales.

Top right. This photograph of the King was probably taken in 1907 or 1908; and was used on postcards celebrating the visit to London in May 1908 of the President of France for the Franco-British Exhibition at Wembley.

Middle right. This photograph, by Lafayette of Dublin, was first published in August, 1893, when Queen Alexandra was Princess of Wales.

Lower right. A photograph of King Edward VII taken in 1905.

Opposite page, right. A photograph by Landhams, taken in 1901.

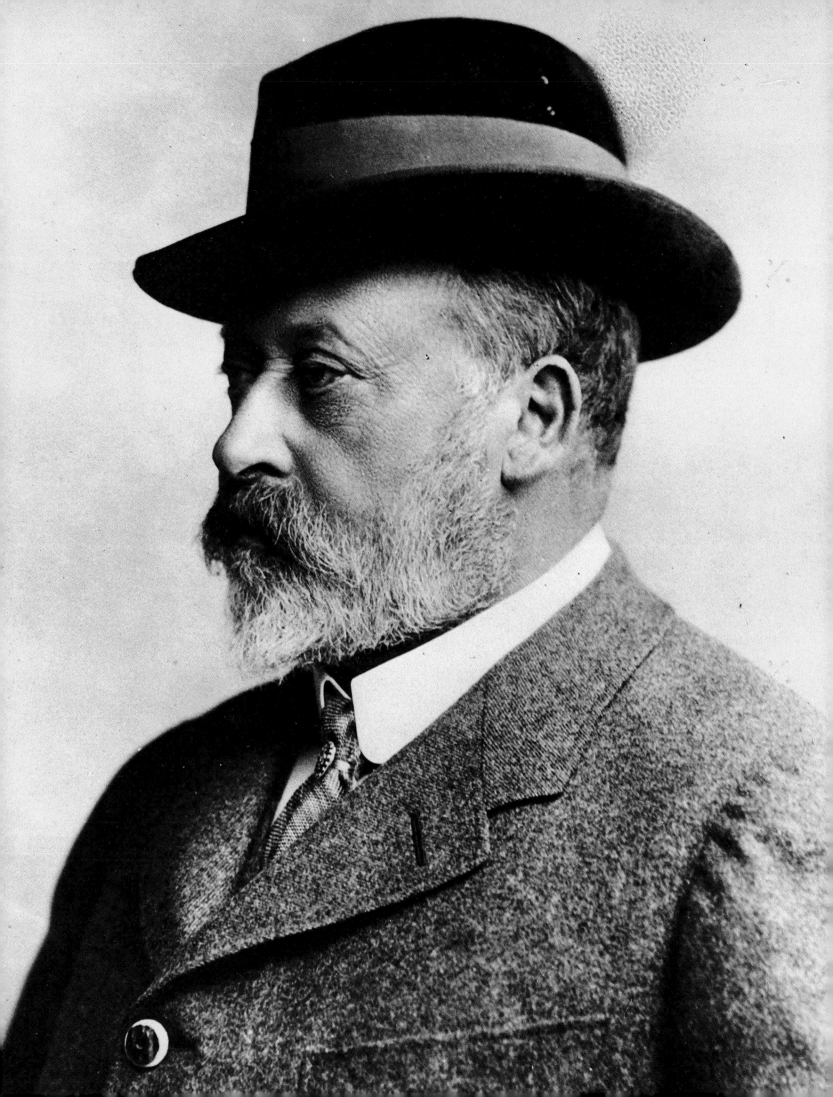

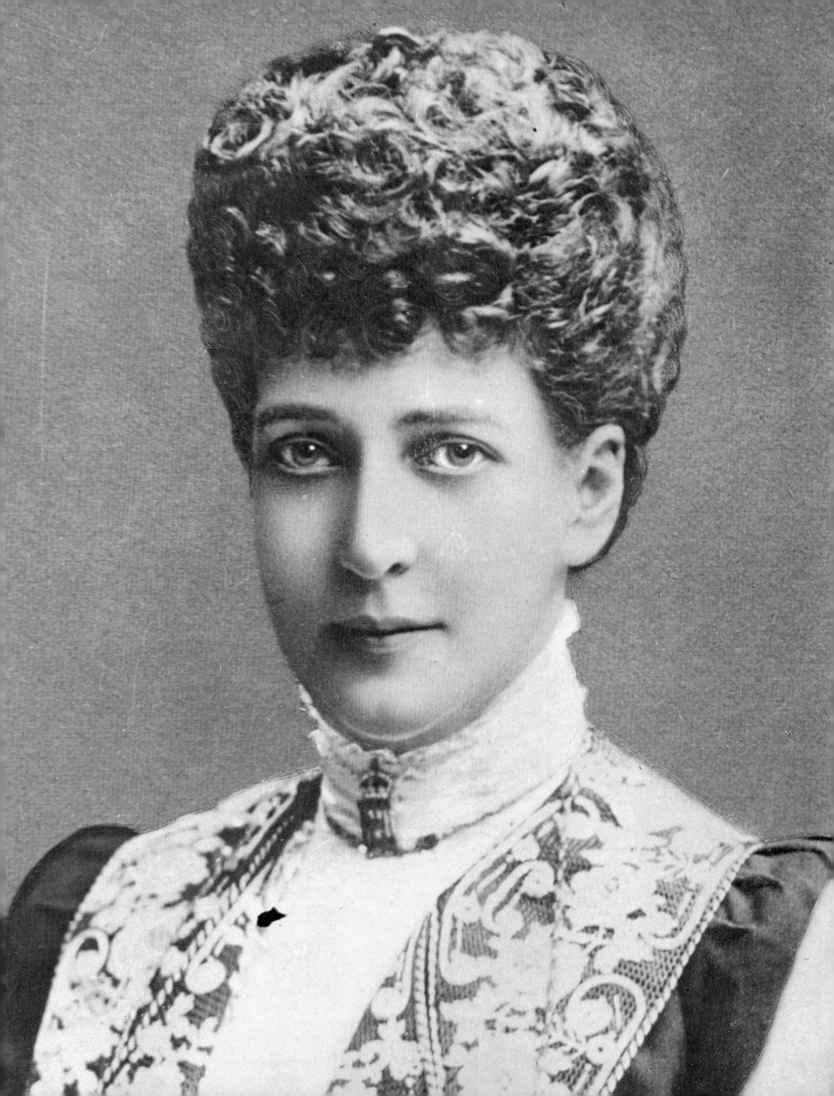

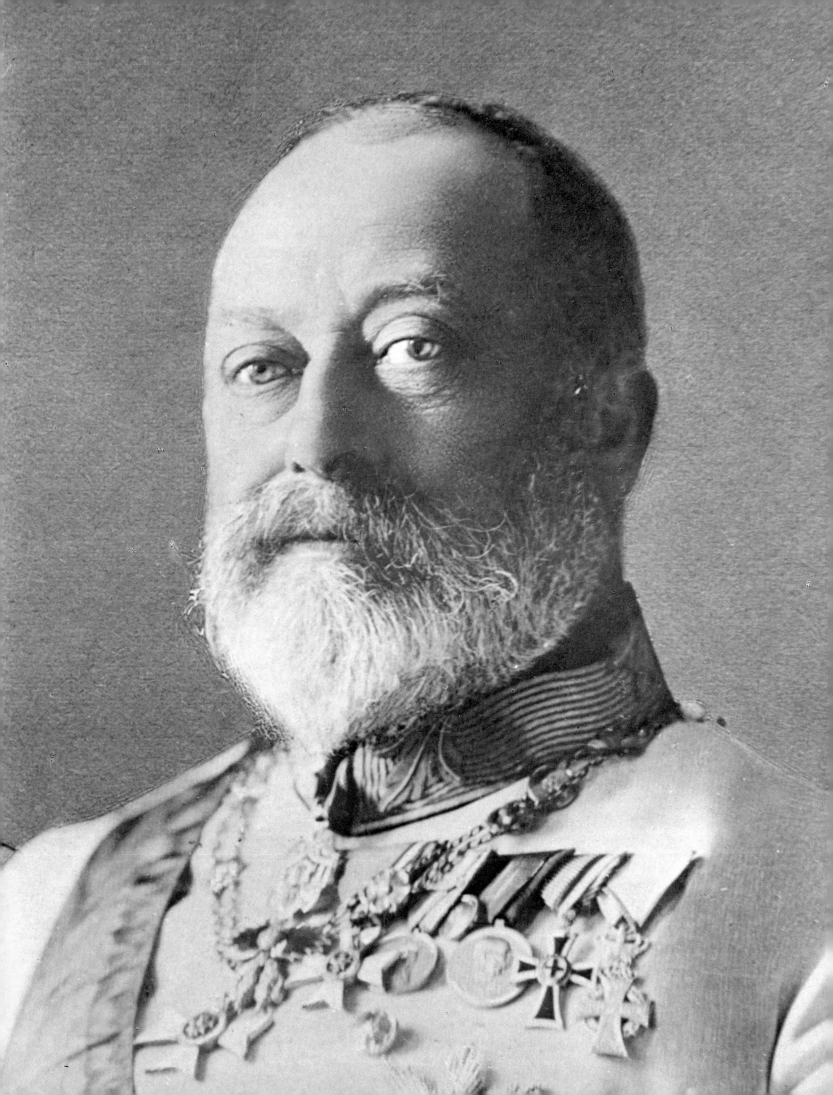

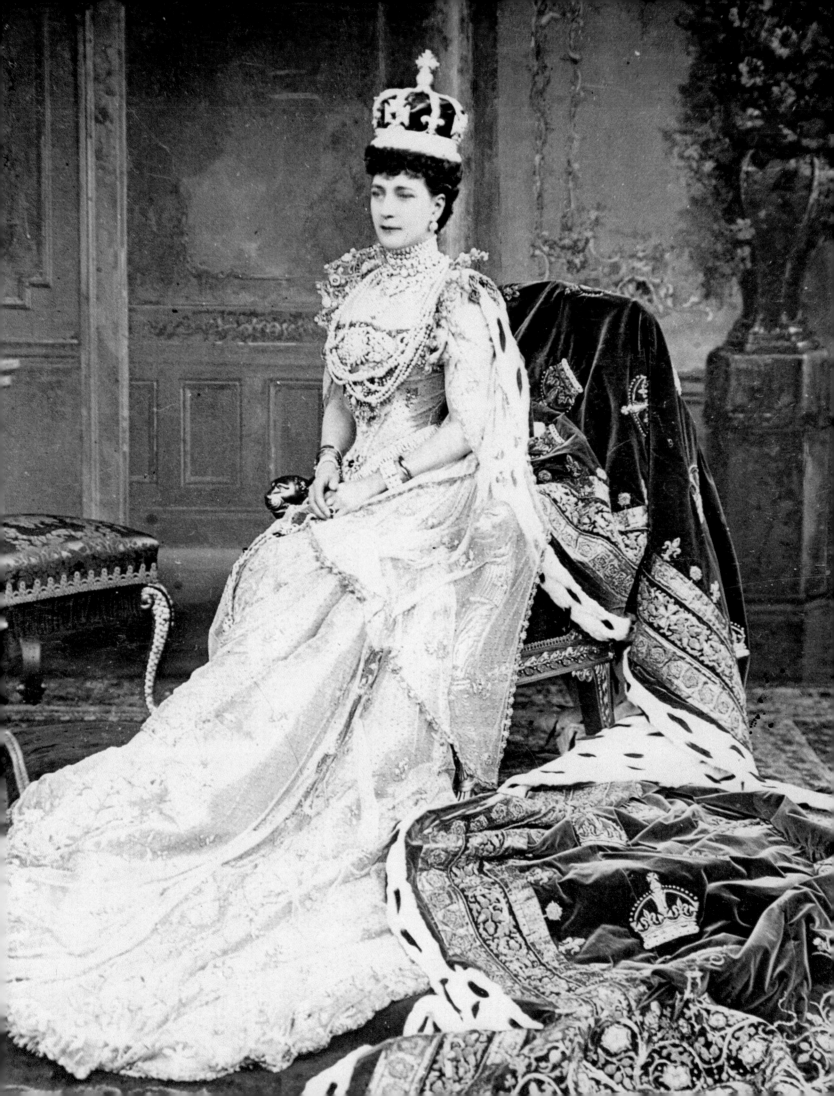

King Edward VII and Queen Alexandra

Previous page. King Edward VII and Queen Alexandra.

Opposite page, left, and below. Queen Alexandra photographed in her coronation robes; taken on Coronation Day, 9th August, 1902. Her six pages, *bottom left,* included the Marquis of Stafford, the Hon Edward Lascelles, the Earl of Macclesfield, Viscount Torrington and the Hon Robert Palmer.

Bottom right. The King in coronation robes; a photographic impression showing Edward VII wearing the Imperial Crown.

Right. A photograph of Queen Alexandra taken in 1904.

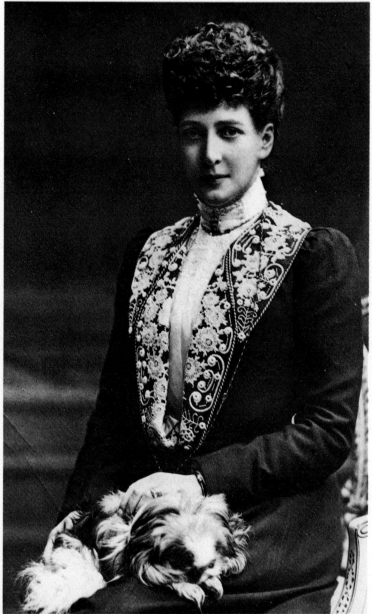

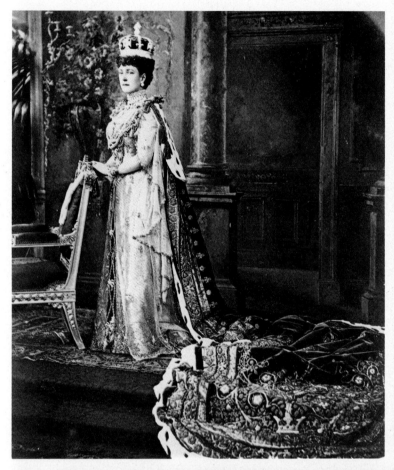

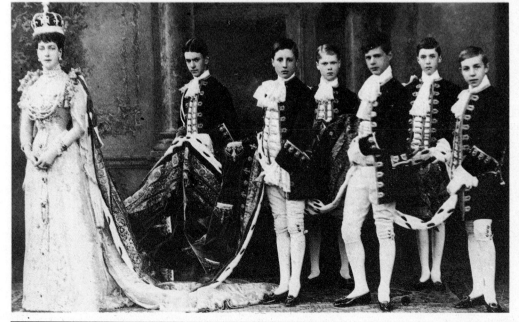

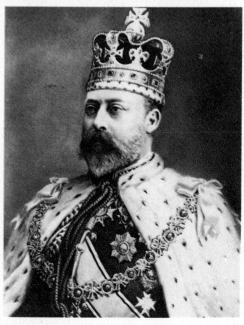

Great Britain

King Edward VII and Kaiser Wilhelm II of Germany, photographed together, *above right,* at Cowes in 1903. Another photograph of uncle and nephew, *below,* taken on 9th February, 1909, at the beginning of King Edward's State Visit to the Kaiser in Berlin.

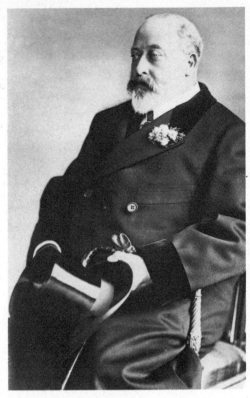

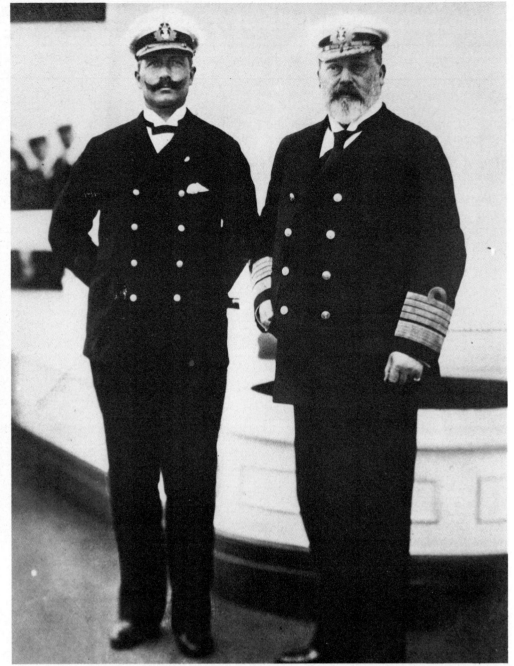

Above. A photograph of King Edward VII taken in November 1907.

Opposite page, right. King Edward and Queen Alexandra, photographed in 1908.

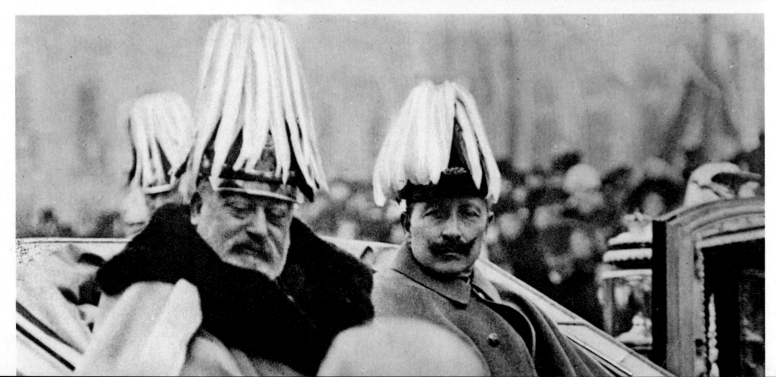

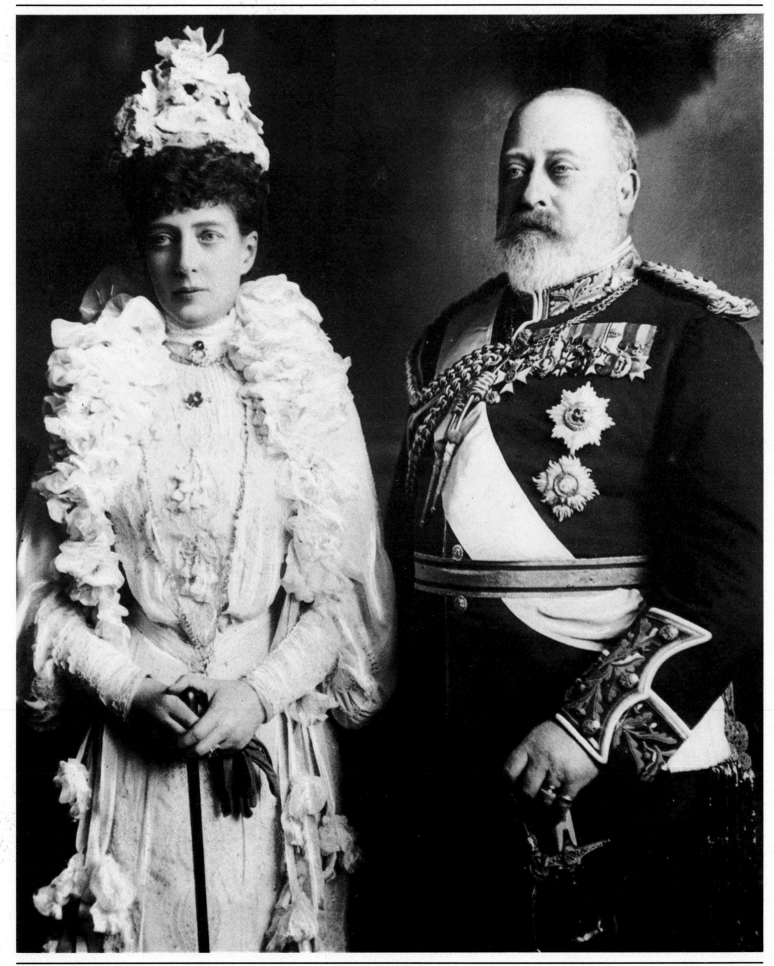

Great Britain

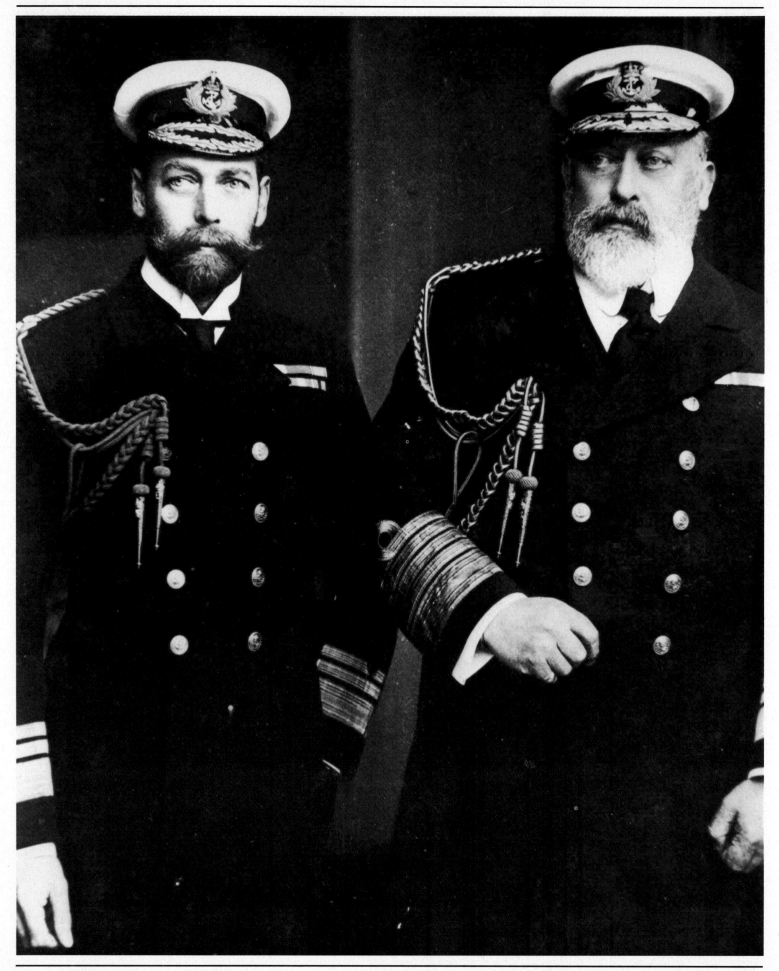

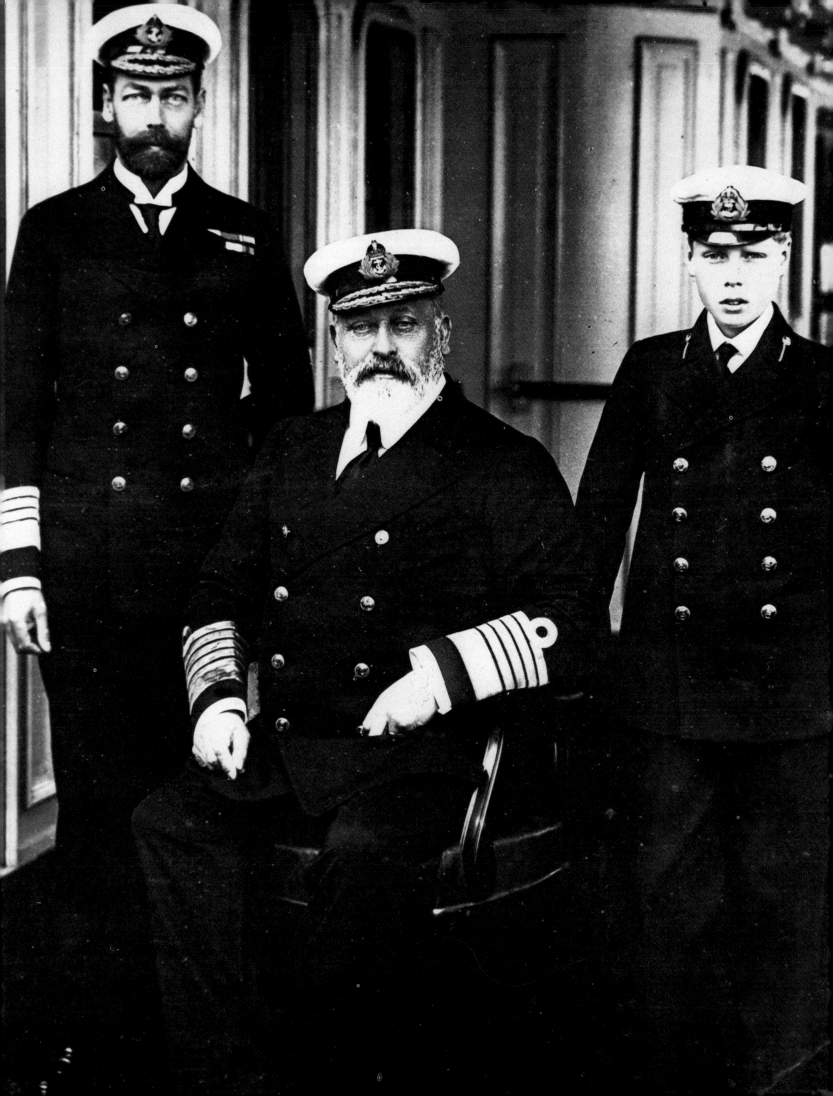

Great Britain

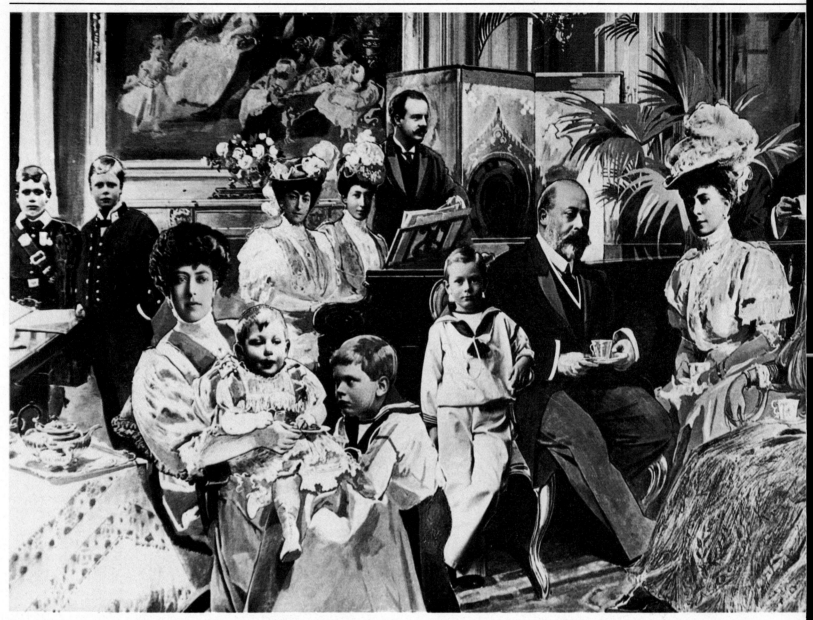

Previous page, left. A photograph taken in the mid-1900's of King Edward VII and the heir apparent, George, Prince of Wales.

Previous page, right. King Edward VII with his son George, the Prince of Wales; and his grandson, Prince Edward of Wales (the future King Edward VIII).

Above. This somewhat whimsical composition of photographs and art-work was apparently put together in about 1910 and shows King Edward VII with his family complete, with three exceptions, to the third generation.

The first generation is represented by King Edward VII himself (1841-1910) seated in the middle, and his wife Queen Alexandra (1844-1925) sitting two places further right.

The second generation is represented by their surviving children, namely Queen Maud of Norway (1869-1938) and Princess Louise, Duchess of Fife (1867-1931) at the piano, Princess Victoria (1868-1935) in the left foreground, and Prince George (King George V, 1865-1936) standing directly behind Queen Alexandra. Queen Maud's husband, King Haakon VII of Norway (1872-1957) stands on the extreme right of the picture; Princess Louise's husband, Alexander, Duke of Fife (1849-1912) stands by her at the piano; and Prince George's wife, the future Queen Mary (1867-1953) sits between King Edward and Queen Alexandra.

The third generation is represented by the children of King George V and Queen Mary: Prince Albert (King George VI, 1895-1952) and Prince Edward (King Edward VIII, 1894-1972) stand at the extreme left; Prince John (1905-1919) sits on Princess Victoria's knee, watched by Prince George (later Duke of Kent, 1902-1942). Prince Henry (later Duke of Gloucester, 1900-1974) leans against King Edward VII, and Princess Mary (later Princess Royal and Countess of Harewood, 1897-1965) stands on the right holding her dog. Only Prince Olav of Norway and the two daughters of the Duke and Duchess of Fife are missing.

Above right. The youngest of King Edward VII and Queen Alexandra's children was Princess Maud; she married Prince Carl of Denmark (1872-1957) who was Queen Alexandra's nephew – a son of her brother King Frederick VIII of Denmark.

Prince Carl and Princess Maud had only one child, Prince Alexander, born in 1903. In 1905, Prince Carl was invited to

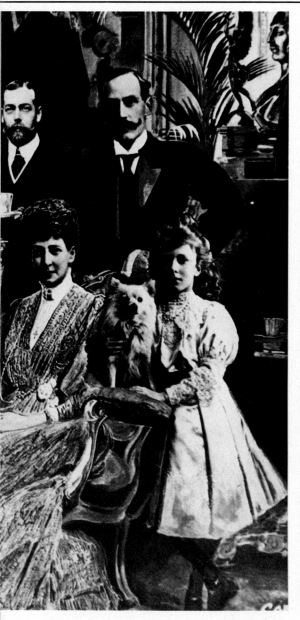

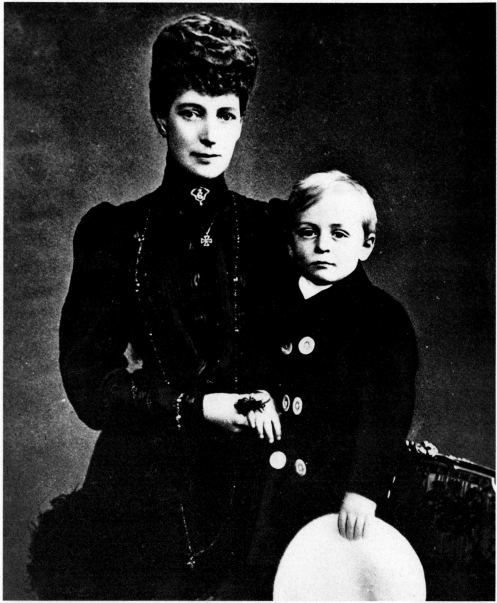

the throne of the newly independent kingdom of Norway, and was enthroned as King Haakon VII. Prince Alexander became Crown Prince Olav of Norway in consequence. In 1929 he married Princess Martha of Sweden (1901-1954) a granddaughter of King Oscar II of Sweden, during whose reign Sweden had ceded Norway its independence. They had three children. Princess Ragnhild (b. 1930), Princess Astrid (b. 1932) and Prince Harald (b. 1937), the present heir to the Norwegian throne. All three children married commoners.

The photograph was taken in 1906, and shows Prince Olav with his grandmother, Queen Alexandra.

Right. King Edward VII, aged 67.

Far right. A photograph of King Edward VII taken in 1896, when he was Prince of Wales.

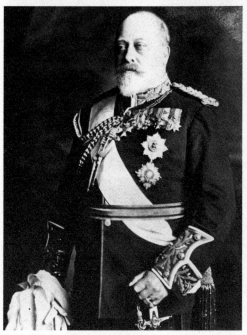

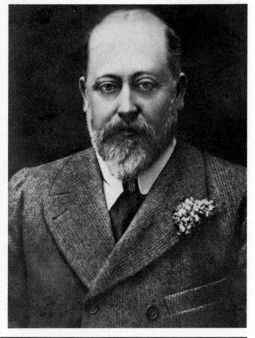

Great Britain

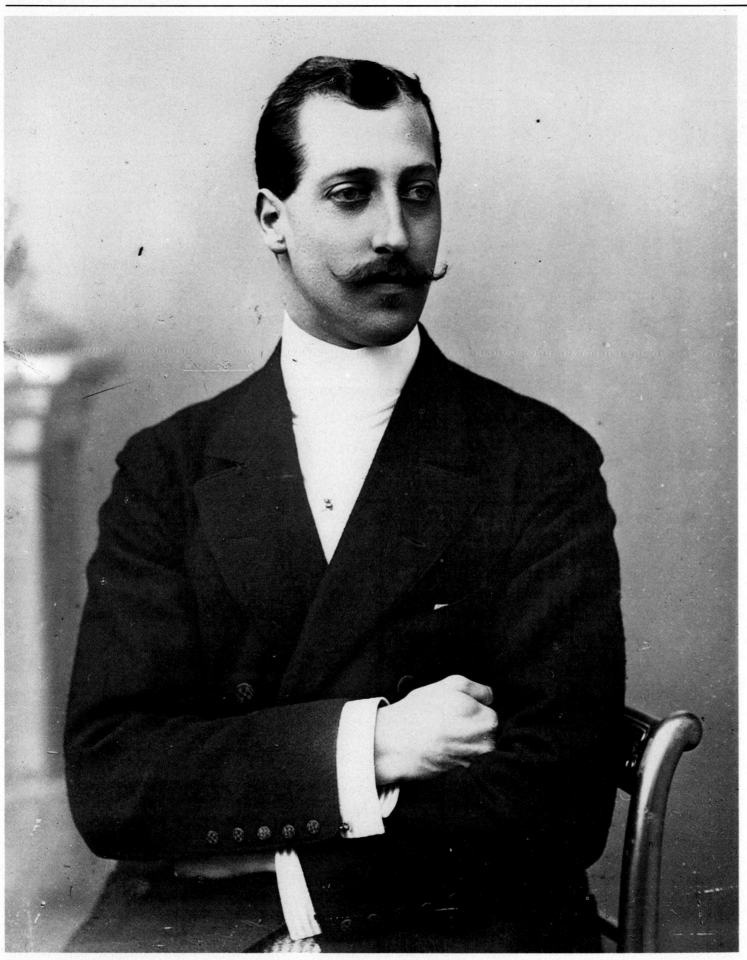

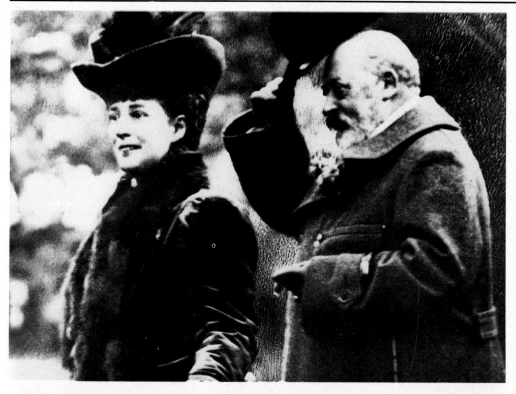

Prince Albert Victor of Wales

Prince Albert Victor, *opposite page, left*, was born in 1864, the eldest child of King Edward VII. He is photographed at the time of his engagement to Princess Victoria Mary of Teck (1867-1953) in 1891, a month before his death at the age of 28.

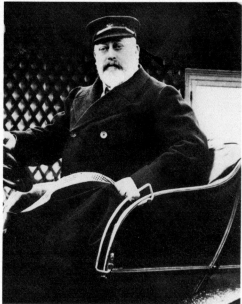

Above. A photograph of King Edward VII, probably taken at Abergeldie, in 1903.

Above left. This photograph was taken at the meet of the Norfolk Hunt at Gayton Hall on King Edward's sixty-seventh birthday: 9th November, 1908.

Left. Queen Alexandra with Queen Amelie of Portugal, photographed in November 1907, at Windsor. Queen Amelie (1865-1951), was formerly Princess Amelie of Bourbon-Orleans, a daughter of Prince Louis-Phillippe of Orleans and a great granddaughter of the last King of the French, Louis-Phillippe. In 1886 she married Prince (later King) Carlos of Portugal, who was assassinated in 1908, along with their eldest son.

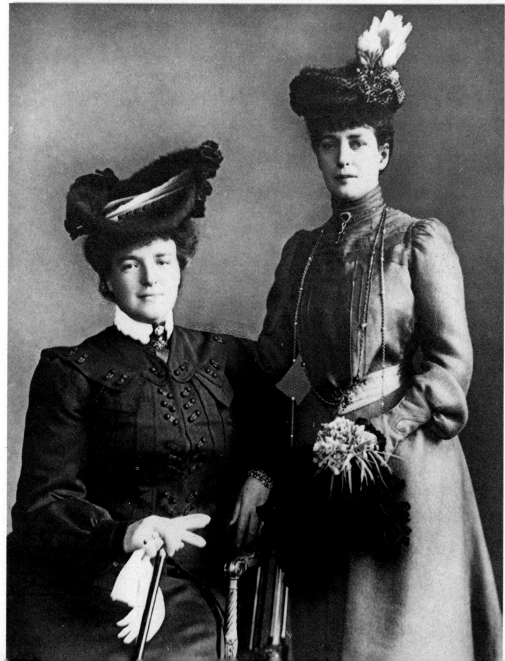

Overleaf. A photograph showing King Edward VII (sitting, front centre) with a shooting party at Crichel, Dorset, in 1909.

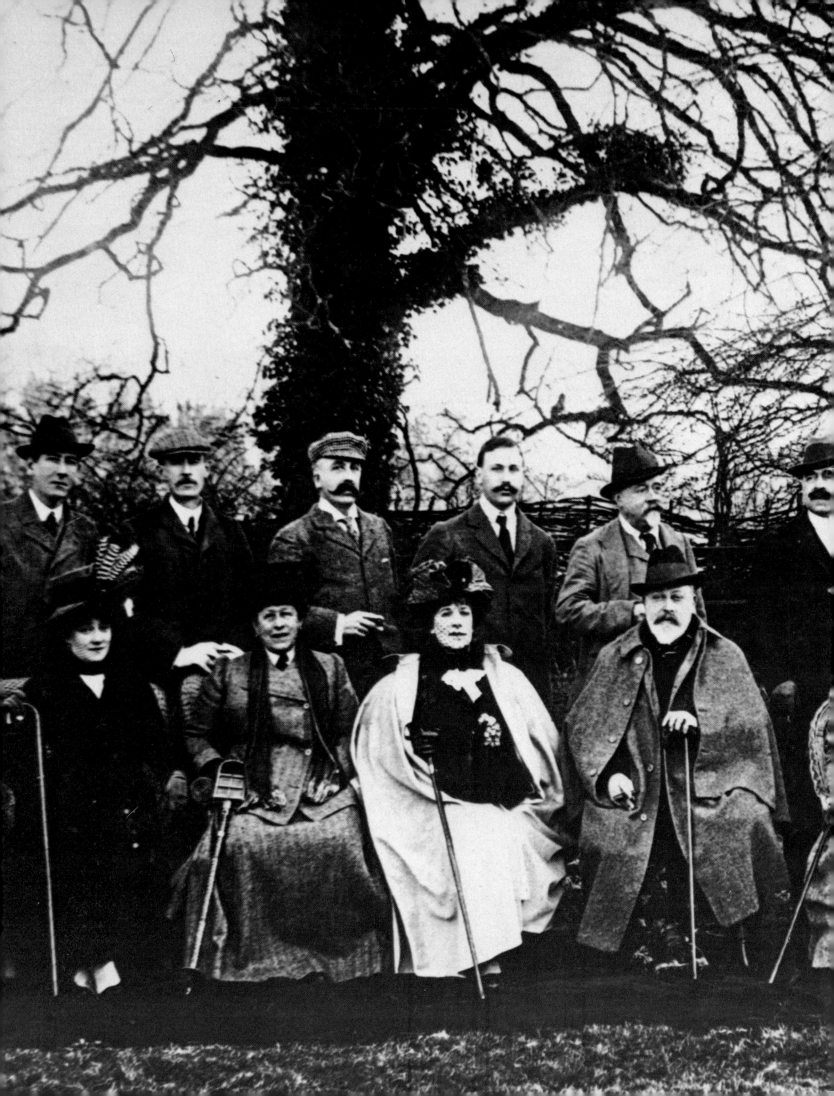

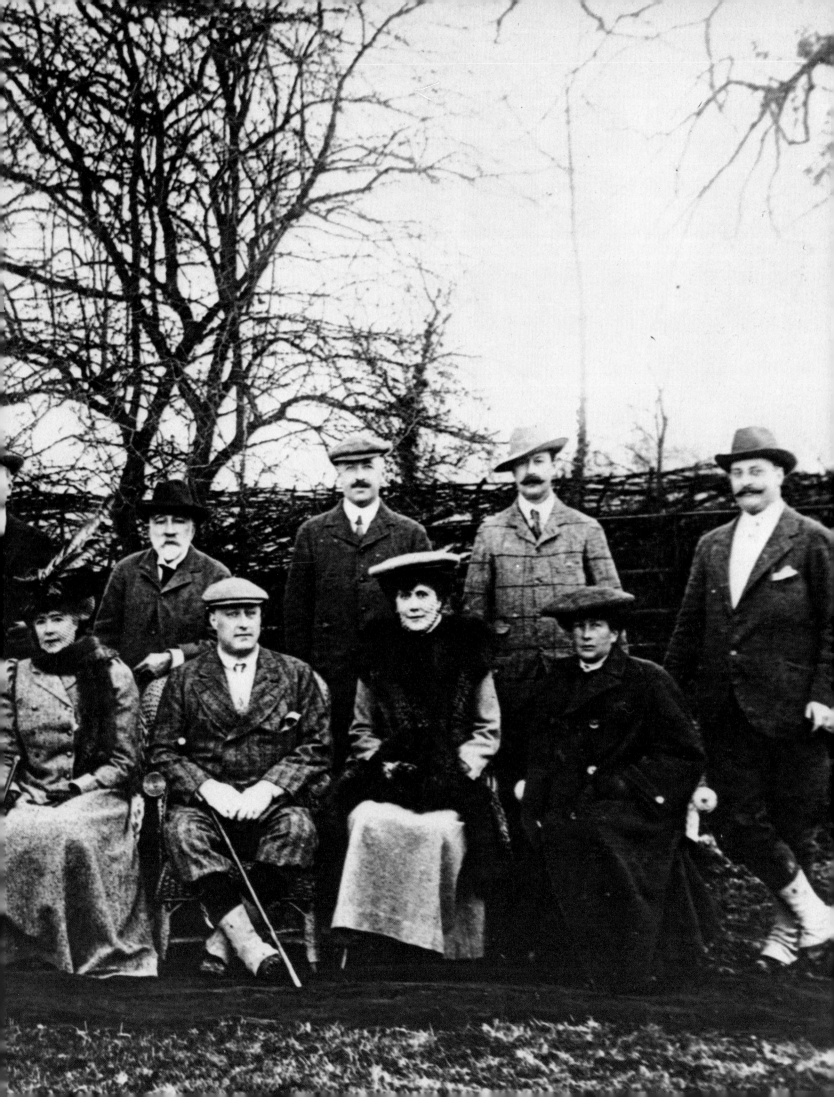

Great Britain

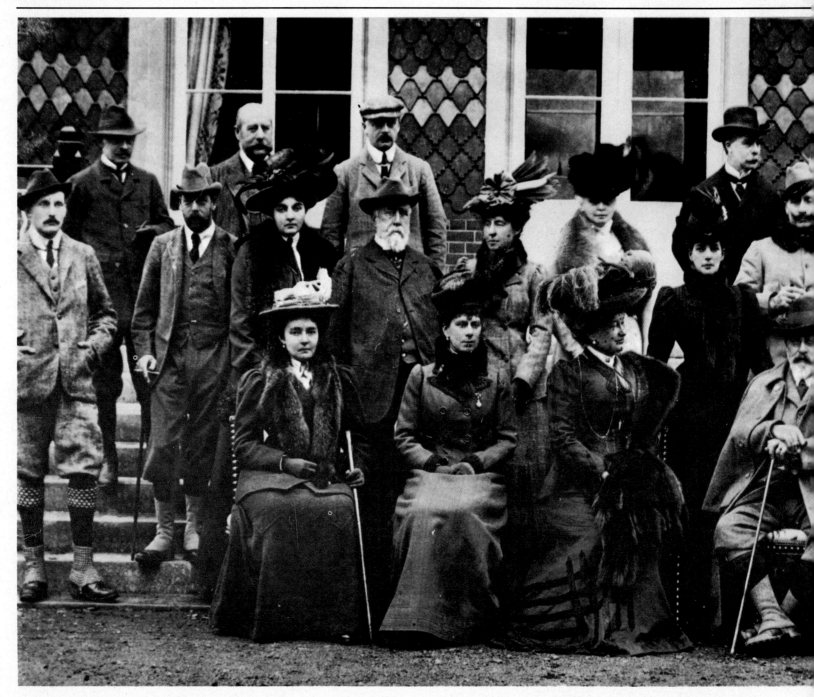

Above, King Edward VII with his family and guests at a shooting party at Holly Grove, Windsor, in 1904.

Standing (left to right).

Prince Arthur of Connaught (1883-1938).

Baron von Marschall, German diplomat.

Prince George, Prince of Wales (1865-1936), who succeeded as King George V in 1910.

Sir Walter Campbell, Deputy Ranger of Windsor Great Park, who lived at Holly Grove.

Princess Patricia of Connaught (1886-1974), sister of Prince Arthur.

Mr. Halsey.

Prince Christian of Schleswig-Holstein (1831-1917), husband of Princess Helena.

Countess von Keller.

Lady Alice Stanley.

Queen Alexandra (1844-1925).

Baron von dem Knesebeck.

Kaiser Wilhelm II of Germany (1859-1941). Eldest son of Emperor Frederick III of Germany and Victoria, Princess Royal (1840-1901), the eldest daughter of Queen Victoria. Married Princess Augusta of Schleswig-Holstein (1858-1921) in 1881.

Lady Landsdowne, wife of the then British Foreign Secretary.

Princess Victoria (1868-1935), second daughter of King Edward VII and Queen Alexandra.

The German Ambassador to England.

Colonel Henry Legge, Equerry to King Edward VII

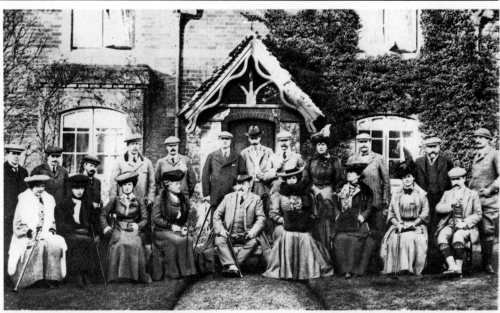

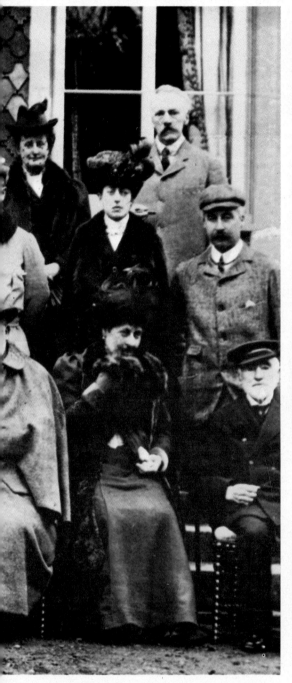

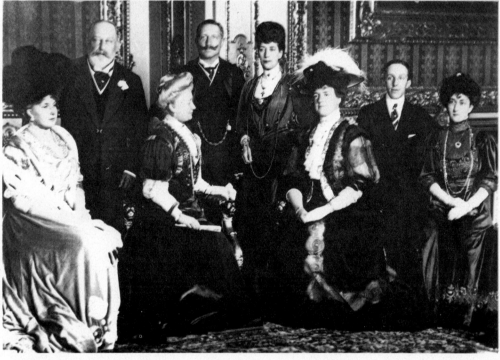

Seated in front

The Duchess of Connaught (1860-1917).

Princess Victoria Mary, Princess of Wales (1867-1953), later Queen Mary.

Empress Augusta of Germany (1858-1921), formerly Princess of Schleswig-Holstein, wife of Kaiser Wilhelm II.

King Edward VII (1841-1910).

Princess Louise (1867-1931), eldest daughter of King Edward VII and Queen Alexandra.

Captain Welch.

Above, right. A photograph showing King Edward VII (centre front) at a house party at Crichel, 1908.

Below, right. King Edward VII and Queen Alexandra with their Royal guests at Windsor, 17th November, 1907.

Left to right.

Queen Victoria Eugenie of Spain (1887-1969). Formerly Princess Victoria Eugenie of Battenberg, only daughter of Princess Beatrice (daughter of Queen Victoria and sister of King Edward VII) and Prince Henry of Battenberg.

King Edward VII.

Empress Augusta of Germany.

Kaiser Wilhelm II of Germany.

Queen Alexandra.

Queen Amelie of Portugal.

King Alfonso XIII of Spain (1886-1941). Only son of King Alfonso XII of Spain and Queen Maria-Christina.

Queen Maud of Norway (1869-1938).

Great Britain

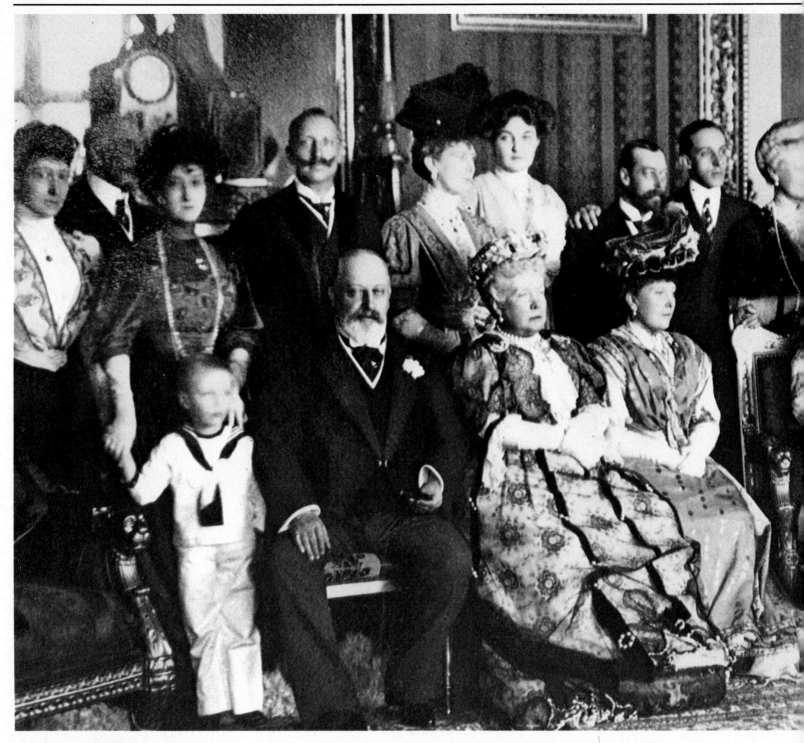

King Edward VII and Queen Alexandra with their Royal guests at Windsor; 17th November, 1907. They are:

King Edward VII, *seated extreme left:* and his wife . . .

Queen Alexandra, *standing sixth from right*. Then their second son . . .

George, Prince of Wales, later King George V, *standing seventh from left:* and his wife . . .

Victoria Mary, Princess of Wales, later Queen Mary, *standing fifth from left*.

Then King Edward's three daughters . . .

Louise, Princess Royal and Duchess of Fife (1867-1931), *standing extreme left:*

Princess Victoria, *standing second from right:*

Queen Maud of Norway, *standing third from left,* holding before her her son, Crown Prince Olav. Then . . .

Prince Arthur, Duke of Connaught, *standing second from left:* and his wife . . .

Princess Louise, Duchess of Connaught, *standing third from right*. Then their only son . . .

Prince Arthur of Connaught, *standing seventh from right:* and his sister . . .

Princess Victoria Patricia of Connaught, later Lady Patricia Ramsay, *standing sixth from left*.

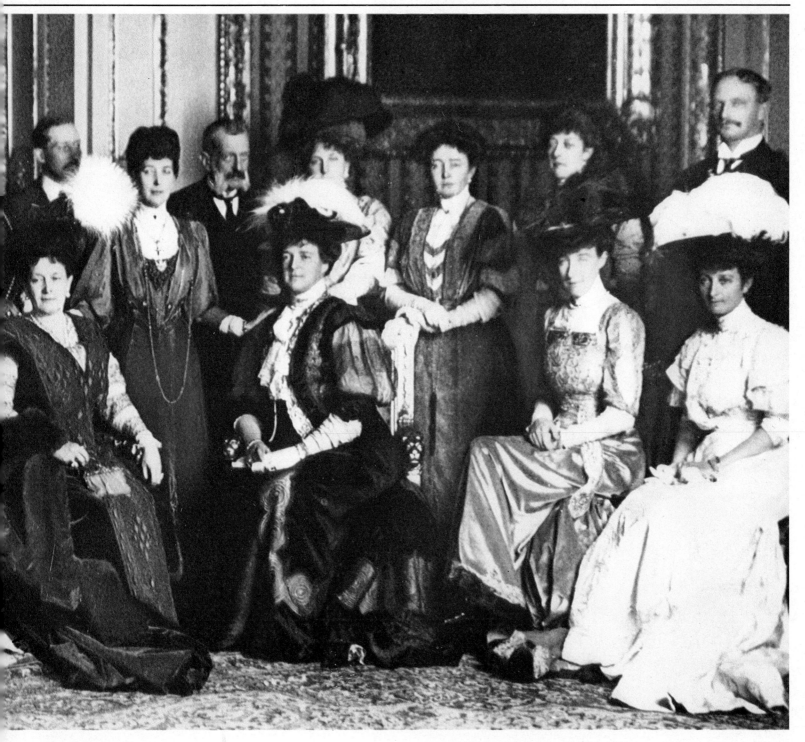

Then King Edward's sister . . .

Princess Henry of Battenberg, formerly Princess Beatrice, *standing third from left:* and her daughter . . .

Queen Victoria-Eugenie of Spain, *standing fourth from right:* and her husband . . .

King Alfonso XIII of Spain, *standing eighth from left:* and his aunt . . .

Infanta Isabella of Spain (1851-1931), *seated second from left.*

Then King Edward's nephew Kaiser Wilhelm II of Germany, *standing fourth from left:* and his wife . . .

Empress Augusta of Germany, *standing eighth from right.*

Grand Duke Vladimir of Russia (1847-1909), brother of Tsar Alexander III, *standing fifth from right:* and his wife . . .

Grand Duchess Vladimir (1854-1920), formerly Duchess Marie of Mecklenburg, *seated centre.*

Queen Amelie of Portugal, *seated third from right:* and her sister . . .

Princess Helene, Duchess of Aosta (1871-1951), *seated second from right.*

Prince Johann-Georg of Saxony (1869-1938), *standing extreme right:* and his second wife . . .

Princess Johann-Georg (1874-1947), formerly Princess Maria-Immaculata of Bourbon-Sicilies, *seated extreme right.*

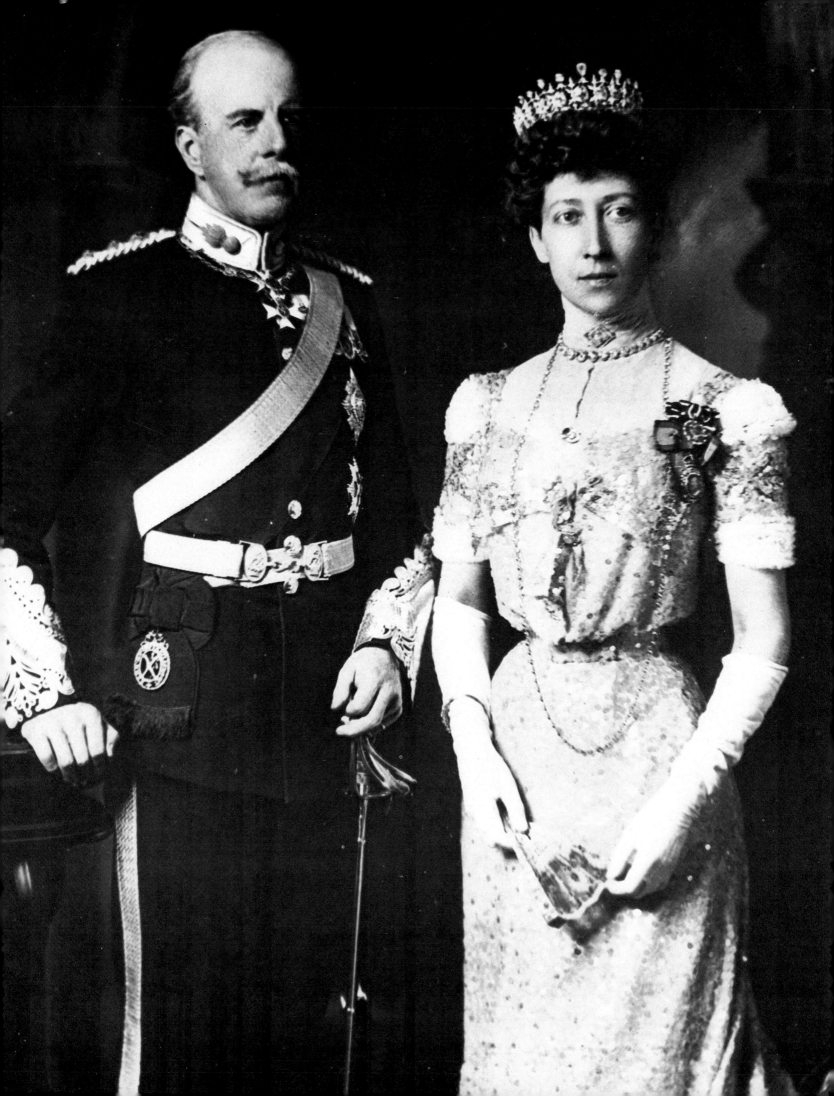

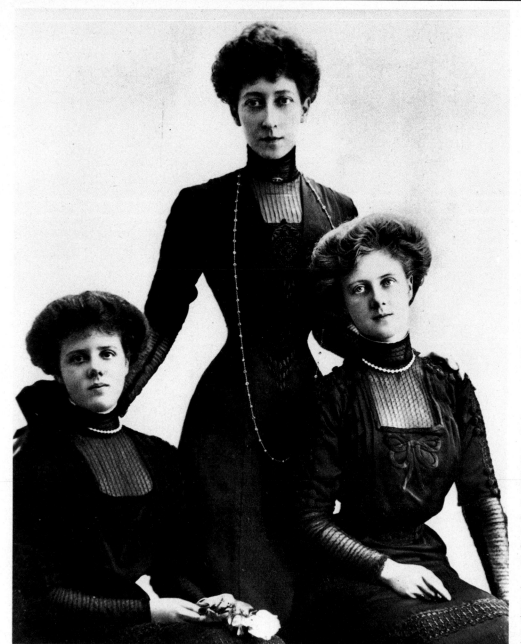

The Duke and Duchess of Fife

Opposite page, left. The Duke and Duchess of Fife. The Duke (1849-1912) was the only son of James, 5th Earl of Fife (1814-1879). Born in 1849, he was christened Alexander William George, and succeeded his father as 6th Earl in 1879. In 1889 he married Princess Louise of Wales and had two children. In 1899 Queen Victoria, his wife's grandmother, raised the Earldom of Fife to a Dukedom and he became the 1st Duke of Fife. By special remainder, his eldest daughter succeeded to the Dukedom on his death in 1912 and became Duchess of Fife in her own right.

The Duchess of Fife (1867-1931) was the eldest daughter of the then Prince and Princess of Wales (later King Edward VII and Queen Alexandra). She was created Princess Royal in 1905, as eldest daughter of the Sovereign and bore this title until her death in 1931.

The photograph was taken about 1911.

Above left. Louise, the Princess Royal (standing) with her two children.

Her elder daughter, Princess Alexandra (seated, right), was born in 1891 and on the death of her father in 1912, inherited the title Duchess of Fife in her own right. In 1913 she married her first cousin once removed Prince Arthur of Connaught (1883-1938) and had one child, Alistair, Earl of Macduff (1914-1943).

Princess Maud of Fife (seated, left), was the younger child of the Princess Royal. She was born in 1893 and married the 11th Earl of Southesk (b. 1893) in 1923. Princess Maud died in 1945, and the Earl of Southesk, who is still living, remarried. Their only child, James, Lord Carnegie, was born in 1929.

This photograph was taken early in 1912, the three Princesses in heavy mourning after the death of the Duke of Fife in Egypt in January 1912.

Far left. The 6th Earl of Fife: a photograph probably taken at the time of his engagement to Princess Louise early in 1889.

Left. The elder daughter of the 6th Earl of Fife, Princess Alexandra, who inherited her father's title. The photograph was taken in 1907.

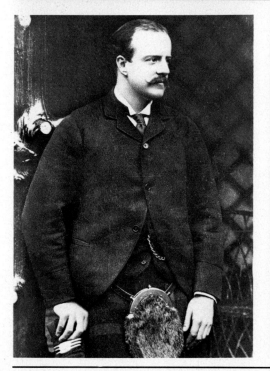

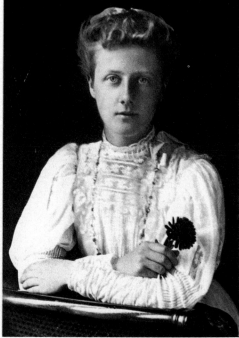

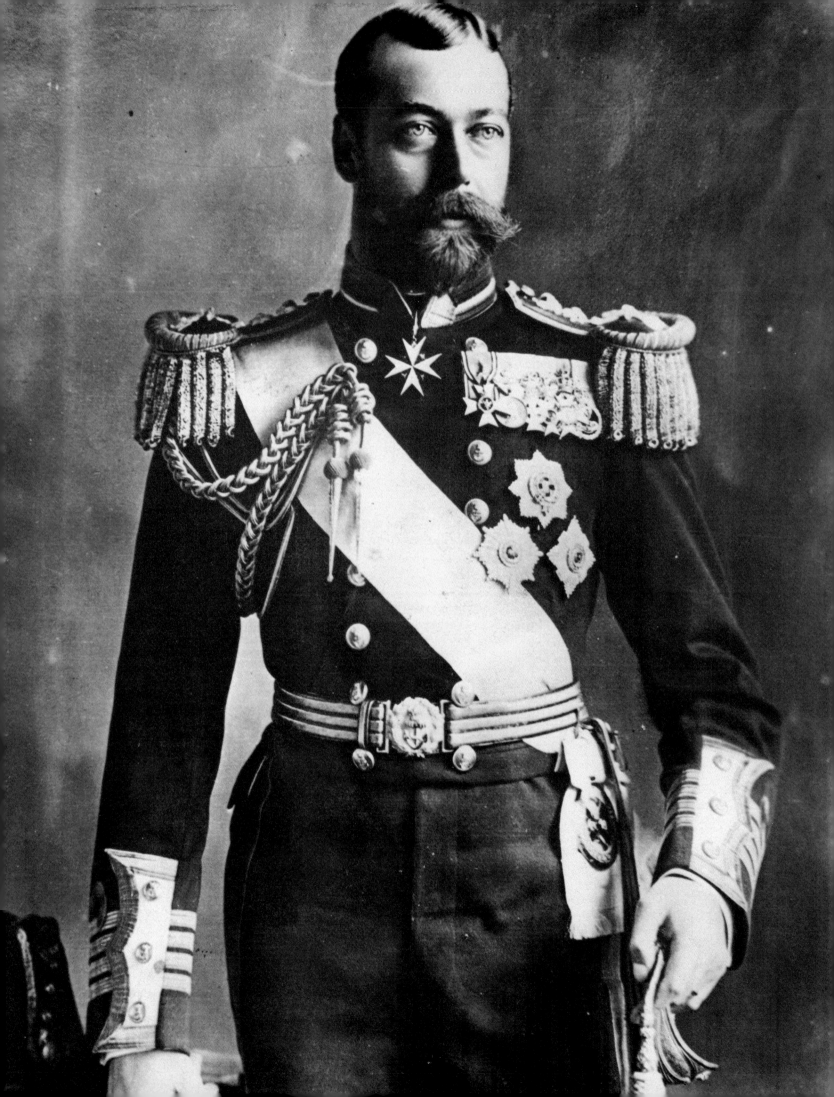

King George V and Queen Mary

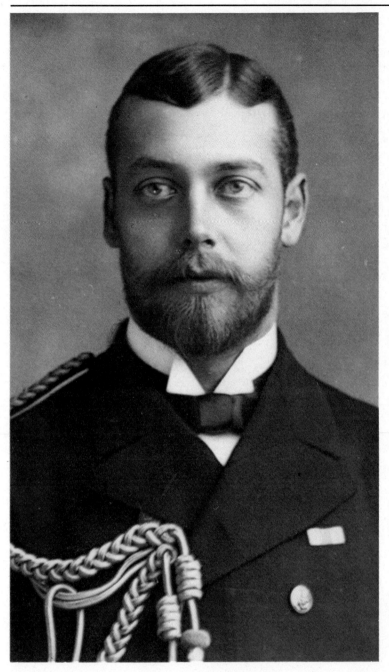

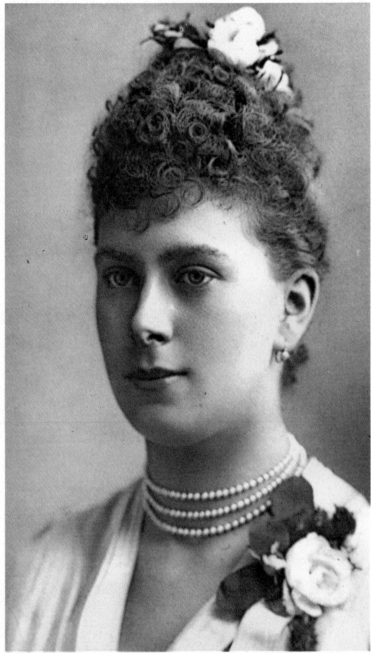

King George V (*above left,* aged 25; and *left,* aged 27) was born Prince George of Wales in 1865, the second son of Albert Edward, Prince of Wales – later King Edward VII – and the Princess of Wales – later Queen Alexandra.

When his elder brother, Prince Albert Victor, Duke of Clarence, died in 1892, Prince George became direct heir, after his father, to the throne of England which was then occupied by Queen Victoria (1819-1901). He was created Duke of York that year, and in 1893 married his second cousin once removed, Princess Victoria Mary of Teck (1867-1953).

They had six children, of whom the first two became kings: these were Edward VIII (1894-1972) and George VI (1895-1952). The remaining four were Princess Victoria Mary (1897-1965) who married the 6th Earl of Harewood (1882-1947); Prince Henry, Duke of Gloucester (1900-1974); Prince George, Duke of Kent (1902-1942), and Prince John (1905-1919).

King George V came to the throne on the death of his father in 1910 (having been created Prince of Wales during his father's reign), and died in 1936.

Queen Mary, *above right,* was born in 1867, as Princess Victoria Mary, daughter of Franz, Duke of Teck (kingdom of Wurttemberg) (1837-1900) and of his wife, the former Princess Mary Adelaide of Cambridge (1833-1897) who was a granddaughter of King George III of England and thus a cousin of Queen Victoria. Queen Mary was thus sister to the Earl of Athlone (1874-1957) husband of Queen Victoria's granddaughter, Princess Alice of Albany (1883-1981).

In 1901, she became Princess of Wales, and in 1910 Queen Mary, on her husband's accession as King George V. She continued to be known as Queen Mary throughout her seventeen-year widowhood, which ended with her death in 1953, the second year of the reign of her granddaughter Queen Elizabeth II.

Great Britain

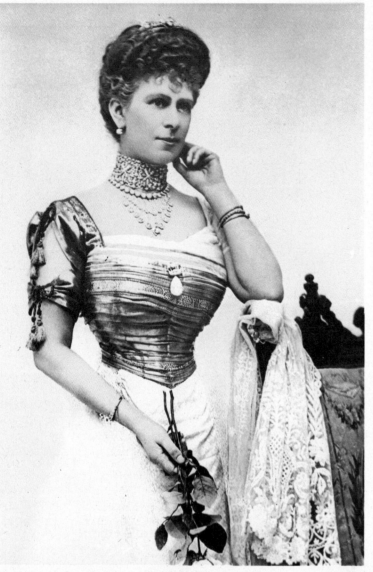

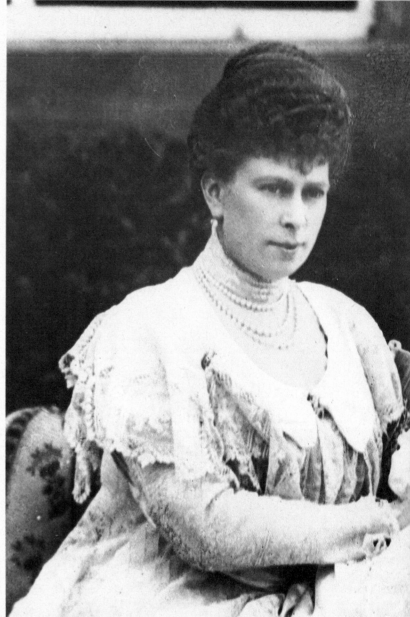

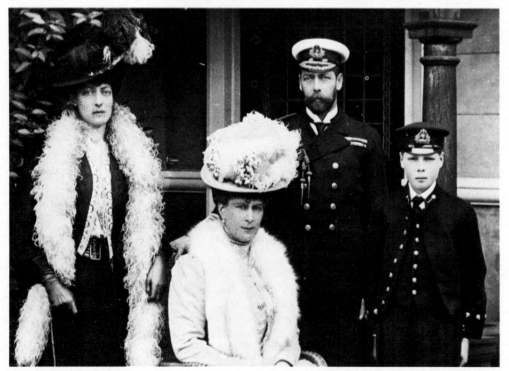

Above, left. A photograph of Queen Mary taken when she was Princess of Wales, in 1906.

Above. Of the six children of King George V and Queen Mary the youngest was Prince John. He was born in 1905. Being frequently ill and subject in particular to epileptic attacks, he was segregated in his early teens from his family and was looked after by his nurse at Wolferton, on the Sandringham Estate. He died in his sleep, at the age of 13, in January 1919.

Opposite page, top. A photograph of Queen Mary taken when she was Princess of Wales, in 1902.

Left. George, Prince of Wales, with the Princess of Wales and their eldest son Edward (who succeeded to the throne in 1936, and abdicated in the same year

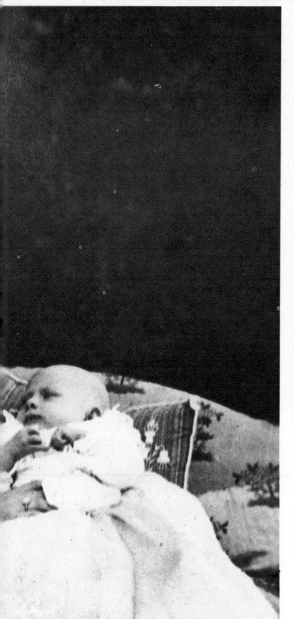

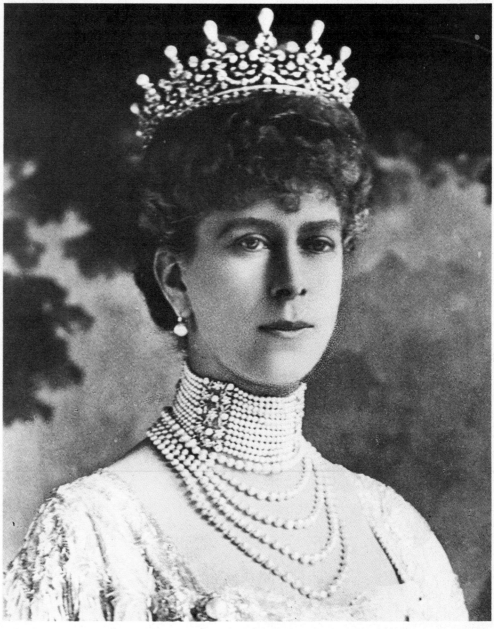

owing to the constitutional difficulties posed by his intended marriage to Mrs Wallis Simpson). The fourth member of the group Princess Victoria (1868-1935), the Prince of Wales' second sister. The photograph was taken in 1907.

Right. George, Prince of Wales with his four eldest children, (left to right): Prince Albert, Princess Mary, Prince Edward, and Prince Henry. This photograph was taken at Sandringham early in 1902, shortly after the return of the Prince and Princess of Wales from their Dominion Tour of 1901-2.

Overleaf. King George and Queen Mary in Coronation Robes, on their Coronation Day, 22nd June, 1911.

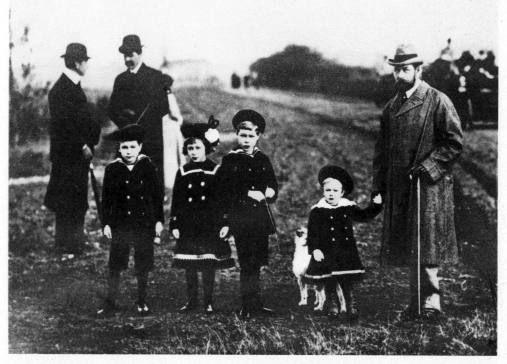

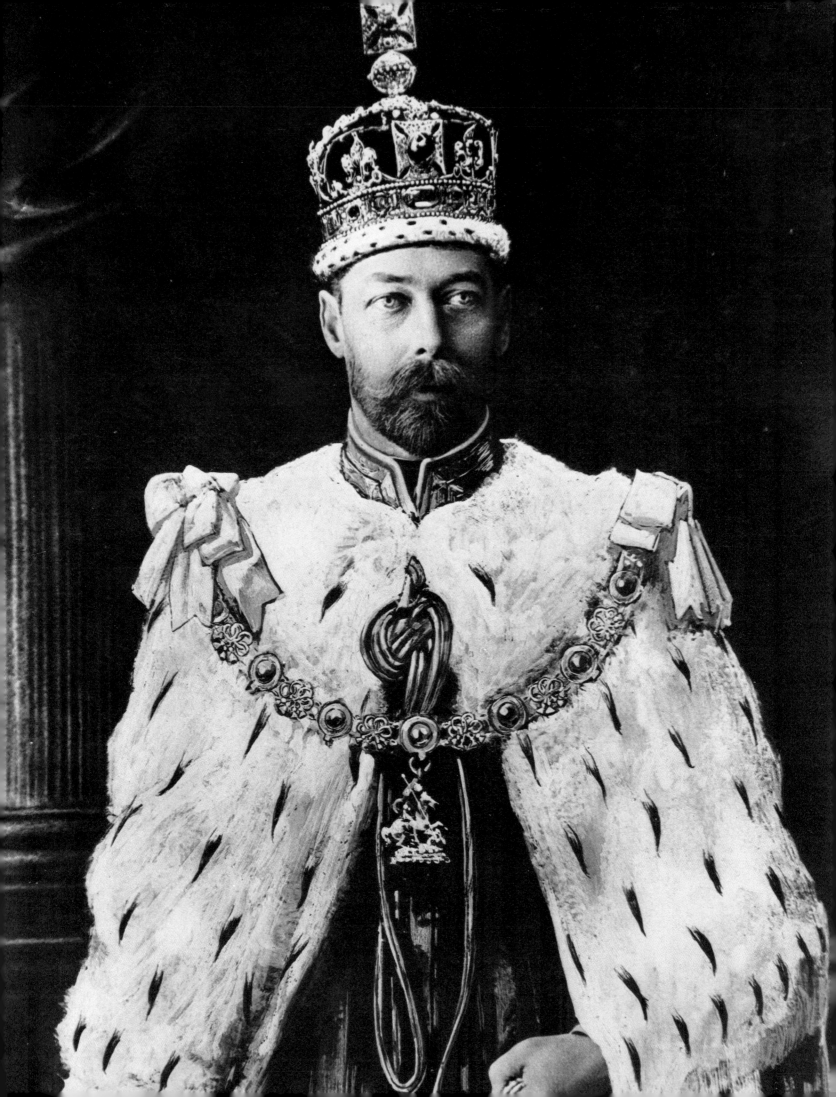

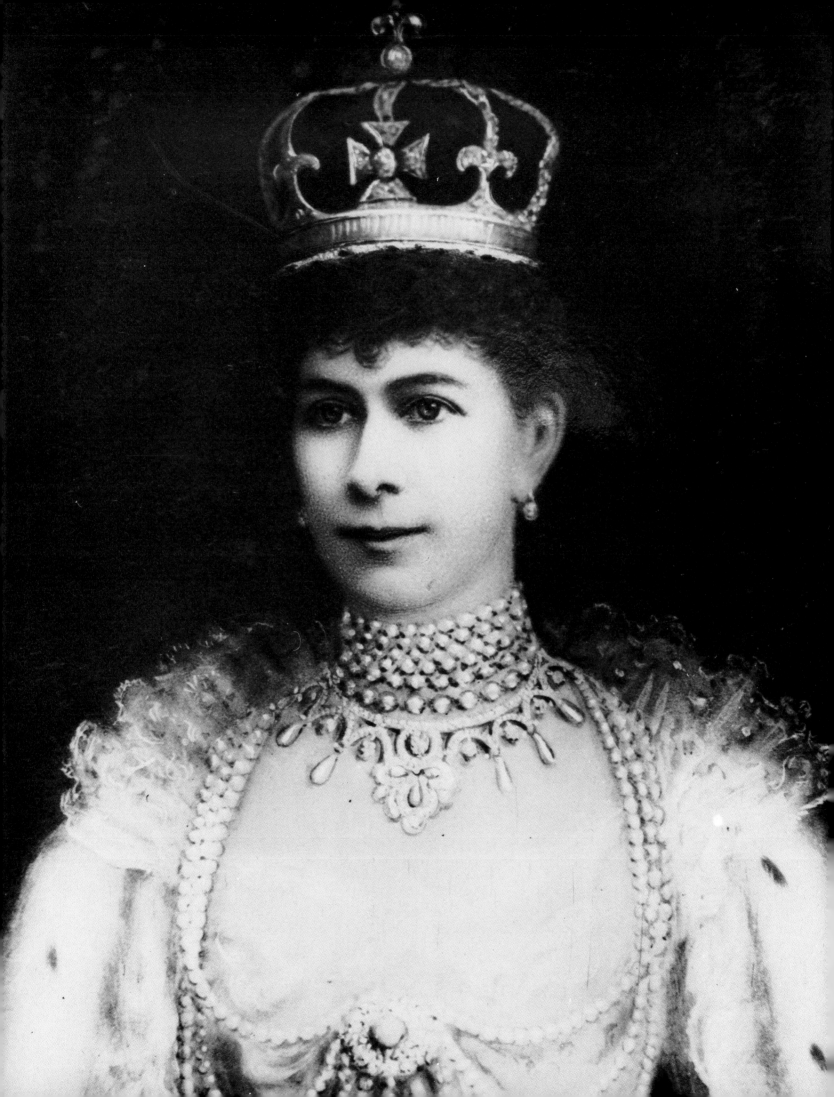

Great Britain

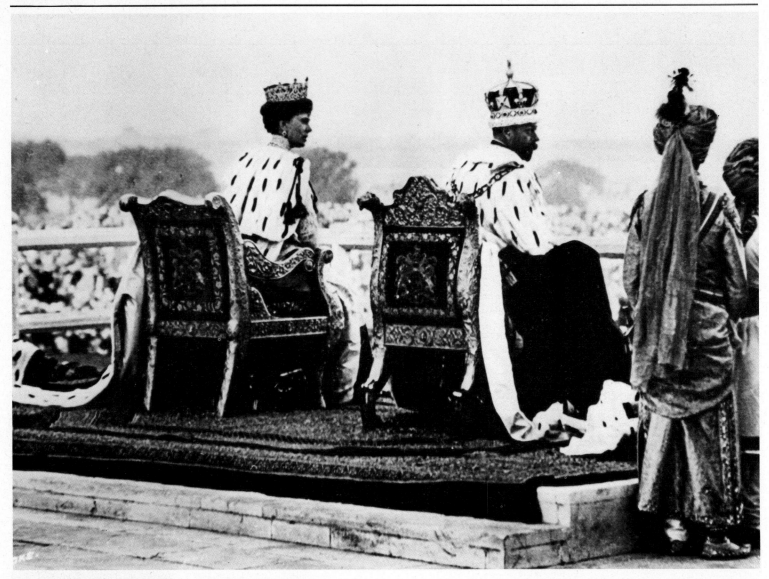

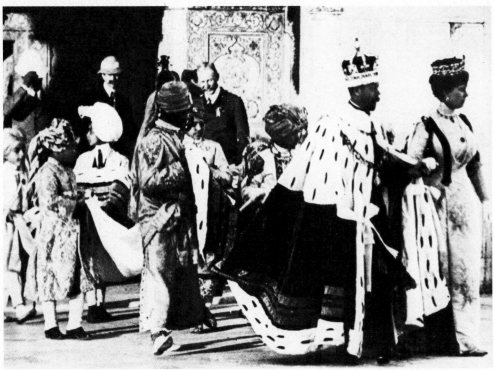

Above, and left. Two photographs taken of the Durbar ceremony during which King George V and Queen Mary were enthroned as Emperor and Empress of India, at Delhi on 12th December, 1911.

Opposite page, right. King George V with Tsar Nicholas II of Russia (1868-1918), the eldest son of Tsar Alexander III of Russia (1845-1894) and his wife, the Empress Marie (1847-1928) who was the sister of King George V's mother, Queen Alexandra. Shortly after his accession in 1894, Tsar Nicholas married Princess Alexandra of Hesse (1872-1918), a daughter of King Edward VII's sister Princess Alice (1843-1878) and the Grand Duke Louis IV of Hesse. They had five children: four daughters and a son.

This photograph of the cousins was taken at Berlin, when they met at the wedding of the only daughter of Kaiser Wilhelm II, Princess Victoria Louise (1892-1980) to the Duke of Brunswick and Luneburg on the 24th May 1913.

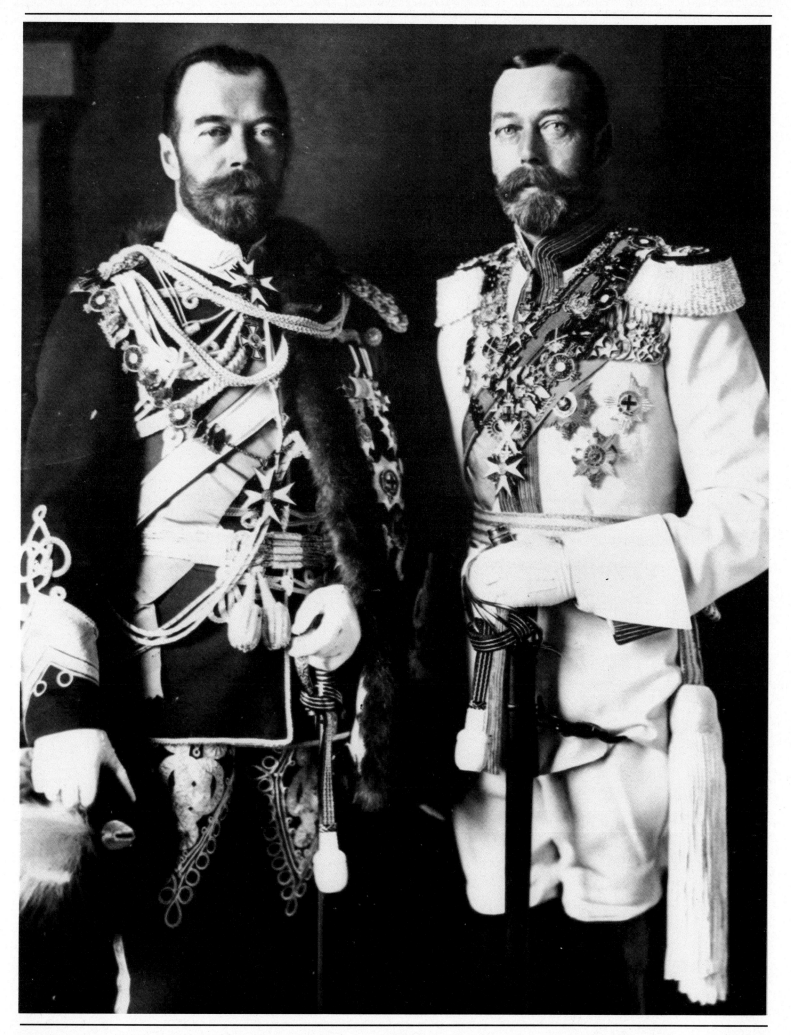

Great Britain

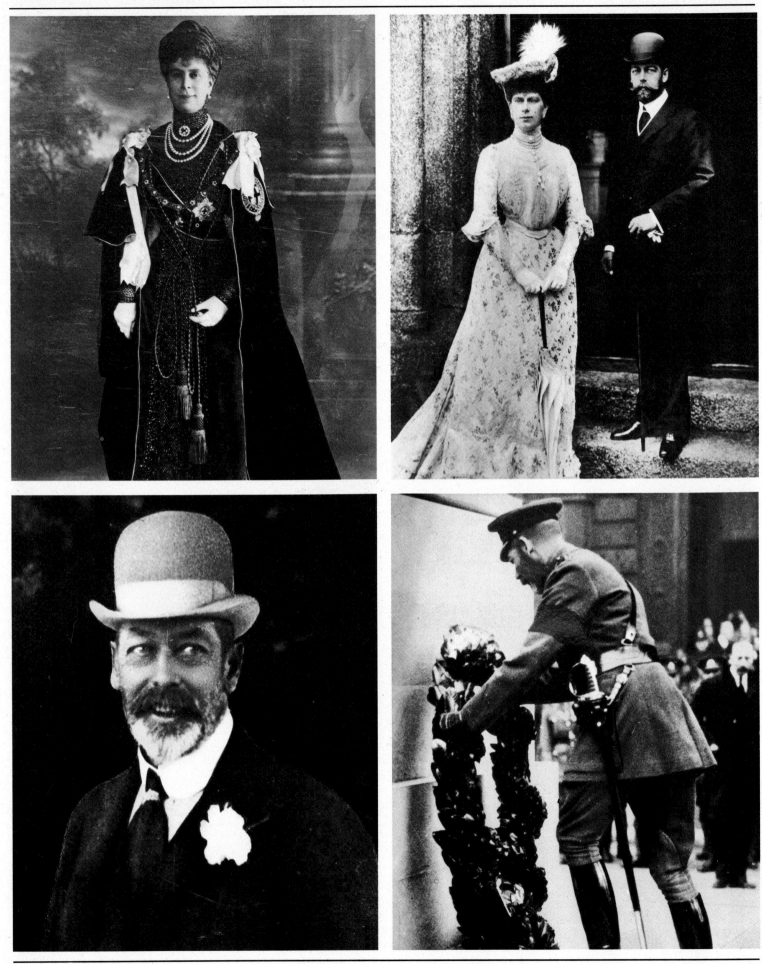

King George V and Queen Mary

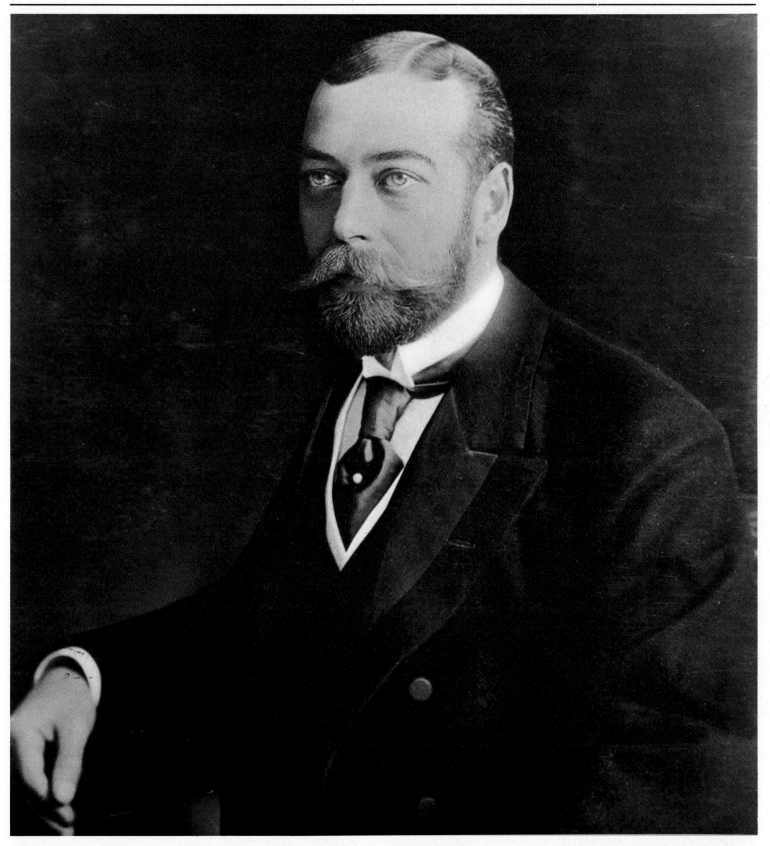

Opposite page, top left. Queen Mary in the robes of a Lady of the Garter, to which Order she was admitted in 1910.

Opposite page, top right. A photograph taken in 1903, whilst King George V and Queen Mary were Prince and Princess of Wales.

Opposite page, lower left. King George V in 1924.

Opposite page, lower right. King George V placing a wreath on the Cenotaph after its unveiling on the first Armistice Anniversary: Whitehall, London; 11th November, 1919.

Above. A photograph of King George V, taken in 1900, when he was Duke of York.

Great Britain

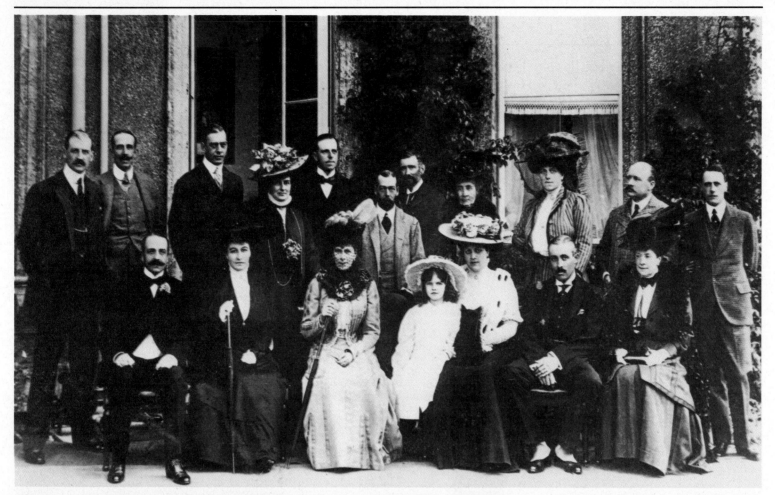

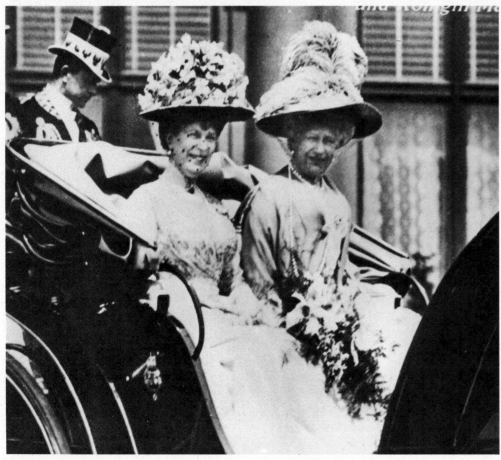

Above. This photograph, showing King George V at the very centre of the group (in the dark cravat tie) and Queen Mary sitting third from left, was taken at a house party at St Giles in about 1912.

Left. Queen Mary with the Empress Augusta of Germany (1858-1921), on the 21st May, 1913 after the arrival of Queen Mary (with King George V) at Berlin for the marriage of Princess Victoria Louise to the Duke of Brunswick and Luneburg.

Opposite page, right, King George V riding to the ceremony of Trooping the Colour at Horse Guards Parade, London, on 4th June, 1933.

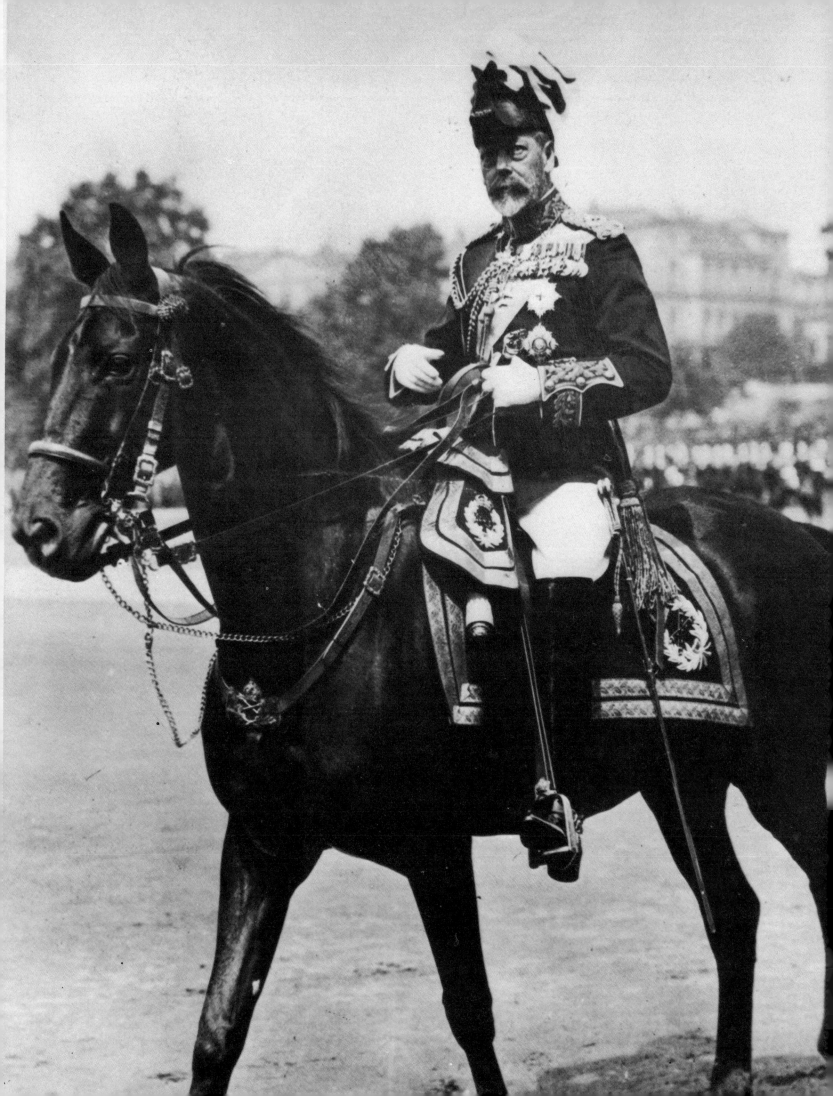

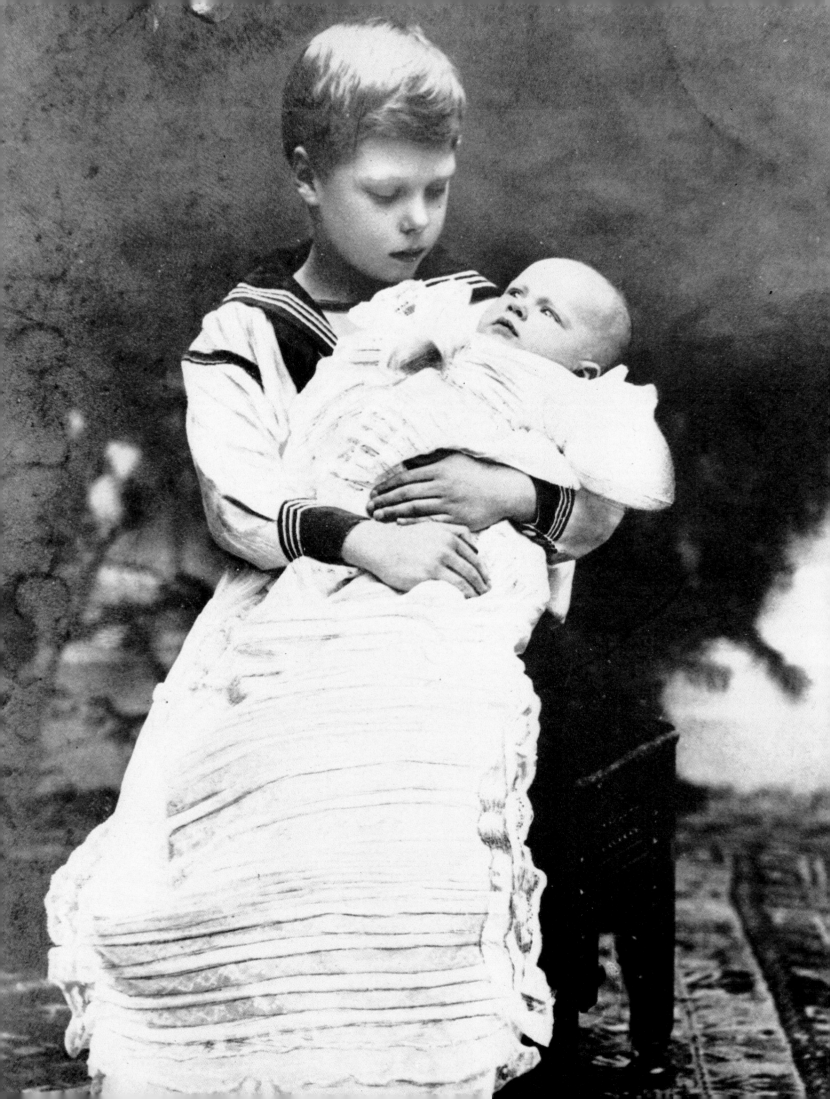

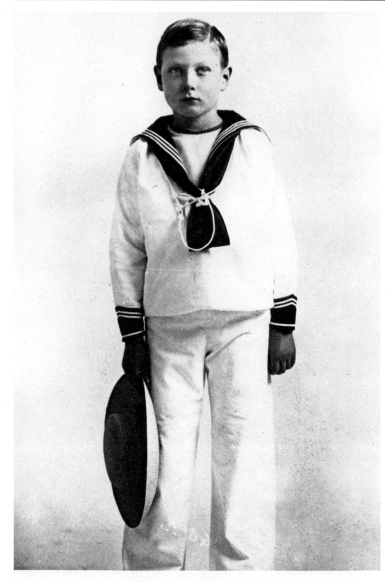

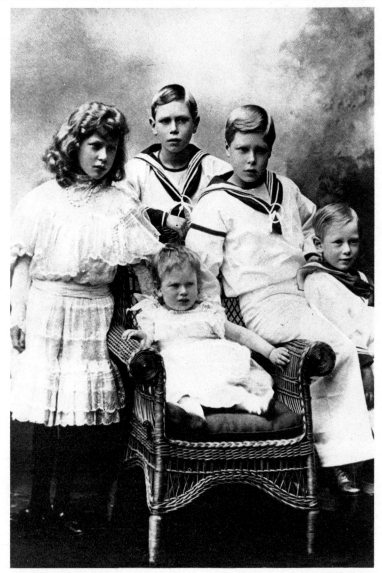

King George V and his wife, Queen Mary, had six children; of whom the first two, Prince Edward and Prince Albert, became Kings.

Prince Edward (1894-1972) – *opposite* holding his baby brother George in 1903 – was the eldest son and heir, and succeeded to the throne on the death of his father in 1936. Following his abdication in December of that year he was created Duke of Windsor in 1937, the year he married Mrs. Wallis Simpson (b. 1896).

Prince Albert, the second child, was born in 1895 and was created Duke of York in 1920. In 1923 he married Lady Elizabeth Bowes-Lyon (b. 1900), youngest daughter of the 14th Earl of Strathmore and Kinghorne, and who is the present Queen Mother. Their children are the present Queen Elizabeth II (b. 1926) and Princess Margaret (b. 1930). Prince Albert succeeded to the throne as King George VI on the abdication of his brother King Edward VIII in 1936, and died in 1952.

Princess Victoria Mary, the third child, was born in 1897. In 1922 she married Henry, Viscount Lascelles (1882-1947), elder son of the 5th Earl of Harewood, and had two children; George, the present (7th) Earl, born in 1923, and Gerald, born in 1924.

Princess Victoria Mary was created Princess Royal in 1932.

Prince Henry (1900-1974) was the fourth child. Created Duke of Gloucester in 1928, he married Lady Alice Montagu-Douglas-Scott, (b. 1901), third daughter of the 7th Duke of Buccleuch, in 1935. He had two sons, Prince William, (1941-1972) and Prince Richard, the present Duke of Gloucester.

Prince George (1902-1942), the fifth child, was created Duke of Kent in 1934. In that year he married Princess Marina (1906-1968), daughter of Prince Nicholas of Greece (1872-1938) and his wife, formerly Grand Duchess Helen of Russia. Their three children are Prince Edward (b. 1935) Princess Alexandra (b. 1936) and Prince Michael (b. 1942).

Prince John (1905-1919) – *above left,* in about 1913.

Above, right. The five eldest children of the then Prince and Princess of Wales. They are (left to right): Princess Victoria Mary, Prince Albert, Prince George (seated) Prince Edward, and Prince Henry.

Great Britain

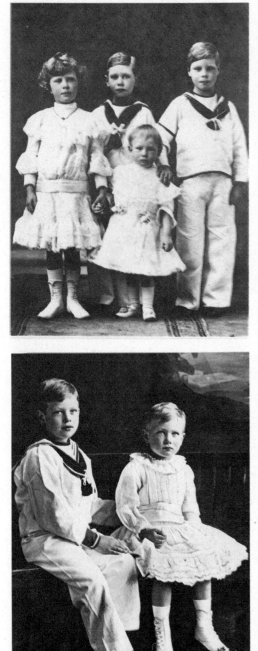

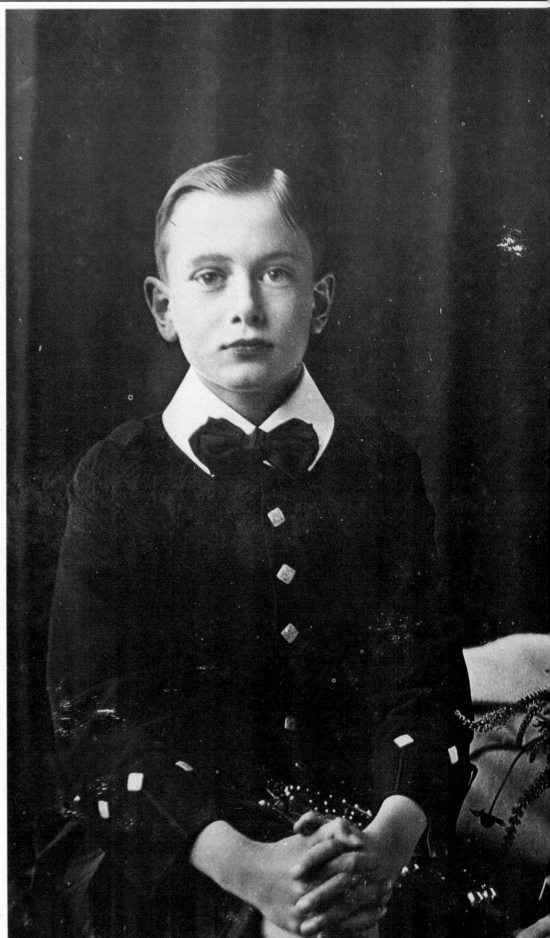

Above, top. Princess Victoria Mary, Prince Albert, Prince Henry and Prince Edward – the four eldest children of King George V and Queen Mary – in 1905.

Above. A photograph taken by Speaight in about 1909, showing Prince George and Prince John.

Right. Prince Henry, Princess Victoria Mary, Prince John and Prince George – the four youngest children of King George V – photographed in 1910 by Lafayette.

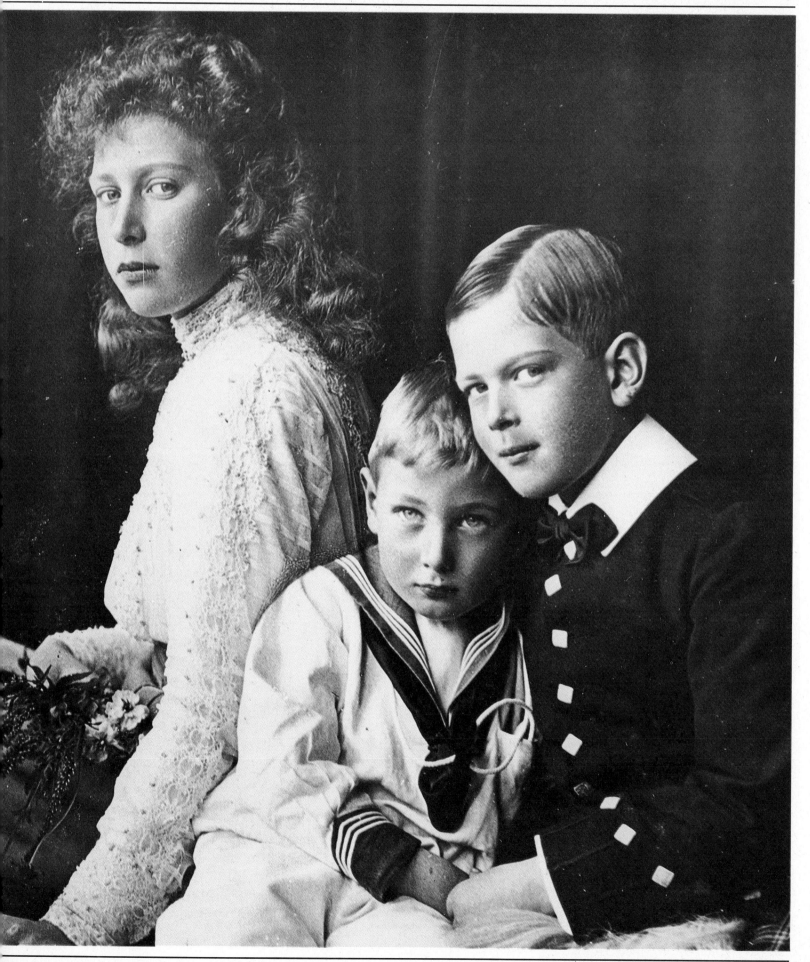

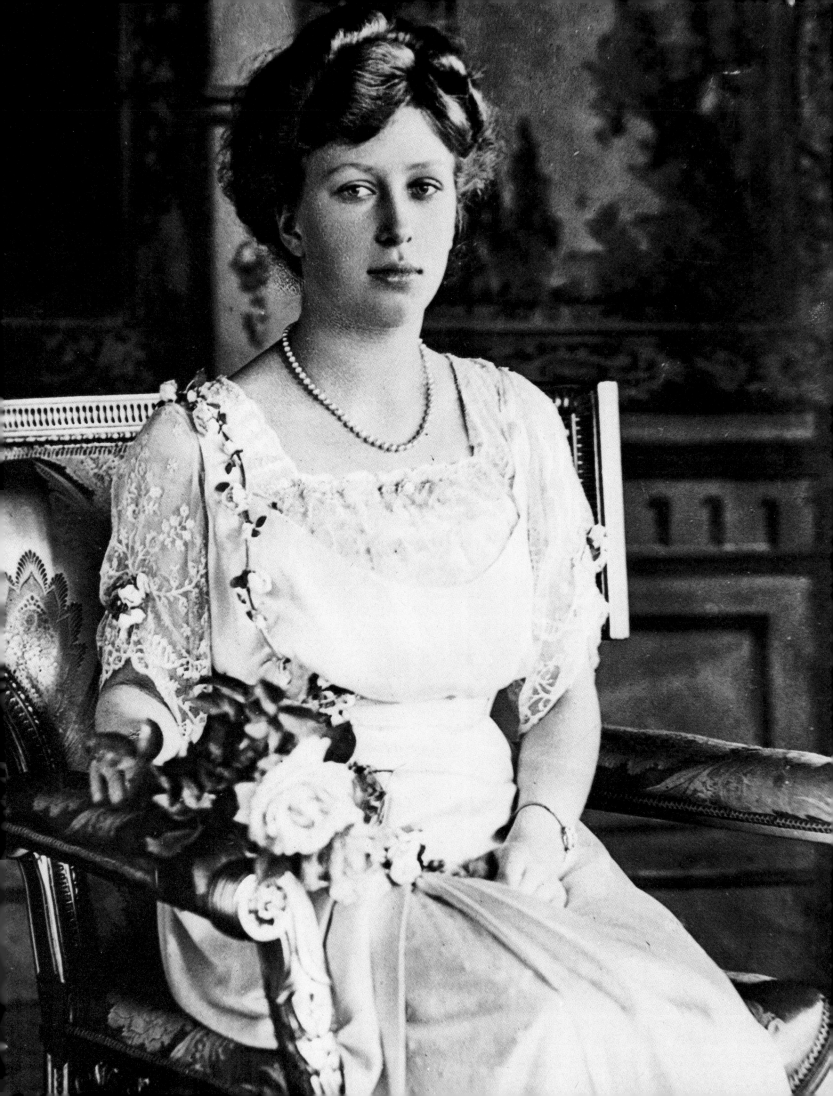

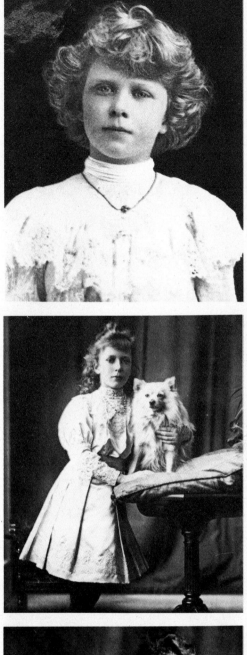

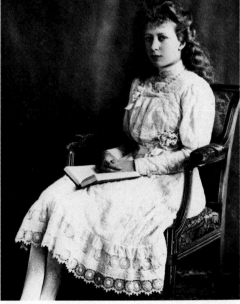

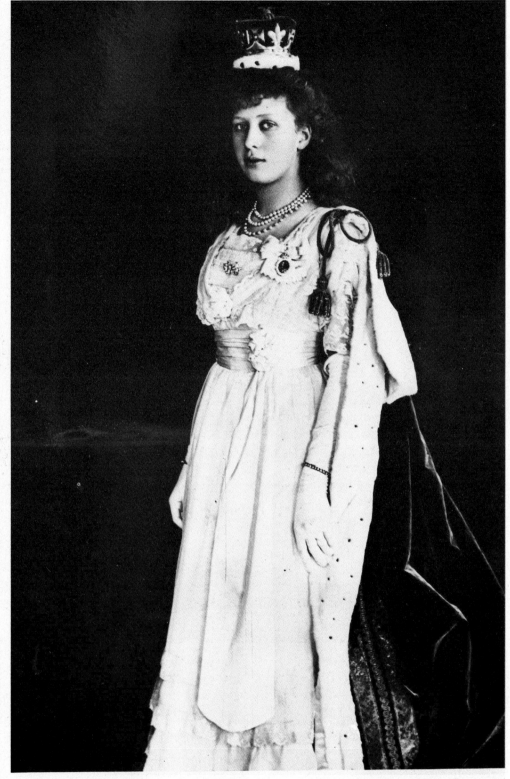

Princess Mary (1897-1965), King George V's only daughter, was formerly known as Princess Victoria Mary of York. She became Princess Victoria Mary of Wales when her father became Prince of Wales in 1901 and was later known simply as Princess Mary.

Left, top. A photograph taken in 1902.

Left, middle. Princess Mary in 1906.

Left. A photograph taken in about 1910.

Above. Princess Mary in the robes she wore at the Coronation of her parents.

Opposite page, left. A photograph of her taken in 1914.

Great Britain

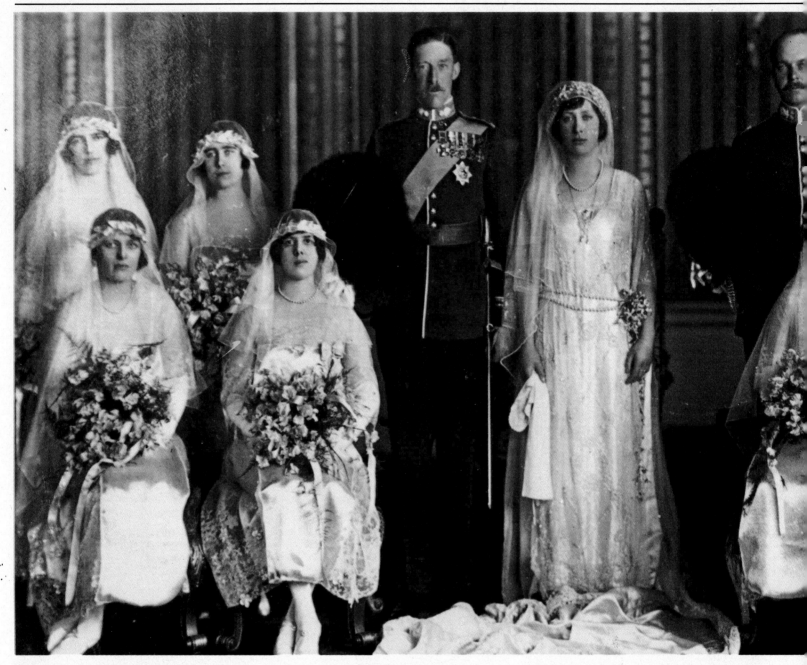

In 1922 Princess Mary married Henry, Viscount Lascelles (1882-1947), the elder son of the 5th Earl and Countess of Harewood, who succeeded to the title as 6th Earl in 1929. Princess Mary was therefore successively Viscountess Lascelles and the Countess of Harewood, and in 1932 she was created Princess Royal, a title held since 1905 by the eldest daughter of King Edward VII, Princess Louise (1867-1931).

Above. The wedding group of Princess Mary and Viscount Lascelles, taken by Vandyk on 28th February, 1922. The group consists of (left to right):

Lady Doris Gordon-Lennox (b. 1896), daughter of the 8th Duke of Richmond;

Lady Mary Cambridge (b. 1897), formerly Princess Victoria of Teck, daughter of the 2nd Duke of Teck (a brother of Queen Mary), and future Duchess of Beaufort.

Lady Elizabeth Bowes-Lyon (b. 1900), daughter of the 14th Earl of Strathmore and Kinghorne. Married Prince Albert, Duke of York (King George VI) in 1923; now the Queen Mother.

Princess Maud of Fife (1893-1935),

younger daughter of Edward VII's eldest daughter Louise, Princess Royal (1867-1931) and the Duke of Fife (1849-1921).

Viscount Lascelles.

Princess Mary.

Major Sir Victor Mackenzie, best man.

Lady Rachel Cavendish (b. 1902) daughter of the 9th Duke of Devonshire.

Lady Diana Bridgeman (b. 1907); eldest daughter of the 5th Earl of Bradford, and niece of Viscount Lascelles.

Lady Mary Thynne (b. 1895), daughter of the 5th Marquess of Bath.

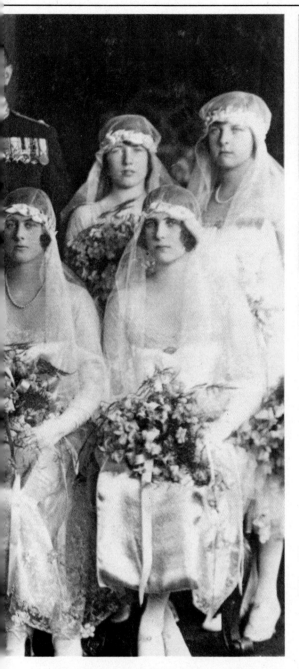

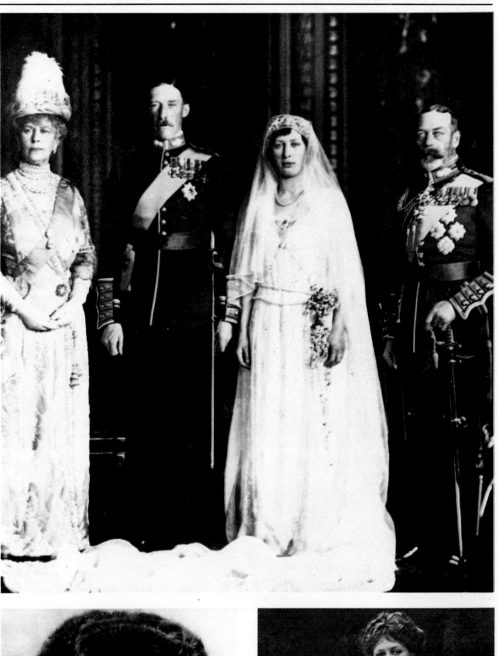

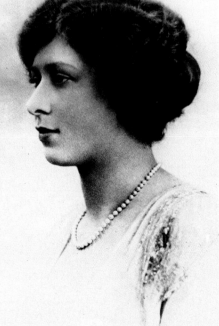

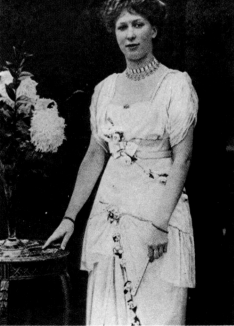

Lady Mary Cambridge (b. 1906) only daughter of the 1st Earl of Athlone, formerly Prince Alexander of Teck (1874-1957) whose sister Queen Mary was the bride's mother.

Right, top. Queen Mary, Viscount Lascelles, his bride Princess Mary, and King George V at Buckingham Palace after the wedding on 28th February, 1922.

Right. A photograph of Princess Mary, taken in about 1921.

Far right. Princess Mary aged about 18.

Great Britain

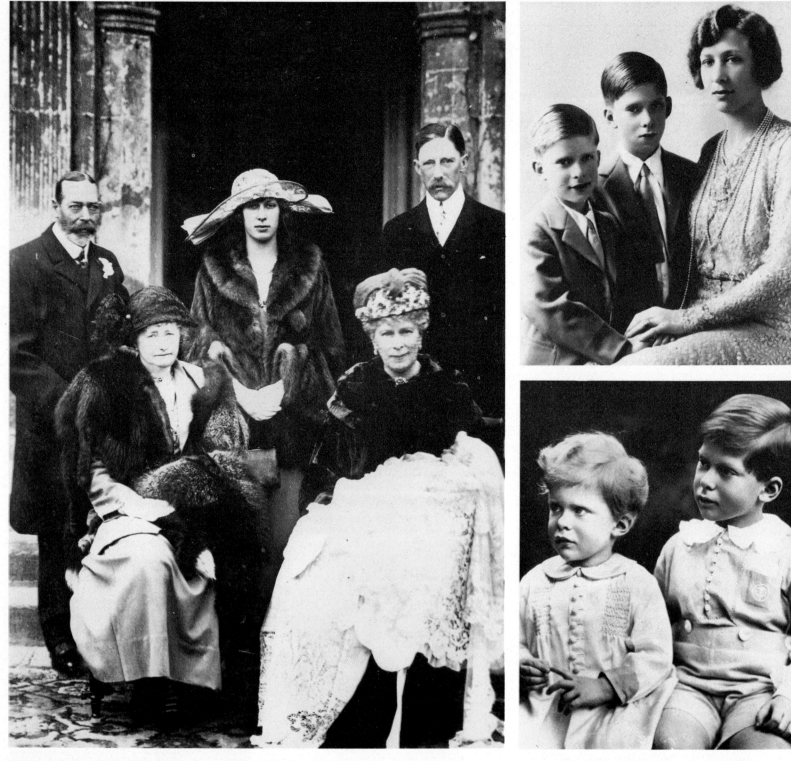

Above, left. This family group was photographed at Goldsborough Hall on the occasion of the christening of the Hon. George Lascelles on 25th March, 1923. It shows (left to right) King George V, the Countess of Harewood, Princess Mary, Queen Mary holding her grandchild, and Viscount Lascelles.

Above right, top. Princess Mary with her two children. The eldest was the Hon. George Lascelles (in the centre of the photograph), born in 1923. He married Miss Marion Stein (b. 1927) in 1949, two years after becoming the 7th Earl of Harewood on the death of his father. He had three children by her – David, Viscount Lascelles (b. 1950), James (b. 1953) and Robert (b. 1955). The couple were divorced in 1967 and the Earl married Miss Patricia Tuckwell in the same year. He had already had a child by her (now the Hon. Mark Lascelles) in 1964.

The second of Princess Mary's children was the Hon. Gerald Lascelles. He was born in 1924 and married Miss Angela Dowding in 1952. He has one son by her – Henry, born in 1953. They were divorced in 1978. The photograph was taken in about 1931.

Above right. A photograph of Princess Mary's children, taken in about 1927.

Opposite page, right. A photograph taken in October 1924, at the time of the christening of the Lascelles' second son, Gerald.

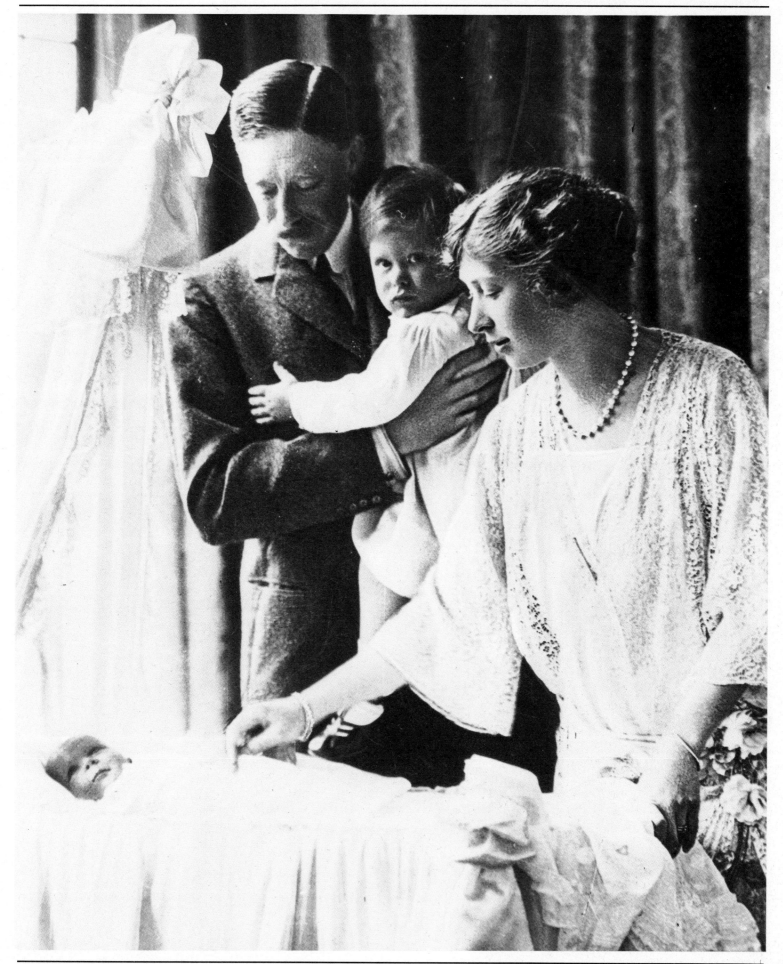

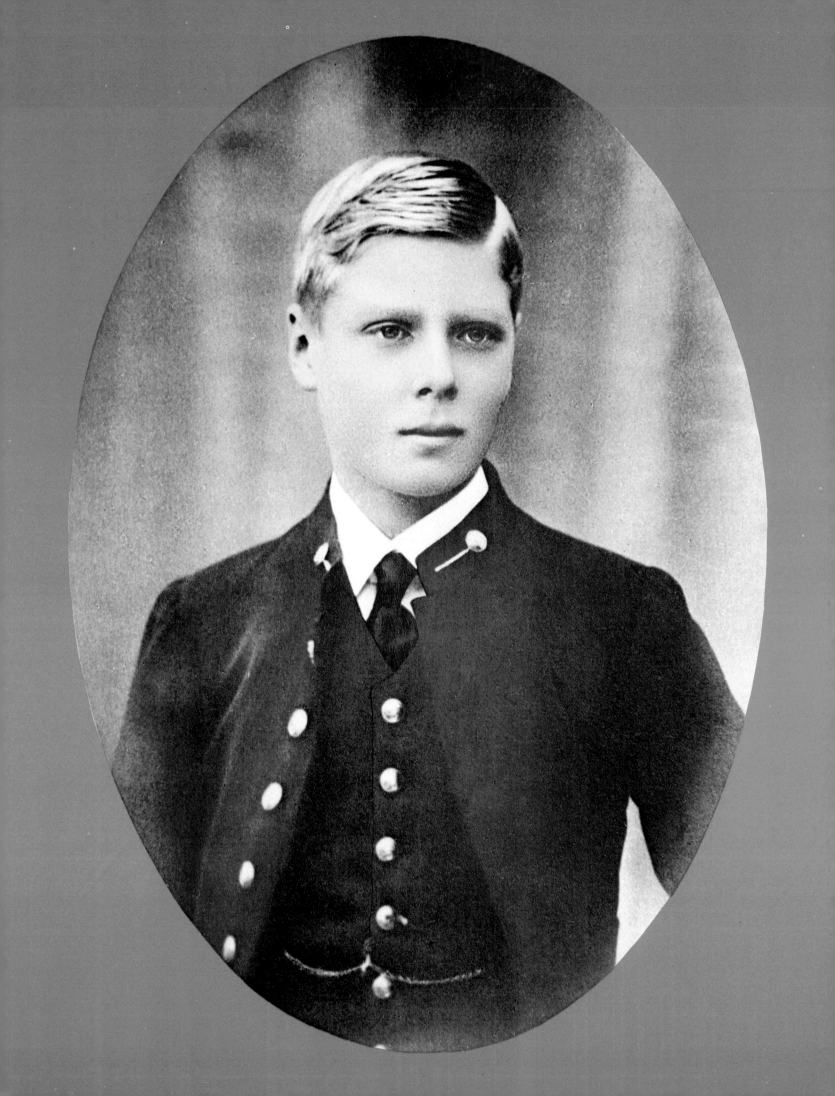

King Edward VIII (*opposite page, left, aged about 15*) was born in 1894, the eldest son of King George V and Queen Mary who were then Duke and Duchess of York. At the time of his birth he was third in direct line to the throne of England, then occupied by his great-grandmother, Queen Victoria.

Born to the title Prince Edward of York, he became Prince Edward of Wales in November 1901, when his grandfather, King Edward VII (1841-1910) conferred the title Prince of Wales on his father; and succeeded his father as Prince of Wales in 1910 following the latter's accession as King George V. He ultimately succeeded as King Edward VIII in 1936 when his father died.

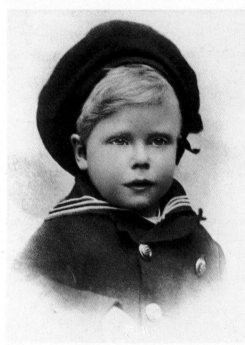

At the end of 1936 and at the culmination of a constitutional crisis precipitated by his anticipated marriage to Mrs. Wallis Simpson (b. 1896) he abdicated in favour of his brother King George VI (1895-1952). He was created Duke of Windsor in 1937 and later that year married Mrs. Simpson who became the Duchess of Windsor. There were no children of the marriage, and the Duke of Windsor died in 1972.

Above. A photograph of King Edward VIII as Prince Edward of York, taken in about 1898.

Right. A photograph taken in about 1910, the year in which Prince Edward became Prince of Wales.

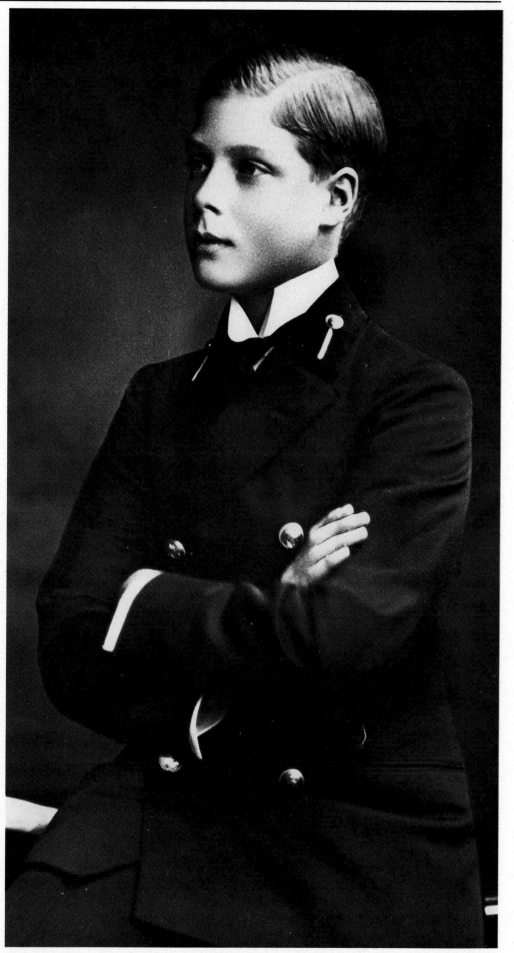

Great Britain

Below. Edward, the Prince of Wales, 1911.
Opposite page, right. This photograph of King Edward VIII as Prince of Wales was taken by Swayne on the occasion of the marriage of King George VI (then Duke of York) to Lady Elizabeth Bowes-Lyon (now the Queen Mother) on 26th April, 1923.

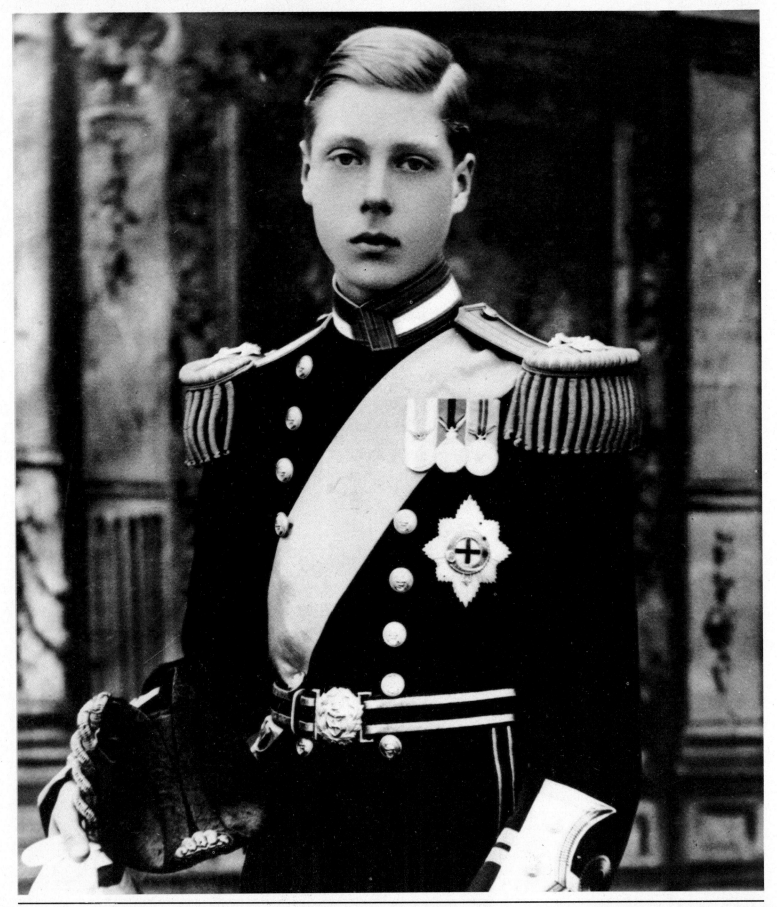

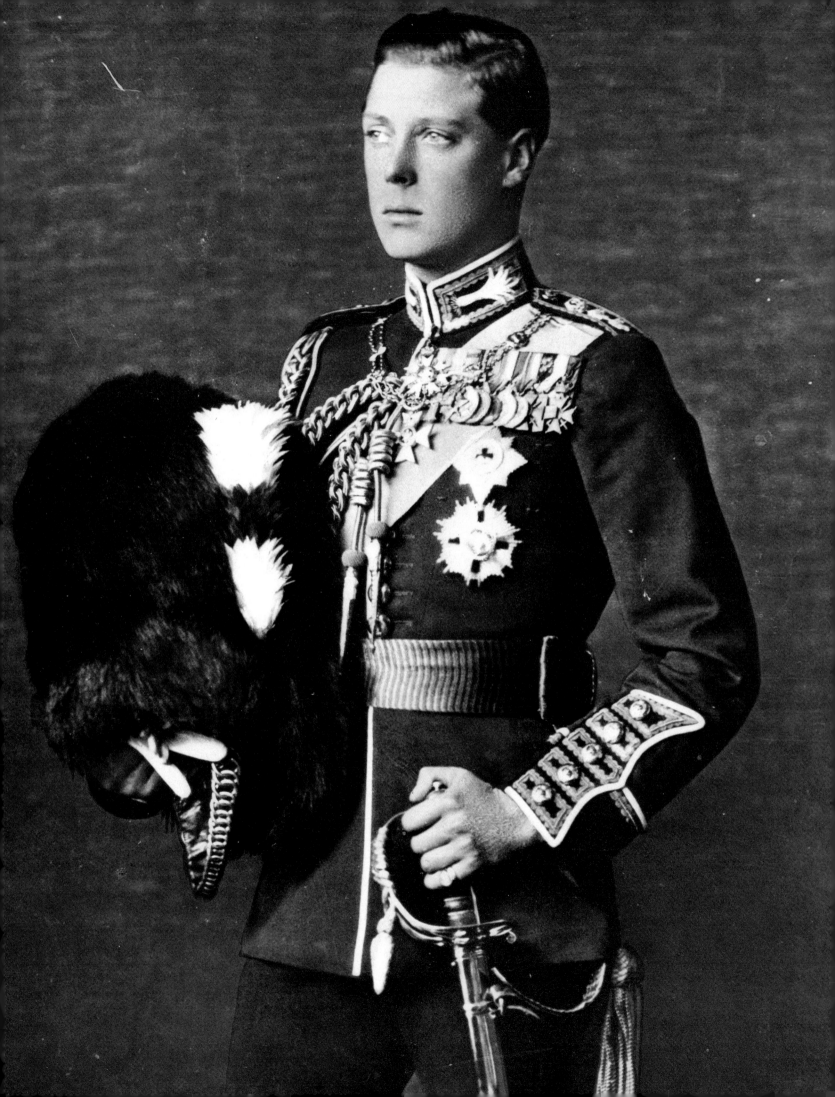

Great Britain

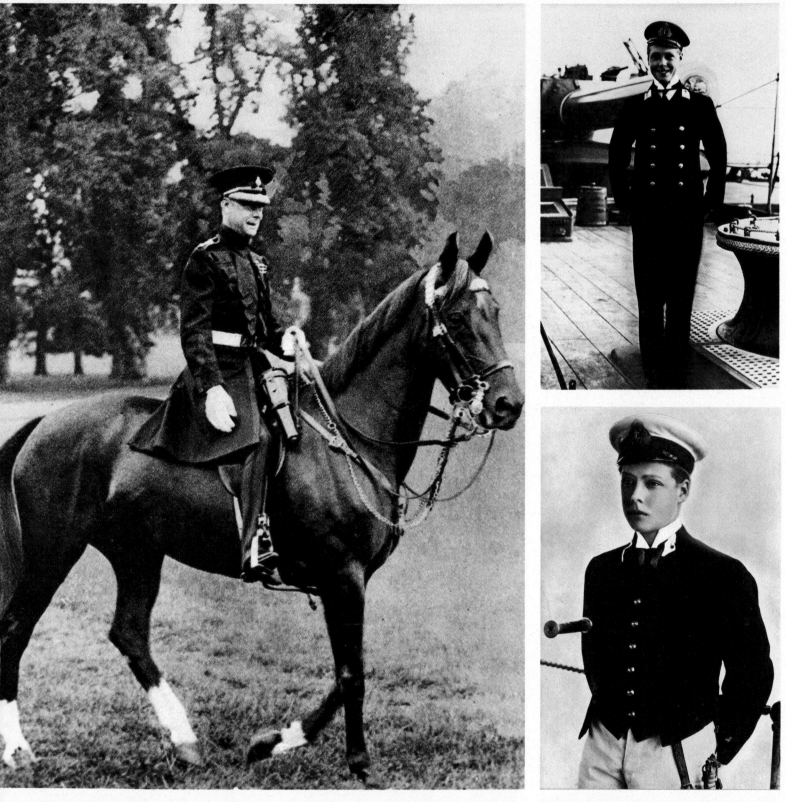

Above, left. King Edward VIII at Windsor in 1936 during his brief reign.

Above right, top. A photograph taken on board HMS *Hindustan*, the ship on which King Edward VIII, then Prince of Wales, served in the late summer of 1911.

Above right. King Edward VIII, in about 1909.

Opposite page, above left. This photograph was taken during the visit of the then Prince of Wales to Wellington, New Zealand in May 1920, as part of his Australasian Tour.

Opposite page, above right. A formal photograph of Prince Edward and his sister Princess Mary, dressed in their robes for the Coronation of King George V on

22nd June, 1911; it was taken by Campbell Grey.

Opposite page, lower left. A photograph of King Edward VIII in about 1925, taken at St. James's Palace.

Opposite page, lower right. This photograph was taken during the visit of the then Prince of Wales to Canada in 1919.

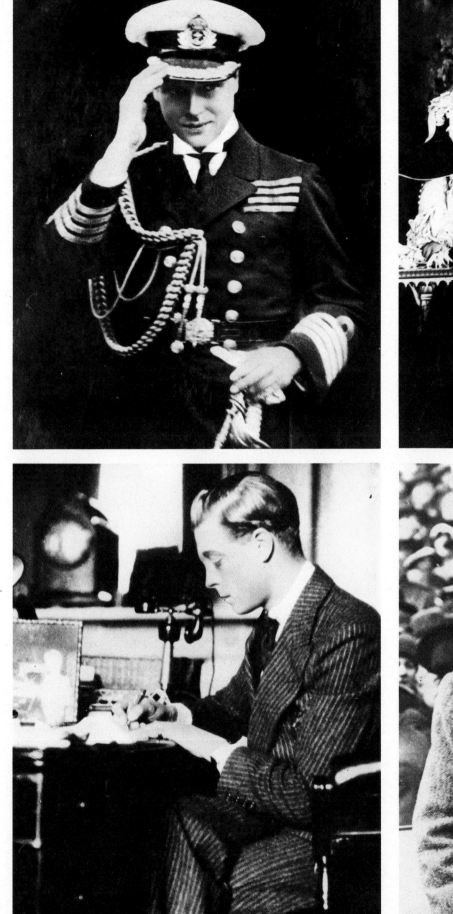

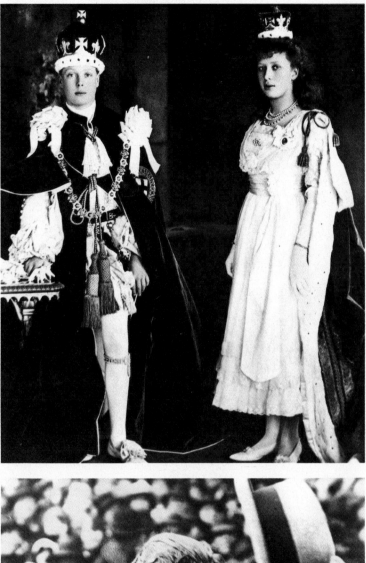

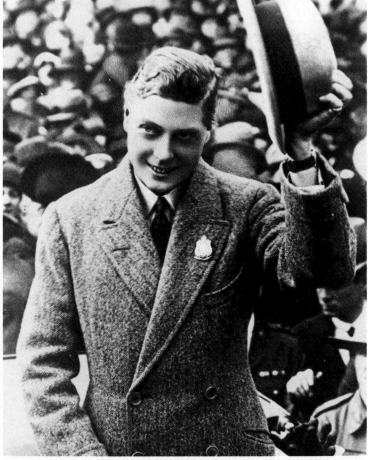

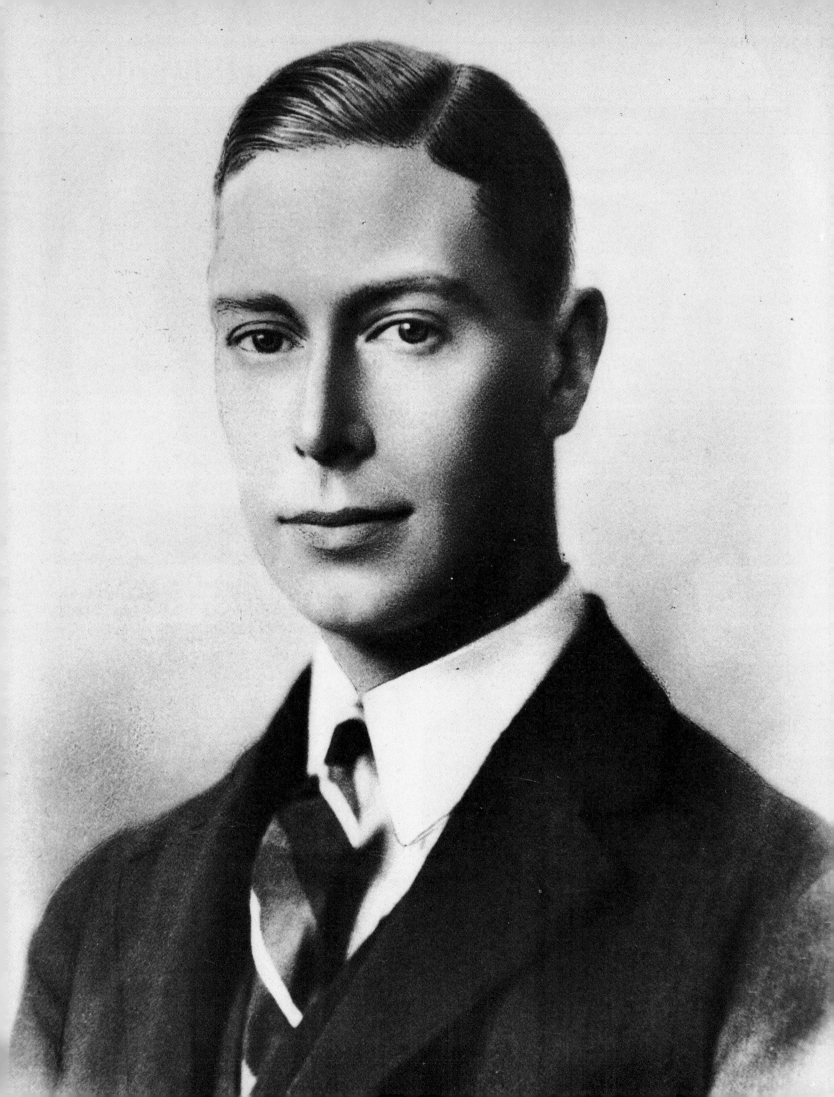

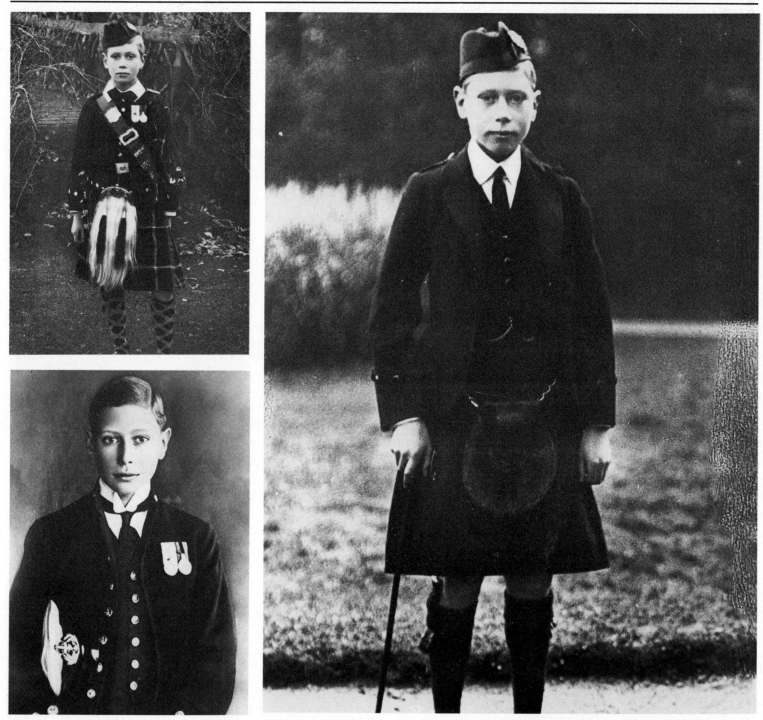

Prince Albert, the second son of King George V and Queen Mary, was born in 1895, and was created Duke of York in 1920.

In 1923 he married Lady Elizabeth Bowes-Lyon (b. 1900), the present Queen Mother. They had two children, the present Queen Elizabeth II (b. 1926) and Princess Margaret Rose (b. 1930).

In 1936 the Duke of York became King on the abdication of his elder brother King Edward VIII and took the title King George VI. He reigned until his death in 1952 when he was succeeded by Queen Elizabeth II.

Opposite page, left. A photograph taken in 1920 – the year King George VI was created Duke of York.

Above right. A photograph taken at Abergeldie in 1906.

Above, top left. This photograph of King George VI as Prince Albert was taken at Balmoral in September 1910.

Above, left. A photograph of King George VI in 1911.

Overleaf. A photograph of King George V and Queen Mary, surrounded by their children. It was taken on 26th April, 1923, the day of the marriage between Prince Albert and Lady Elizabeth Bowes-Lyon. The group are (left to right): Edward, Prince of Wales; Princess Mary; Prince Henry; King George V; Prince Albert, Duke of York; Queen Mary, and Prince George.

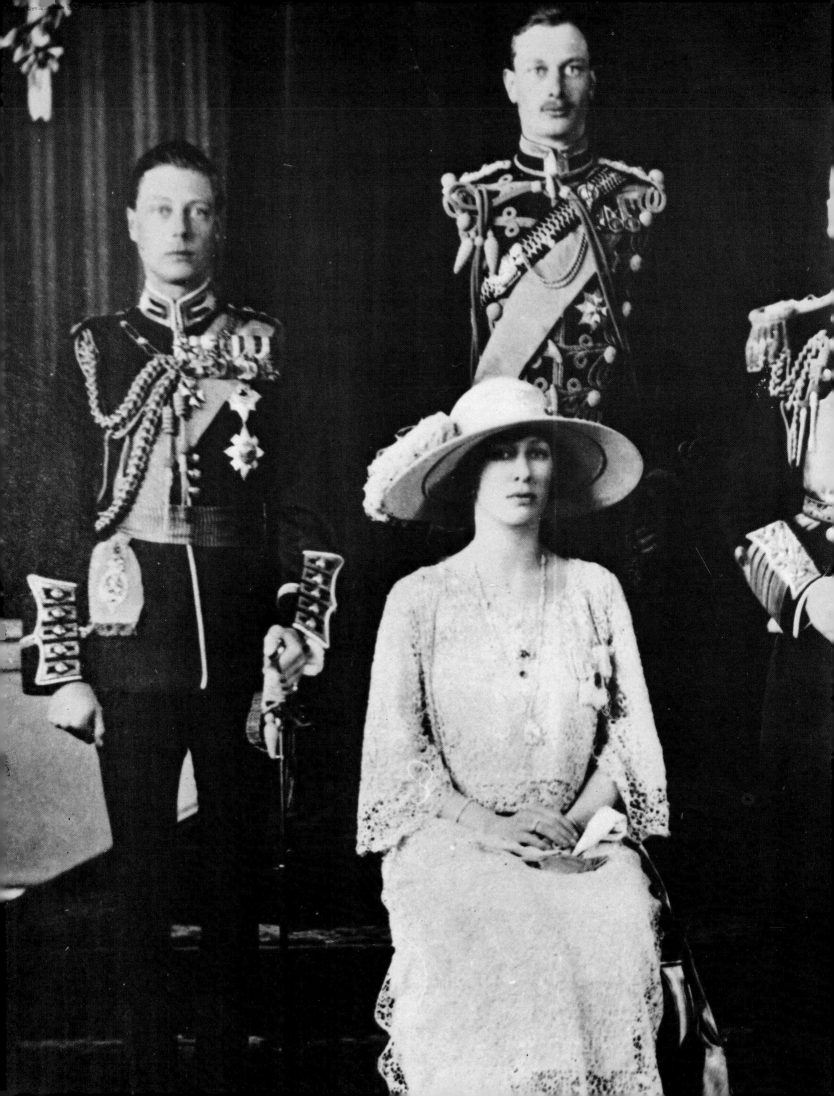

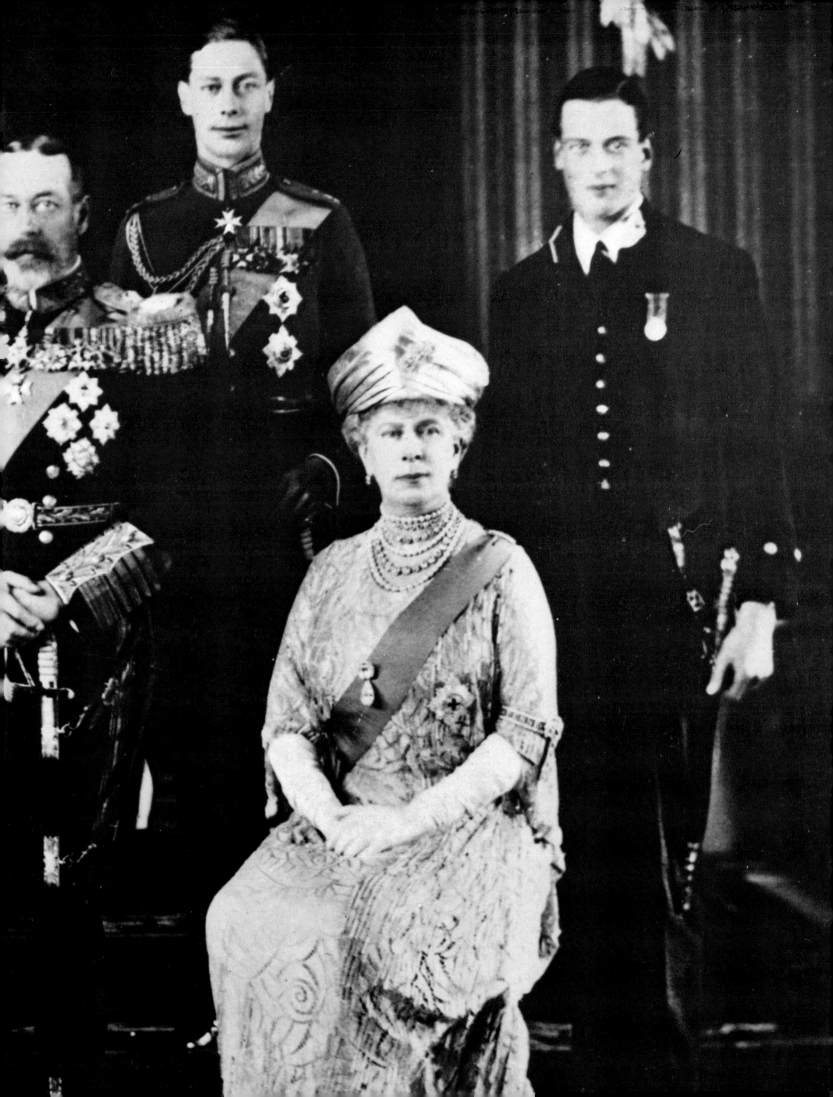

Great Britain

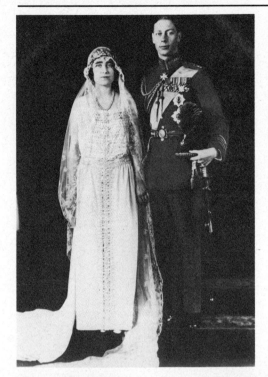

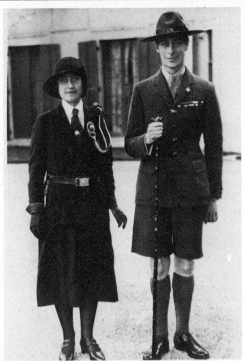

Left. This photograph of the Duke and Duchess of York (the future King George VI and Queen Elizabeth) was taken during an inspection of Scouts and Girl Guides at Adelaide, South Australia, in April 1927.

Far left. The Royal couple on the occasion of their marriage; 26th April, 1923.

Princess Elizabeth of York (*lower left,* c 1929), now Queen Elizabeth II, the elder daughter of King George VI and Queen Elizabeth.

She became heir presumptive to the throne when, in 1936, her uncle, King Edward VIII abdicated in favour of her father. In 1947 she married her fourth cousin Prince Philip of Greece (b. 1921), the only son of Prince Andrew (1882-1944) – a son of King George I of Greece – and his wife, formerly Princess Alice of Hesse (1885-1969), a great-grand-daughter of Queen Victoria. She came to the throne on the death of her father in 1952.

She has four children, Charles, Prince of Wales (b. 1948), Princess Anne (b. 1950), Prince Andrew (b. 1960) and Prince Edward (b. 1964).

The photograph, *opposite page, right,* was taken by Marcus Adams in July 1928 at 145 Piccadilly, the London home of Princess Elizabeth and her parents.

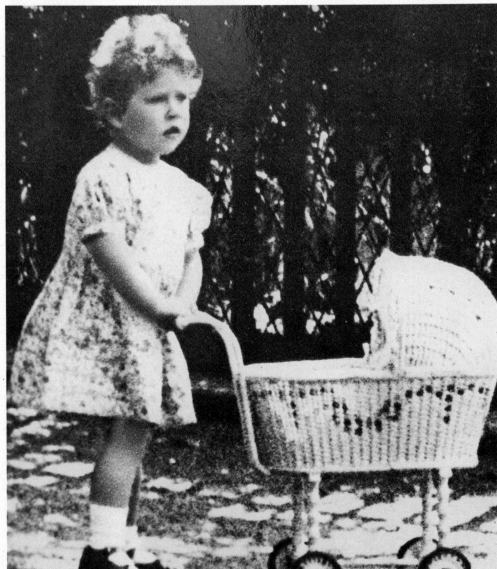

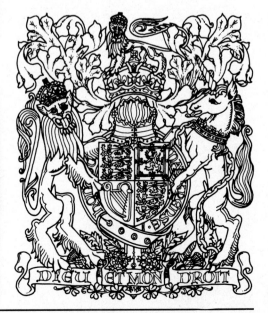

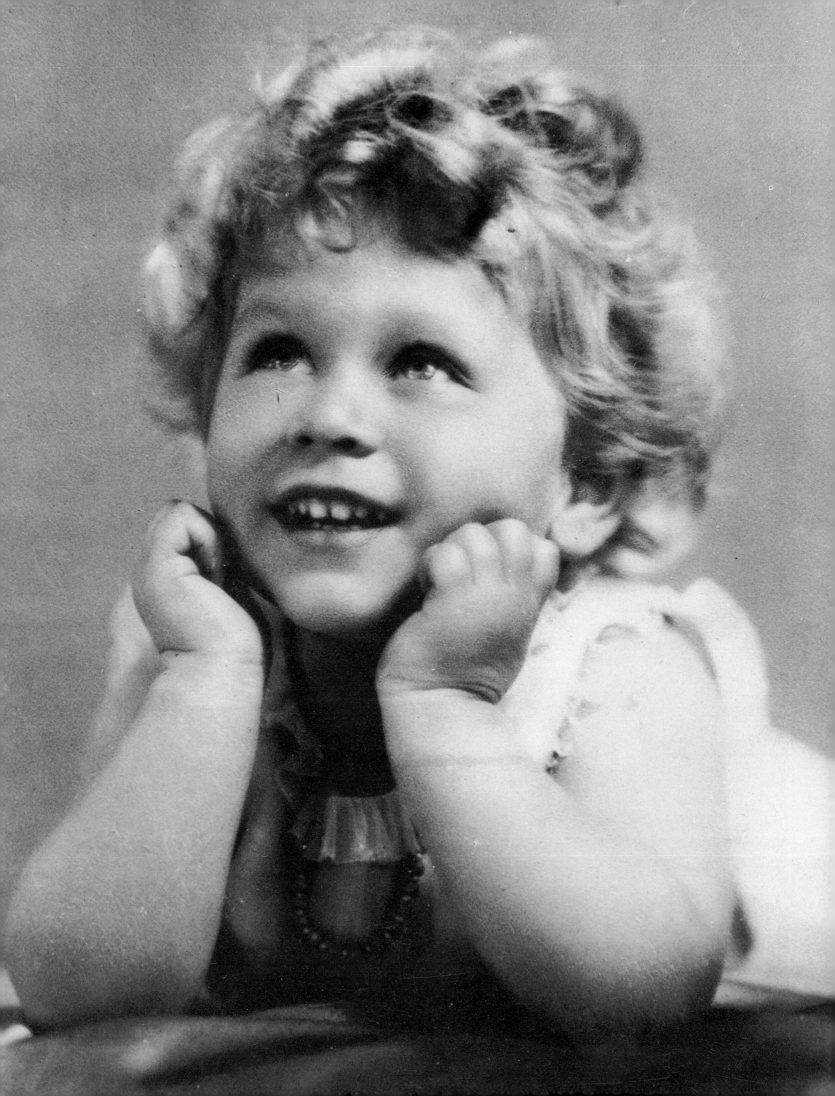

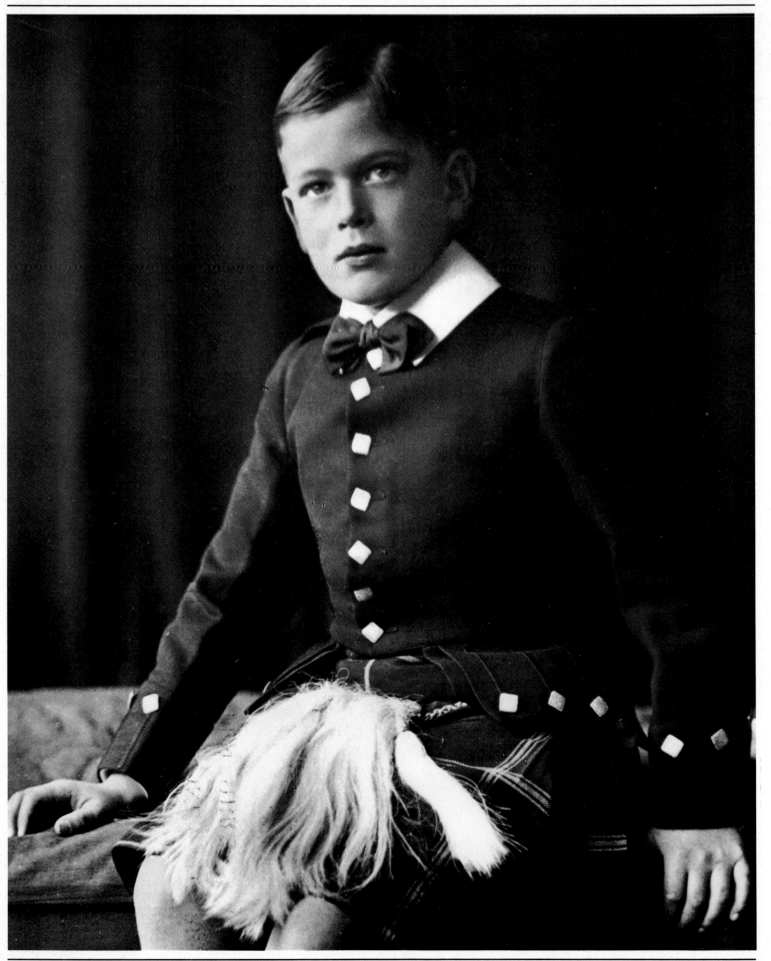

Prince Henry and Prince George

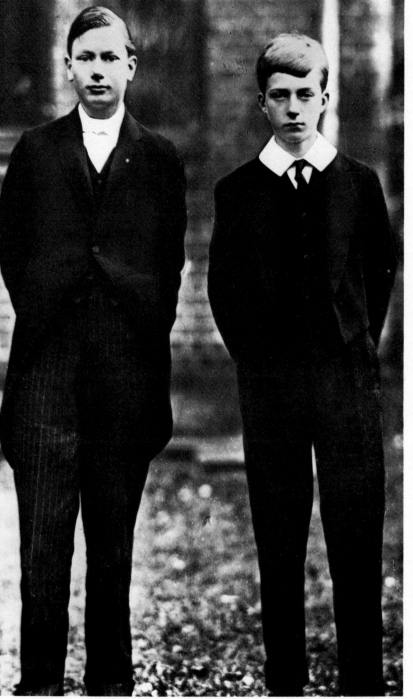

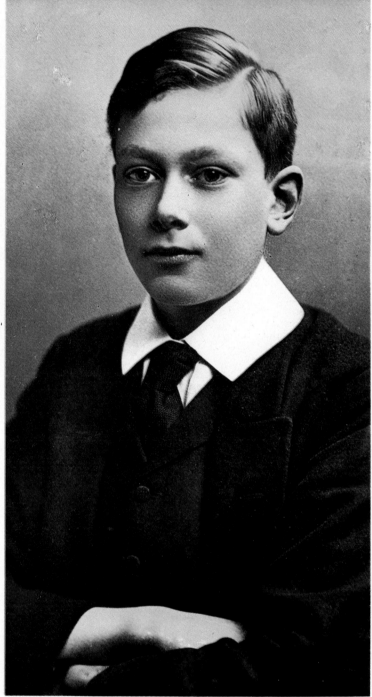

Opposite page, left. Prince George (1902-1942) was the fifth of six children of King George V and Queen Mary. He was created Duke of Kent in 1934, six weeks before his marriage to Princess Marina (1906-1968), the daughter of Prince Nicholas of Greece (1872-1938), a granddaughter of King George I of Greece, and sister-in-law to the wartime Regent Prince Paul of Yugoslavia.

They had three children: Prince Edward (b. 1935), the present Duke of Kent who married Miss Katharine Worsley (b. 1933) in 1961; Princess Alexandra (b. 1936) who married Mr. Angus Ogilvy (b. 1928) in 1963; and Prince Michael (b. 1942) who married Baroness Marie-Christine von Reibnitz in 1978. Prince Michael was born seven weeks before Prince George was killed on active service in Scotland in August 1942.

The photograph was taken in about 1910 by Lafayette.

Above right. Prince Henry, Prince George's elder brother, was born in 1900, and became Prince Henry of Wales after November 1901 when his father was created Prince of Wales. In 1928 he was created Duke of Gloucester.

He married in 1935 Lady Alice Christabel Montagu-Douglas-Scott (b. 1901), the present Princess Alice Duchess of Gloucester, by whom he had two children, Prince William (1941-1972), who was killed in an aircraft accident, and Prince Richard (b. 1944), the present Duke.

Prince Henry died in 1974, the last survivor of King George V's six children. The photograph was taken in about 1912.

Above left. Prince Henry with Prince Leopold of Belgium; a photograph dated about 1914, and taken at Eton where the two princes studied together.

Battenberg (Mountbatten)

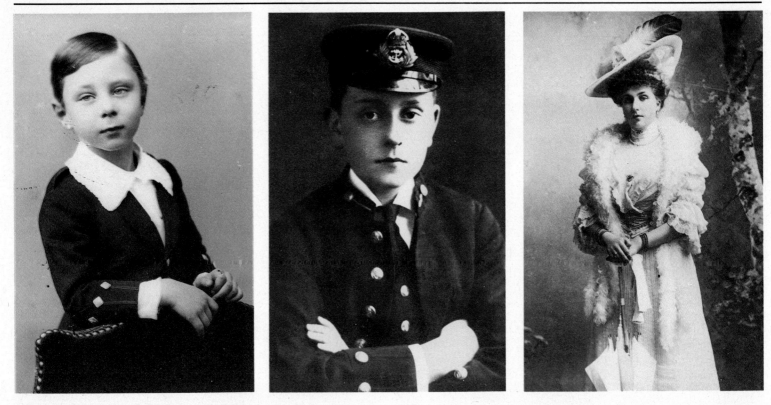

Opposite page, right. Prince Louis of Battenberg (1854-1921) was one of four sons of Prince Alexander of Hesse and by Rhine (Hesse-Darmstadt) (1823-1888) and his morganatically married wife Countess Julia von Hauke (1825-1895): she was created Countess of Battenberg, from which her children took their titles. Prince Louis' brothers included Prince Henry (1858-1896) the husband of Queen Victoria's youngest daughter Princess Beatrice (1857-1944) and father of Queen Victoria-Eugenie of Spain (1887-1969); and Prince Alexander (1857-1893) who was for a short time Sovereign Prince of Bulgaria.

Prince Louis married in 1884 Princess Victoria of Hesse (1863-1950) the eldest daughter of Queen Victoria's third child Princess Alice (1843-1878) by her husband Grand Duke Louis IV of Hesse, and a sister of the ill-fated Tsarina Alexandra of Russia (1872-1918).

Of their four children, the eldest, Princess Alice (1885-1969) married Prince Andrew of Greece (1882-1944) and became the mother of the present Duke of Edinburgh; the second child, Princess Louise (1889-1965) became the second wife of King Gustav VI of Sweden (1882-1973); the third, Prince George (1892-1938) succeeded his father as Marquis of Milford Haven in 1921, and married Nadjeda (1896-1963) the younger daughter of the Grand Duke Michael of Russia; the fourth child was Earl Mountbatten of Burma (1900-1979).

In 1917, consequent upon the Royal Proclamation which discontinued the use of German styles and titles in respect of British subjects, Prince Louis of Battenberg took the title Marquis of Milford Haven and Earl of Medina, and the family assumed the Anglicised surname of Mountbatten.

This photograph was taken in about 1905.

Above, left. Prince Alexander (1886-1960) was the eldest son of Prince Henry of Battenberg (1858-1896) and Princess Beatrice (1857-1944), the youngest of the nine children of Queen Victoria and the Prince Consort. When the German title of Battenberg was relinquished, he was created Marquess of Carisbrooke, on 18th July, 1917.

On the following day, he married Lady Irene Denison (1890-1956) the only daughter of the 2nd Earl of Londesborough, and there was one child of the marriage, Lady Iris Mountbatten (b. 1920). She has married three times, and has a child, Robin (b. 1957), by her second husband, Mr. Michael Bryan.

This photograph was taken when Prince Alexander was aged about six.

Above, centre. Prince George (1892-1938), the elder son and third child of Prince Louis of Battenberg.

Prince George took his father's courtesy title Earl of Medina in 1917. The previous year he had married Countess Nadjeda de Torby (1896-1963), younger daughter of the Grand Duke Michael, a distant cousin of Tsar Nicholas II of Russia. They had two children; Tatiana, born in 1917, and David (1919-1970), the 3rd Marquess of Milford Haven and father of the present (4th) Marquess.

The picture was taken in 1905, the year when Prince George became a Naval Cadet.

Above, right. Princess Victoria-Eugenie (photographed here in 1905) was the only daughter of Prince Henry of Battenberg and his wife Princess Beatrice of England.

Born in 1887, she married in 1906 King Alfonso XIII of Spain (1886-1941), and was Queen of Spain until the Republic was declared in 1931. As ex-Queen, she lived in exile until her death, in Switzerland, in 1969. Her third son, Prince Juan, Count of Barcelona, is the father of the present King Juan Carlos of Spain.

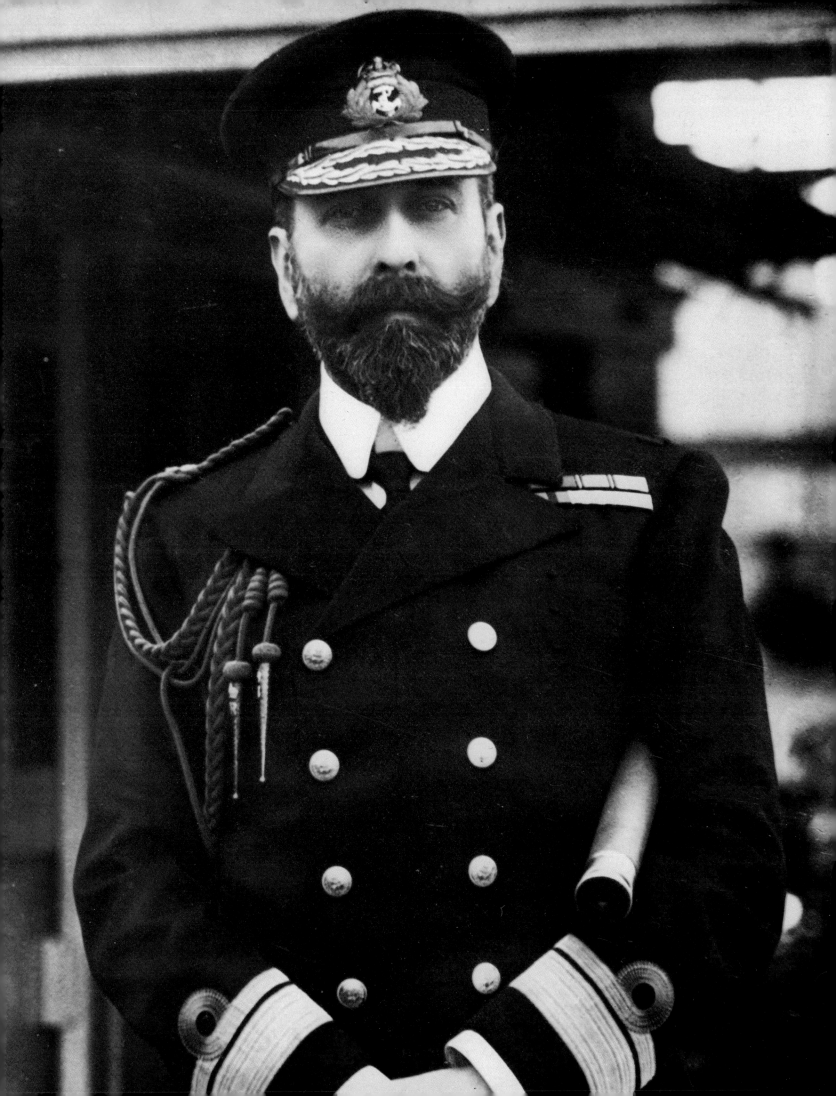

Battenberg (Mountbatten)

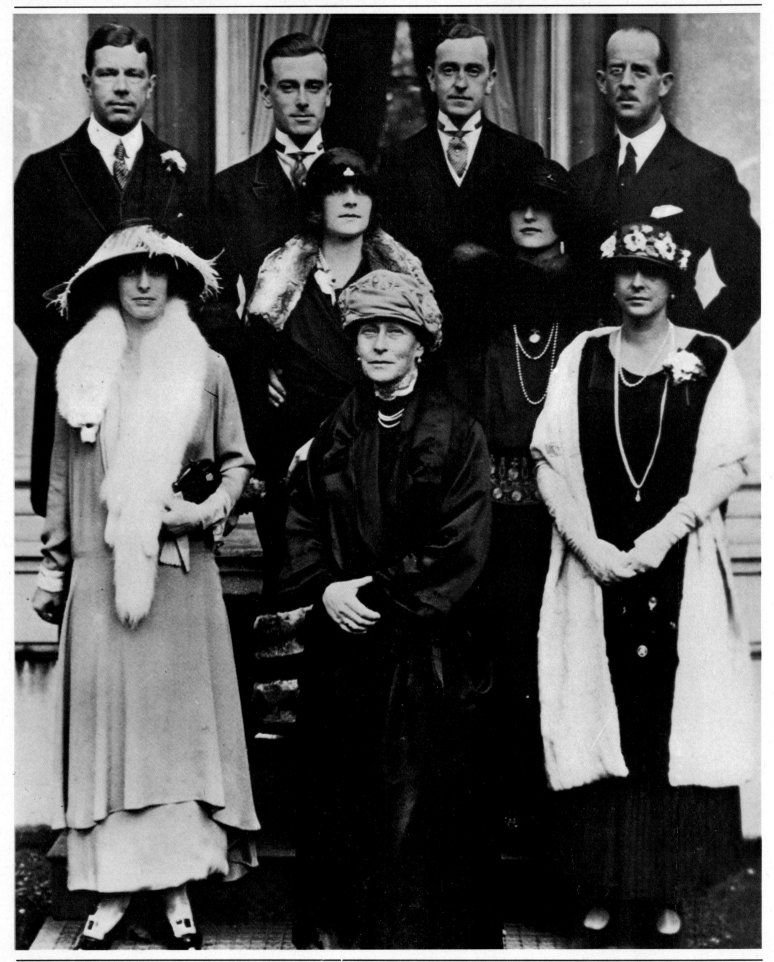

Battenberg

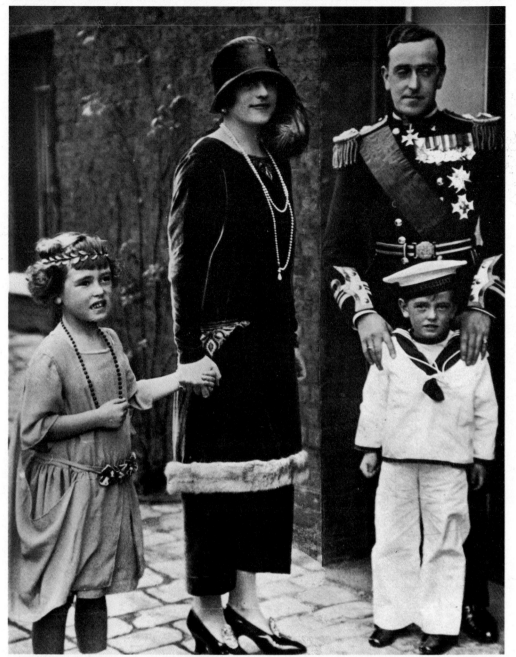

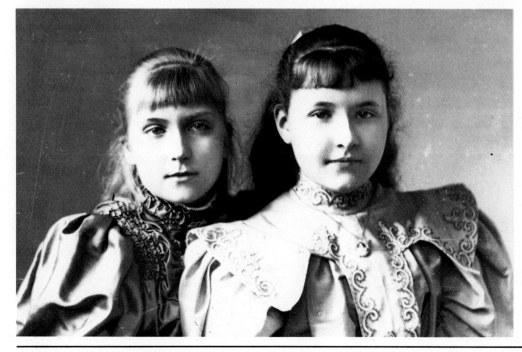

Opposite page, left. The Dowager Countess of Milford Haven (centre of photograph) surrounded by her four children and their spouses.

They are (left to right):

Princess Louise (1889-1965) who married Crown Prince Gustav Adolf (1882-1973), later King Gustav VI of Sweden, and whose only child by him was stillborn in 1925.

Prince Louis (1900-1979), Lord Mountbatten, Earl Mountbatten of Burma, who married Edwina Ashley (1901-1960) in 1922. In 1979 he was assassinated by terrorists of the Irish Republican Army (the IRA).

Prince George (1892-1938) who married Nadjeda (1896-1963) daughter of the Grand Duke Michael of Russia (grandson of Tsar Nicholas I). His eldest grandson George (born 1961) is the present Marquess of Milford Haven.

Princess Alice (1885-1969), who married Prince Andrew (1882-1944), the fourth son of King George I of Greece, and who was the mother of Prince Philip, Duke of Edinburgh (b. 1921).

This family photograph was taken in the garden of Brook House, Park Lane, London, the former home of Sir Ernest Cassel, the grandfather of Lady Edwina Mountbatten, in 1924.

Top left. The 2nd Marquess of Milford Haven and his family, photographed on 18th July, 1922, outside one of the entrances to St Margaret's Westminster on the occasion of the marriage of his brother Lord Louis Mountbatten to Edwina Ashley.

The 2nd Marquess and his wife had two children; Lady Tatiana Mountbatten (born 1917) who has remained unmarried, and Lord David Mountbatten (1919-1970), who became Earl of Medina in 1921 and the 3rd Marquess of Milford Haven in 1938 on his father's death. He was twice married: the first and childless marriage to the American Romaine Dahlgren Simpson lasted from 1950 until divorce in 1954; the second marriage to Janet Bryce (born 1932) produced two children, Lord George Mountbatten (born 1961), the present Marquess, and Lord Ivar Mountbatten (born 1963).

Lower left. A photograph dated 1897 showing Princess Victoria Eugenie of Battenberg (left) with her cousin Princess Marie Elisabeth of Erbach-Schoenberg.

Teck (Athlone)

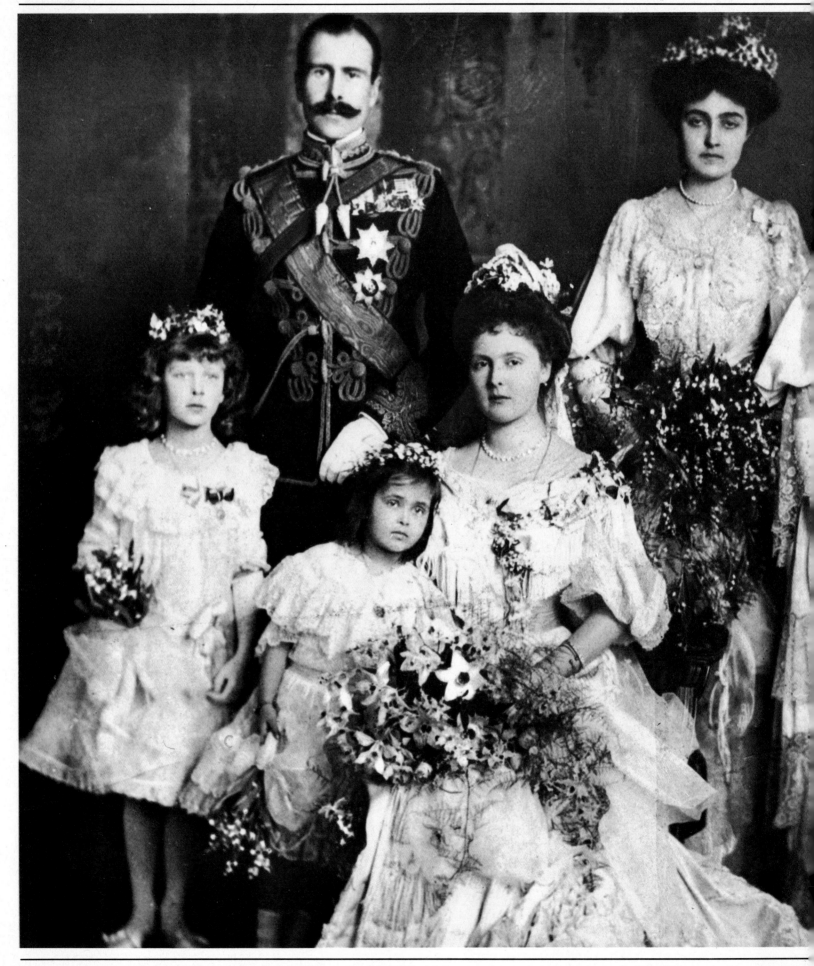

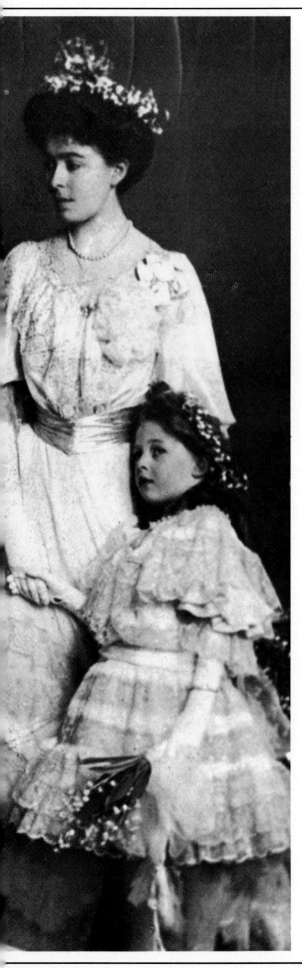

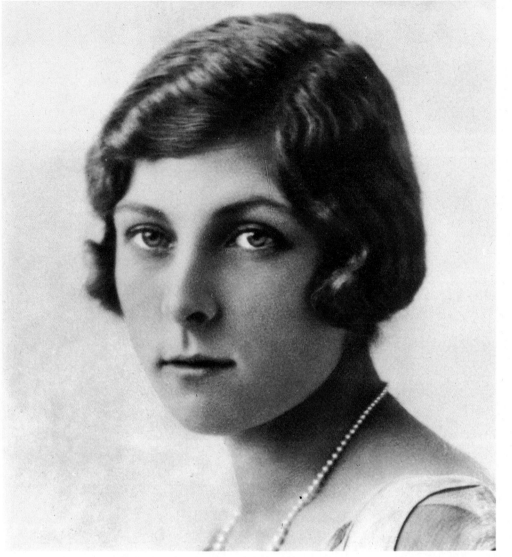

Prince Alexander of Teck (1874-1957) was the youngest child of Franz, Duke of Teck (1837-1900) – only son of the Duke Alexander of Wurttemberg – and the Duchess of Teck, formerly Princess Mary Adelaide of Cambridge (1833-1897), a granddaughter of King George III and a first cousin of Queen Victoria. Prince Alexander's sister was Queen Mary (1867-1953), consort of King George V.

Princess Alice was the only daughter of Prince Leopold Duke of Albany (1853-1884) who was the youngest of Queen Victoria's sons. Princess Alice was born in 1883 and died in January 1981.

They married in 1904, *left*. The wedding group consists of (left to right): Princess Victoria Mary of Wales; Prince Alexander of Teck; Princess Helena of Waldeck-Pyrmont (1899-1948), the bride's first cousin; Princess Alice of Albany; Princess Victoria Patricia of Connaught; Princess Margaret of Connaught; Princess Mary of Teck (b. 1897) – a niece of the bridegroom and the present Duchess of Beaufort.

The eldest of the five bridesmaids are the two daughters of Queen Victoria's third son Prince Arthur Duke of Connaught (1850-1942).

Prince Alexander and Princess Alice had three children, of which two boys died unmarried – Rupert, Viscount Trematon in 1928 at the age of 20, and Maurice at the age of six months in 1910. The only girl, formerly Princess May (b. 1906) (photographed, *above,* in about 1928) was married to Col. Sir Henry Abel Smith in 1931 and has three children.

In 1917, the title of Teck was replaced by English titles and Prince Alexander became the Earl of Athlone.

Greece

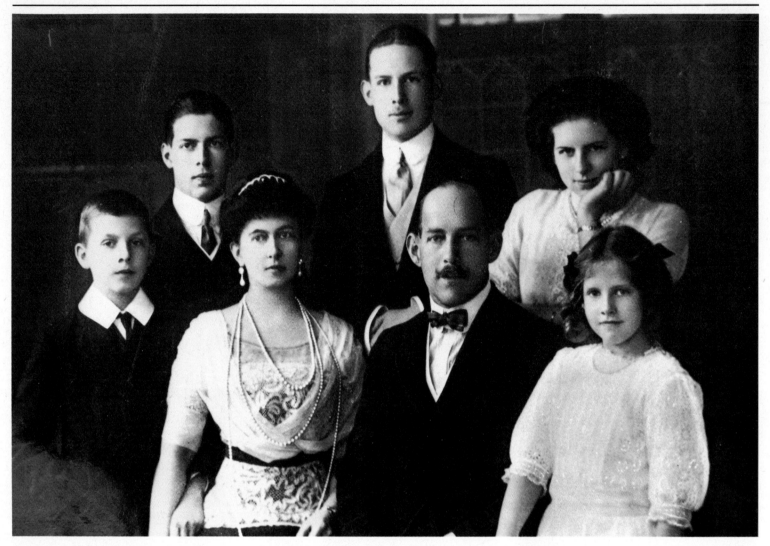

Above. A photograph dated 1912, showing Crown Prince Constantine of Greece and his five eldest children.

Crown Prince Constantine (1868-1923) was the eldest son of King George I of Greece, whom he succeeded in 1913, and Queen Olga (1851-1926) formerly a Grand-Duchess of Russia. In 1889 he married Princess Sophia of Prussia (1870-1932) who is seated next to him in the photograph.

She was a daughter of Emperor Frederick III of Germany (1831-1888) and his wife, formerly Victoria Princess Royal of Great Britain (1840-1901), and a sister of Kaiser Wilhelm II (1859-1941).

They had six children, of whom the eldest five are shown in this photograph:

Prince George (1890-1947) (standing directly behind his father): in 1921 he married Princess Elizabeth (1894-1956), daughter of King Ferdinand of Roumania and Queen Marie (eldest daughter of Queen Victoria's second son Prince Alfred). They had no children and were divorced in 1935. Prince George succeeded as King George II on the abdication of his father in 1922, went into voluntary exile in 1924, was elected back onto the throne in 1935, and reigned until his death in 1947.

Prince Alexander (1893-1920) (second from left): he succeeded to the Greek throne as King Alexander I in 1917 when his father was (in events temporarily) overthrown, and died from a monkey-bite in 1920. In the previous year he had married Aspasia Manos, a Greek commoner (1896-1972) and their only child Princess Alexandra was born in 1921, five months after his death. She married King Peter II of Yugoslavia (1923-1970) and now lives in America.

Prince Paul (1901-1964) (furthest left: he married in 1938 Princess Frederika (1917-1981) daughter of Prince Ernst of Hanover and Princess Victoria Louise, daughter of Kaiser Wilhelm II of Germany. Their three children are ex-King Constantine II (b. 1940) who married Princess Anne-Marie (b. 1946), daughter of King Frederick IX of Denmark; Queen Sophie of Spain (b. 1938), wife of King Juan Carlos (b. 1938); and Princess Irene (b. 1941), unmarried. Prince Paul succeeded his brother George II as King of Greece in 1947.

Princess Helen (b. 1896) (second from right): she married as his second wife King Carol II of Roumania (1893-1953) in 1921 – he was the elder brother of Princess Elizabeth whom Princess Helen's brother, Prince George, married in the same year. Their only child became King Michael of Roumania (b. 1921) and married Princess Anne of Bourbon-Parma (b. 1923).

Princess Irene (1904-1974) (far right): she was married in 1939 to Prince Aimone of Savoy (1900-1948) who was created Duke of Spoleto in 1904, Duke of Aosta in 1942 and was designated King of Croatia as Tomislav II from 1941-1943. They had only one son, Prince Amadeo, (b. 1943) the present Duke of Aosta.

Opposite page, right. Crown Princess Sophie and her children, in 1905. They are (left to right): Princess Helen, Prince Paul, Crown Princess Sophie, Princess Irene, Prince George and Prince Alexander.

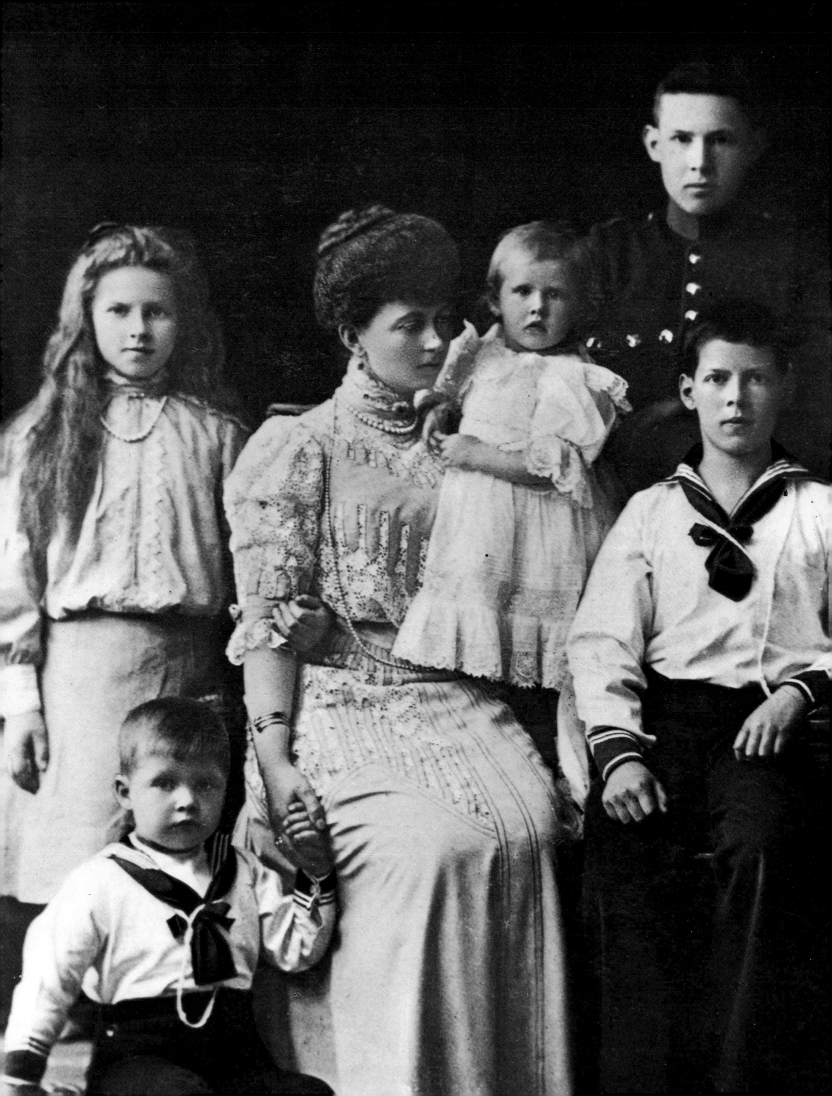

Greece

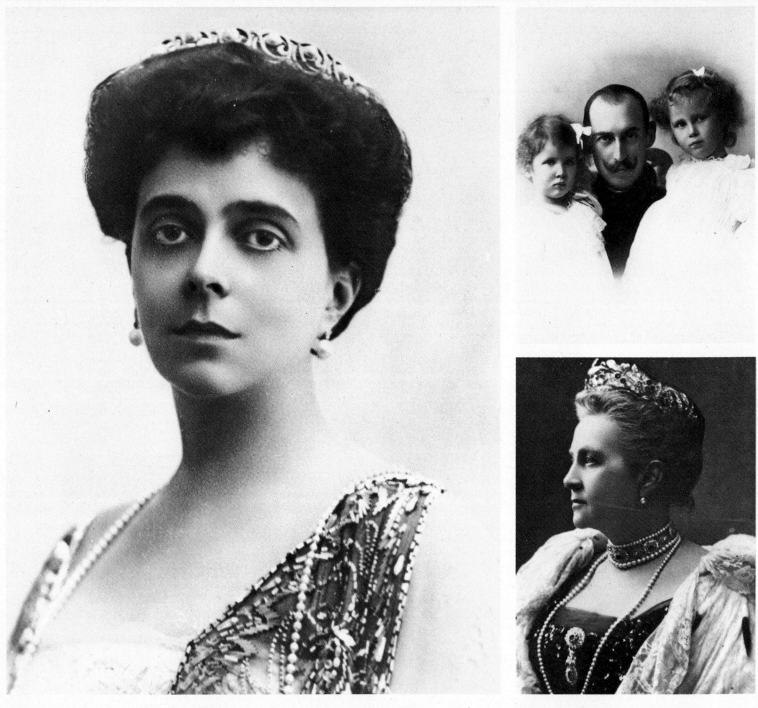

Above left. Princess Nicholas of Greece who married Prince Nicholas (1872-1938), the third son of King George I of Greece and Queen Olga in 1902. She was born in 1882 under the title Grand Duchess Helen of Russia, and was a daughter of the Grand Duke Vladimir (1847-1909), Tsar Alexander III's brother. Her mother was formerly Princess Marie of Mecklenburg-Schwerin (1854-1920), a daughter of Grand Duke Frederick-Franz II of Mecklenburg-Schwerin. One of Grand Duchess Helen's brothers was the Grand Duke Kirill (1876-1938) who married one of Queen Victoria's granddaughters, Princess Victoria Melita of Edinburgh, the daughter of Prince Alfred, Duke of Edinburgh and of Saxe-Coburg-Gotha.

Above, top right. A photograph taken in about 1909 showing Prince Nicholas of Greece with his two youngest daughters, Princess Marina (on the left), and Princess Elizabeth.

Above, right. Queen Olga of Greece (1851-1926) was formerly Grand Duchess Olga, daughter of Grand Duke Constantine of Russia (1827-1892) – he was the eldest brother of Tsar Alexander II – and Princess Alexandra (1830-1911) nee of Saxe-Altenburg.

In 1867, at the age of 16, she married King George I of Greece (1845-1913). Queen Olga survived her husband, who was assassinated at Salonika in 1913, by 13 years; during which time she saw her eldest son, King Constantine I and his two eldest sons, King George II and King Alexander as successive Kings of Greece following several political and constitutional crises in the early 1920's.

The photograph was taken in 1907.

Greece

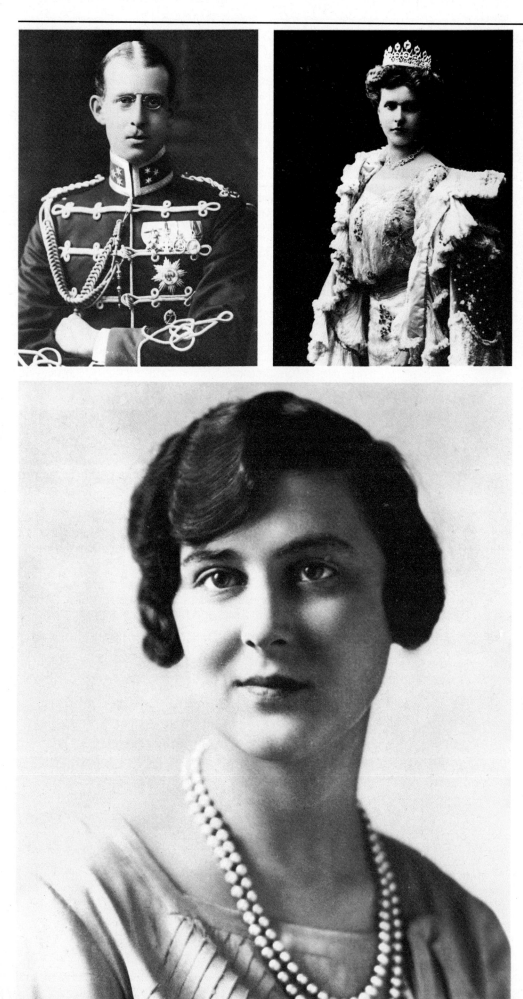

Far left. Prince Andrew, born in 1882, the fourth son of King George I of Greece and Queen Olga.

In 1903 he married Princess Alice, *left,* the eldest child of Prince Louis of Battenberg, and had five children. The only son was Prince Philip (b. 1921) who became Duke of Edinburgh and married Princess (now Queen) Elizabeth of England (b. 1926) in 1947.

Their four daughters were Princess Margharita (b. 1905), wife of Prince Gottfried of Hohenlohe-Langenburg (1897-1960), a grandson of Prince Alfred, second son of Queen Victoria; Princess Theodora (1906-1969), who married Prince Berthold, Margrave of Baden (1906-1963), in 1931; Princess Cecilie (1911-1937), wife of Prince George, Grand Duke of Hesse (1906-1937), grandson of Queen Victoria's second daughter of Princess Alice; and Princess Sophie (b. 1914) who married firstly Prince Christopher of Hesse-Cassel (1901-1943) and secondly Prince George of Hanover (b. 1915), a grandson of Kaiser Wilhelm II of Germany.

Prince Andrew died in 1944, and Princess Alice in 1969.

Lower left. Princess Marina (1906-1968) was the youngest of the three children – all daughters – of Prince Nicholas (1872-1938), third son of King George I of Greece. Their mother, Princess Helen (1882-1957) was a daughter of the Grand Duke Vladimir who was a brother of Tsar Alexander III and a first cousin to Princess Helen's mother-in-law Queen Olga of Greece.

Princess Marina, one of whose sisters, Princess Olga (b. 1903) married Prince Paul of Yugoslavia (1893-1977) who was regent during the minority of King Peter II, herself married, in 1934, Prince George, Duke of Kent (1902-1942), the fourth son of King George V and Queen Mary.

This photograph was taken in about 1930.

Russia

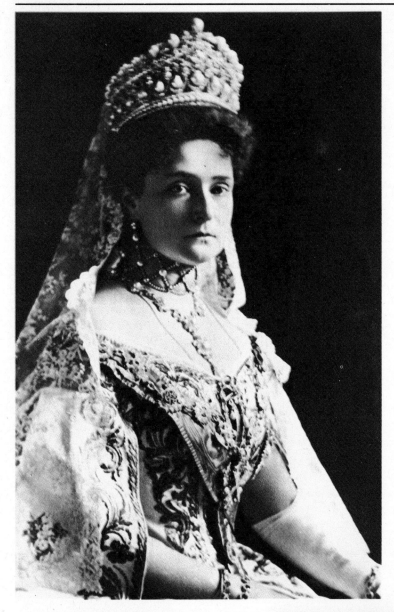

Opposite page, right. Tsar Nicholas II and his heir, Tsarevitch Alexei. Tsar Nicholas II of Russia was the last Tsar of Russia. He was born in 1868, the eldest child of Tsar Alexander III (1845-1894) and Tsarina Marie (1847-1928) formerly Princess Dagmar, second daughter of King Christian IX of Denmark. He was thus a nephew, through his mother's family, of Queen Alexandra of England and King George I of Greece, and a cousin of King George V of England and of King Haakon VII of Norway.

He came to the throne in 1894, on the assassination of his father. In the same year he married Princess Alexandra (1872-1918) (photograph, *left,* c 1900), daughter of the Grand Duke Louis IV of Hesse and Princess Alice – Queen Victoria's second eldest daughter.

Lower, left. Grand Duke Nicholas Nicholaievitch of Russia, born in 1856. His father, also Grand Duke Nicholas Nicholaievitch (1831-1891) was the third son of Tsar Nicholas I (1796-1855). He was therefore a cousin of Tsar Alexander III.

Lower, centre. Grand Duke Sergei, Grand Duchess Marie, and Grand Duke Paul – the youngest children of Tsar Alexander II of Russia (1818-1881), photographed in about 1867.

Grand Duchess Marie (1853-1920) married Queen Victoria's second son Prince Alfred (1844-1900), the Duke of Edinburgh. Her eldest brother, Grand Duke Sergei, married Princess Elizabeth of Hesse-Darmstadt (1864-1918), but their union failed to produce children. In 1905 Grand Duke Sergi was assassinated in Moscow by anarchists, and 13 years later his wife was also murdered – in Alapaievsk, by Bolsheviks.

The youngest of the children, Grand Duke Paul, married Princess Alexandra (1870-1891), the daughter of King George I of Greece: but in 1919 he too fell victim of political execution, at St Petersburg.

Lower, right. Grand Duke Michael, the younger brother of Tsar Nicholas II. He was murdered at Perm in July 1918, shortly before his brother, the Tsar, and his family were executed.

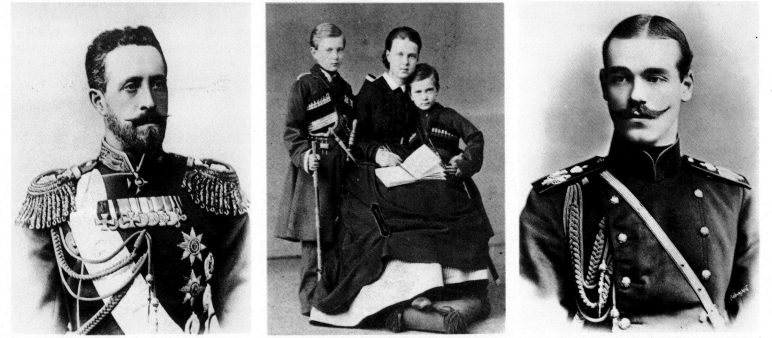

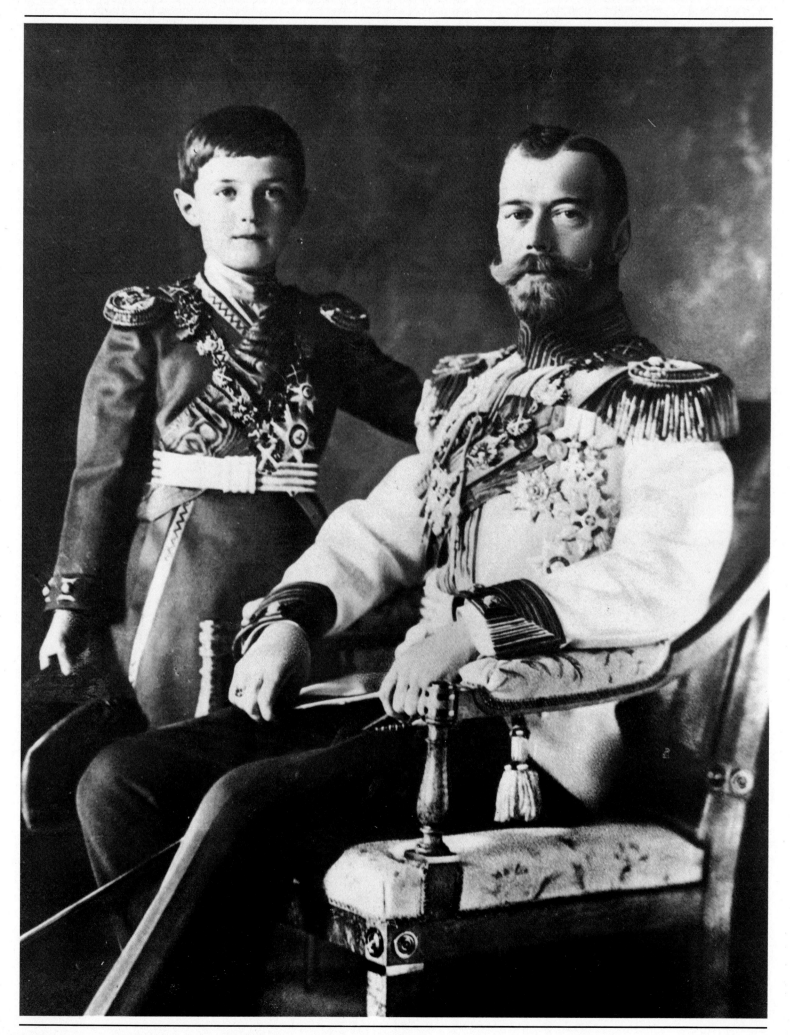

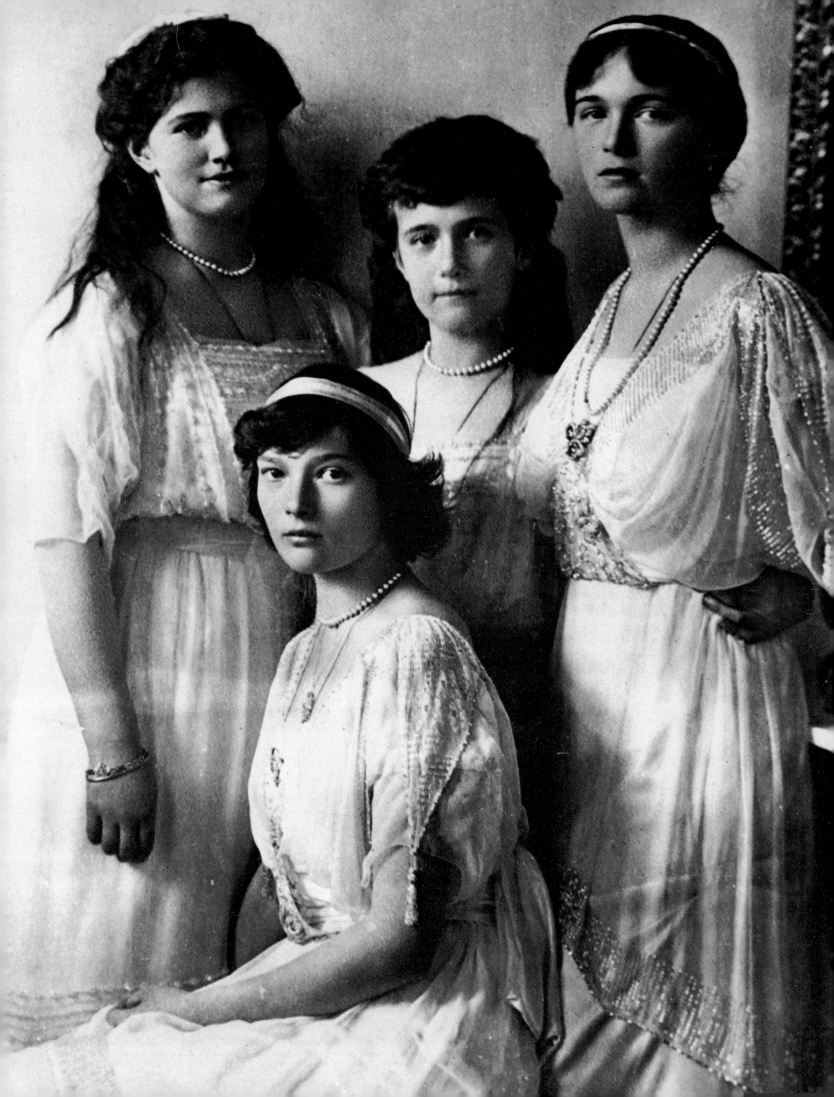

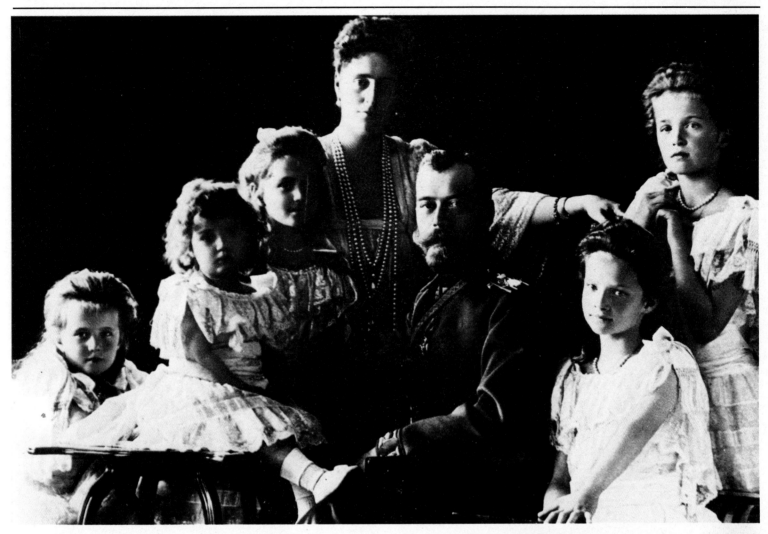

Tsar Nicholas and his wife Princess Alexandra of Hesse (1872-1918), had five children. The first four to be born were all girls – each bearing the style of Grand Duchess. Olga was born in 1895, the year after her parents' marriage; Tatiana was born in 1897; Marie in 1899, and Anastasia in 1901. In 1904 Tsarevitch Alexei was born, the last of their children, and the only male.

The Tsar, Tsarina, their four daughters and the Tsarevitch were all shot at Ekaterinburg in July 1918, a year after the Tsar's abdication.

Above. The Imperial Family of Russia, photographed in 1906. (Left to right): Grand Duchess Anastasia; Grand Duke Alexei; Grand Duchess Marie; Tsarina Alexandra; Tsar Nicholas II; Grand Duchess Tatiana; Grand Duchess Olga.

Opposite page, left. The four daughters of Tsar Nicholas II. (Left to right): Grand Duchess Marie; Grand Duchess Tatiana; Grand Duchess Anastasia, and Grand Duchess Olga. This photograph was taken in 1914.

Right. Another photograph, taken on the same occasion, of the four Grand Duchesses. (Left to right): Grand Duchess Marie; Grand Duchess Tatiana; Grand Duchess Olga, and Grand Duchess Anastasia. None of the four was married.

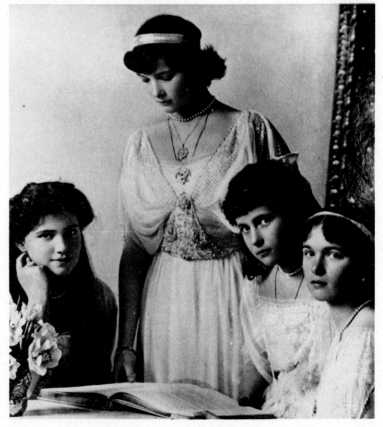

Germany

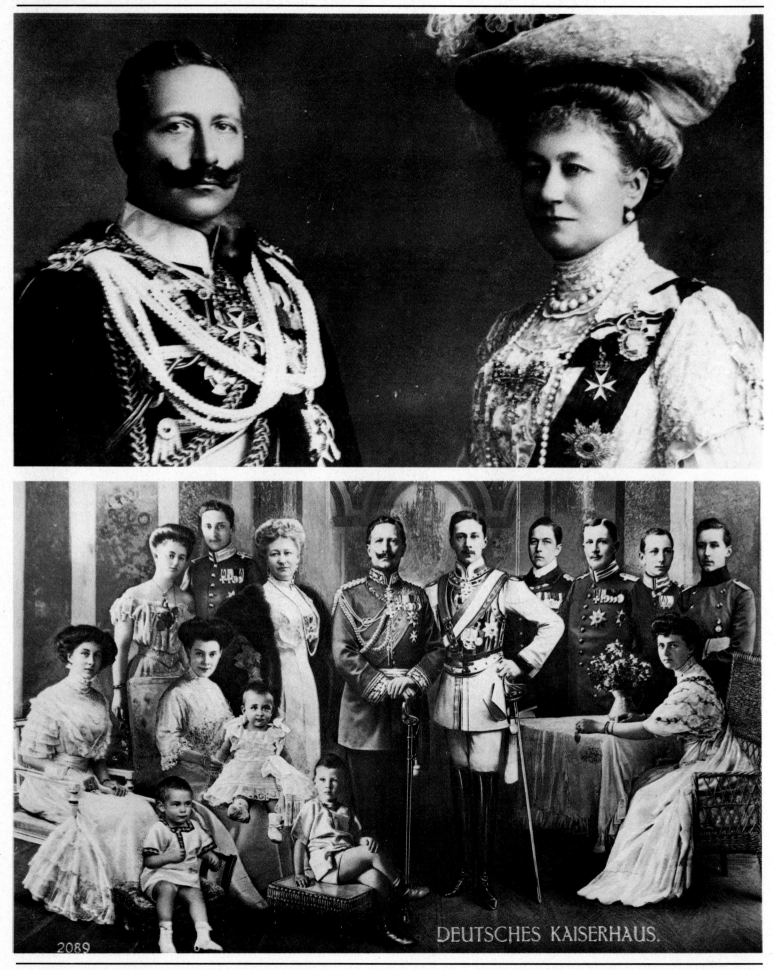

DEUTSCHES KAISERHAUS.

2089

112

Above left. A photograph dated around 1904, showing Kaiser Wilhelm II and his wife, the Empress Augusta.

Kaiser Wilhelm II (1859-1941) was the eldest son of Emperor Frederick III of Germany (1831-1888) and his wife, formerly Victoria, Princess Royal of Great Britain (1840-1901), the eldest daughter of Queen Victoria. He came to the German Imperial throne in 1888 on the death of his father from cancer after a reign of only three months.

In 1881 he had married Princess Augusta-Victoria of Schleswig-Holstein (photographed, *lower right,* in 1912), a daughter of Frederick, Duke of Schlewig-Holstein-Sonderburg-Augustenburg, the head of a junior branch of the royal house of Denmark.

There were seven children of the marriage: Prince Wilhelm (1882-1951) who married Duchess Cecilie of Mecklenburg-Schwerin (1886-1954); Prince Eitel (1883-1942) who married Princess Sophia of Oldenburg; Prince Adalbert (1884-1948) who married Princess Adelaide of Saxe-Meiningen (b. 1891); Prince Augustus Wilhelm (1887-1949) who married Princess Alexandra of Schleswig-Holstein-Sonderburg-Glucksburg (1887-1957), a niece of Empress Augusta; Prince Oscar (1888-1958) who married a Polish Countess; Prince Joachim (1890-1920) who married Princess Maria of Anhalt (b. 1898); and Princess Victoria-Louise (1892-1980) who married Prince Ernst, Duke of Brunswick-Luneburg (1887-1953) and was the grandmother of the present ex-King Constantine of Greece (b. 1940).

Above right. Kaiser Wilhelm II and Empress Augusta with their youngest child – the only daughter – Princess Victoria-Louise. A photograph to celebrate their Silver Wedding in 1906.

Lower left. A photograph of 1910 showing the Imperial German Family to the third generation. (Relationships to the Kaiser are explained above.)

Standing (left to right):
Princess Alexandra, Prince Augustus William, Empress Augusta, Kaiser Wilhelm II, Crown Prince Wilhelm, Prince Adalbert, Prince Eitel, Prince Joachim, Prince Oscar.

Seated (left to right):

Princess Victoria Louise, Prince Louis-Ferdinand (b. 1907), Crown Princess Cecilie, Prince Hubertus (1909-1950), the third son of Crown Prince Wilhelm, with his elder brother Prince Wilhelm (1906-1940), and Princess Sophia.

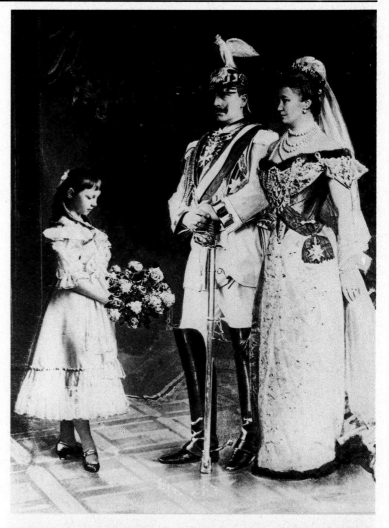

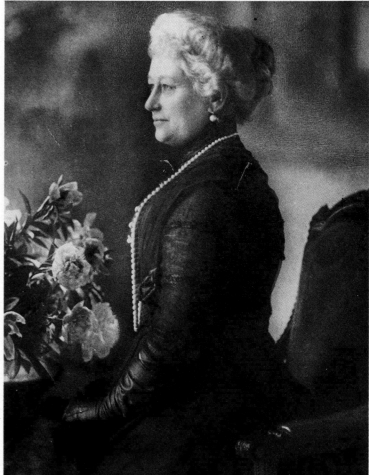

Germany

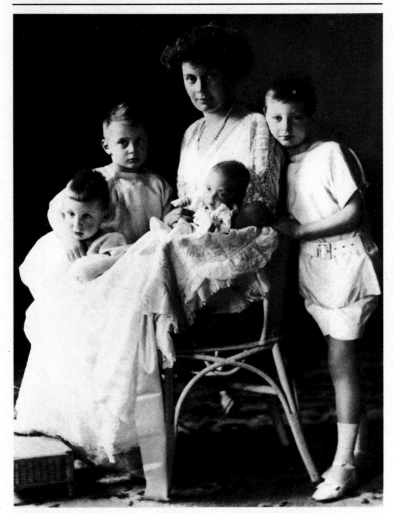

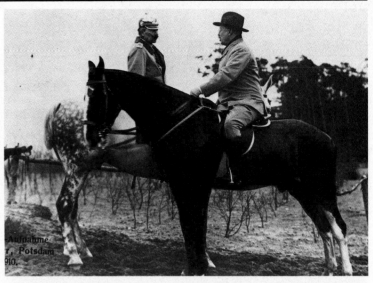

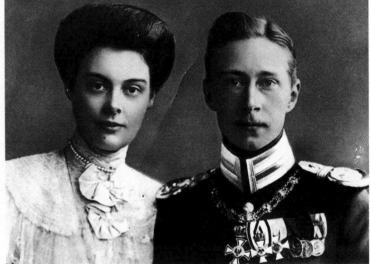

Above right. Kaiser Wilhelm II, with President Theodore Roosevelt of the United States of America (President from 1901-1912) at Döberitz during Roosevelt's tour of Germany in 1910.

Lower right. Crown Prince Wilhelm – the eldest of the Kaiser's seven children – and his wife, the Duchess Cecille of Mecklenburg-Schwerin. He was born in 1882, and succeeded his father as head of the house of Hohenzollern in 1941, twenty-three years after the latter had abdicated as Emperor of Germany.

    Duchess Cecilie was born in 1886, the daughter of Grand Duke Frederick-Franz III of Mecklenburg-Schwerin (1851-1897) and Grand Duchess Anastasia (1860-1922), a niece of Tsar Alexander II of Russi   She was sister to Duchess Alexandrine (1879-1952) who became grandmother to the present Queen of Denmark, Margrethe II (b. 1940). The photograph was taken in May 1905, the year in which the couple were married.

Above left. Crown Prince Wilhelm and Duchess Cecilie had six children. The first four are photographed here with their mother. They are:

Prince Wilhelm (1906-1940) who married a commoner, Dorothea von Salviati (1907-1972) in 1933, renouncing his rights of succession in favour of his eldest brother, and who died of wounds received on active service at Valenciennes in 1940.

Prince Louis Ferdinand (b. 1907). He has been head of the House of Hohenzollern since the death of his father in 1951. In 1938 he married Grand Duchess Kira (1909-1967), daughter of Grand Duke Kirill of Russia, and has seven children.

Prince Hubertus (1909-1950). He contracted a marriage to a commoner in 1941 which ended in divorce in 1943, and to Magdelene, Princess Reuss (b. 1920) in the same year (1943), by whom he had two daughters. He died in South West Africa in 1950.

Prince Frederick (b. 1911). He married Lady Brigid Guinness (b. 1920), daughter of the Earl of Iveagh, by whom he had five children.

The photograph was taken in 1912.

Opposite page, right. A photograph of Princess Victoria Louise taken in about 1909.

    Princess Victoria Louise was the only daughter, and the youngest child, of Kaiser Wilhelm II of Germany. She was born in 1892, and in 1913 married Prince Ernst of Hanover (1887-1953) son of the last Duke of Cumberland (1845-1923) whose wife, Princess Thyra (1853-1933), was the youngest daughter of King Christian IX of Denmark and sister of Queen Alexandra of England. Both Princess Victoria Louise and Prince Ernst were direct descendants of King George III of England – she in the fifth generation; he in the fourth.

    Of their five children, Prince George (b. 1915) is the second husband of Princess Sophie of Greece (b. 1914) who is a sister of Prince Philip, Duke of Edinburgh; and Princess Frederika (1917-1981) married King Paul of Greece (1901-1964) and was the mother of ex-King Constantine II.

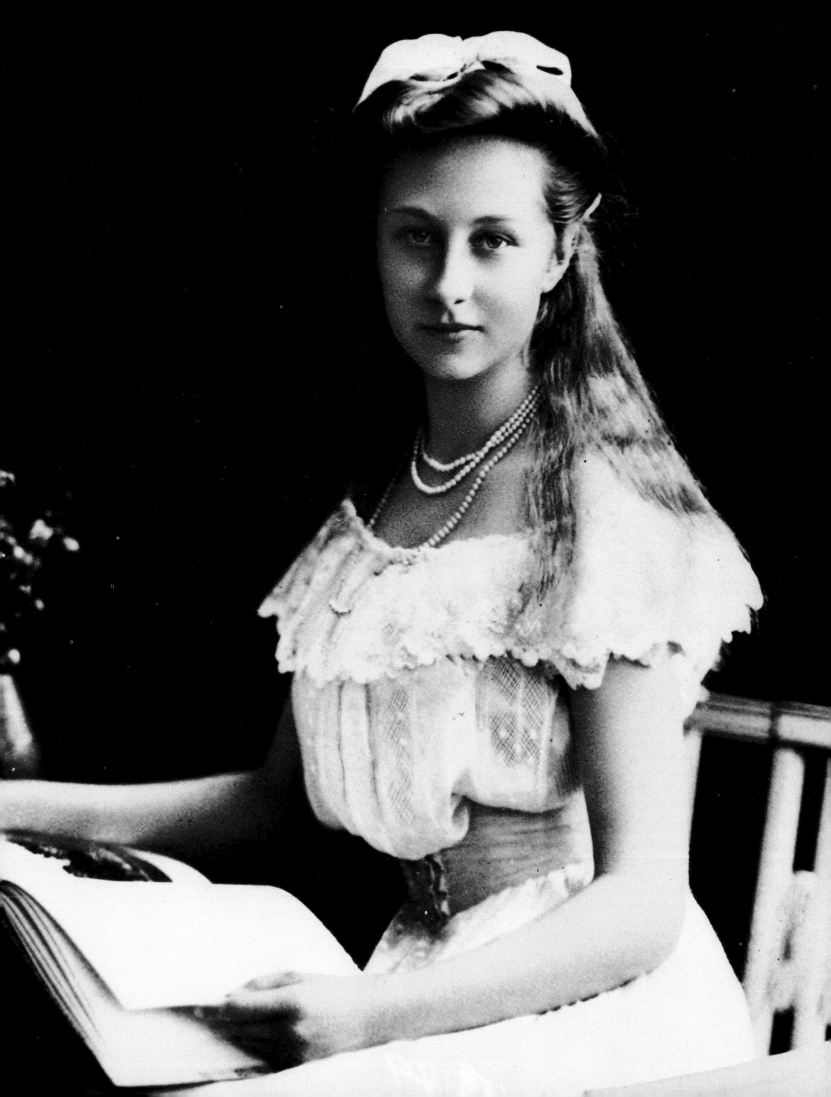

Denmark

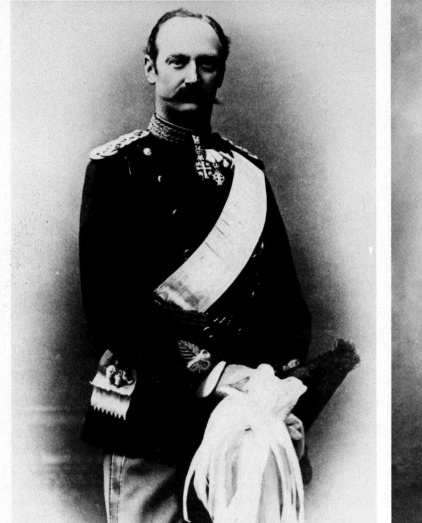

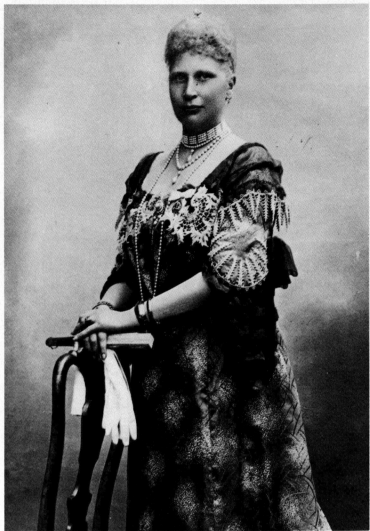

Above, left. King Frederick VIII of Denmark (1843-1912) was the eldest son of King Christian IX (1818-1906) and Queen Louise, formerly Princess Louise of Hesse-Cassel (1817-1898).

In 1869 he married Princess Louise (photographed, *above right,* in 1905), the only daughter of King Carl XV of Sweden (1826-1872) and Queen Louise of Sweden (1828-1871), formerly Princess of the Netherlands, and a first cousin of King William III of the Netherlands of whom the present Queen Beatrix is great-granddaughter. King Carl XV had no sons, and on his death in 1872, the Crown, being subject to Salic law, passed to his brother, King Oscar II, rather than to Princess Louise herself.

King Frederick had eight children, of whom the two most significant dynastically were the eldest, who succeeded his father as King Christian X (1870-1947) and was the grandfather of the present Queen Margrethe of Denmark; and the second son, Prince Carl (1872-1957) who married Princess Maud (1869-1938), youngest daughter of King Edward VII and Queen Alexandra, and who in 1905 became the first King of newly independent Norway when it was ceded by Sweden. He reigned as Haakon VII for 52 years, and his only son is now King Olav V (b. 1903).

King Frederick VIII came to the throne of Denmark on the death of his father in 1906 and died six years later.

Opposite page, right. Crown Princess Alexandrine and the two sons of King Christian X, taken in about 1909, three years before his succession to the Danish throne.

King Christian X was the eldest son of King Frederick VIII and in 1898 married Crown Princess Alexandrine, the eldest daughter of Grand-Duke Frederick-Francis III of Mecklenburg Schwerin (1851-1897).

King Christian X's and Crown Princess Alexandrine's first son, Prince Frederick (1899-1974) (standing in the photograph) married Princess Ingrid (b. 1910), daughter of King Gustav VI of Sweden, in 1935; they had three children, the present Queen Margrethe II (b. 1940), Princess Benedikte (b. 1944), who married Prince Richard of Sayn-Wittgenstein, and Princess Anne-Marie (b. 1946) who married King Constantine II, (now ex-King) of Greece.

Their second son, *seated,* Prince Knud (1900-1976) married his first cousin, Princess Caroline Mathilda (b. 1912) the daughter of Prince Christian's brother Prince Harald (1876-1949), in 1933.

In 1912 on the accession of King Christian X, Alexandrine became Queen. Christian X died in 1947 and was succeeded by the elder son Frederick IX.

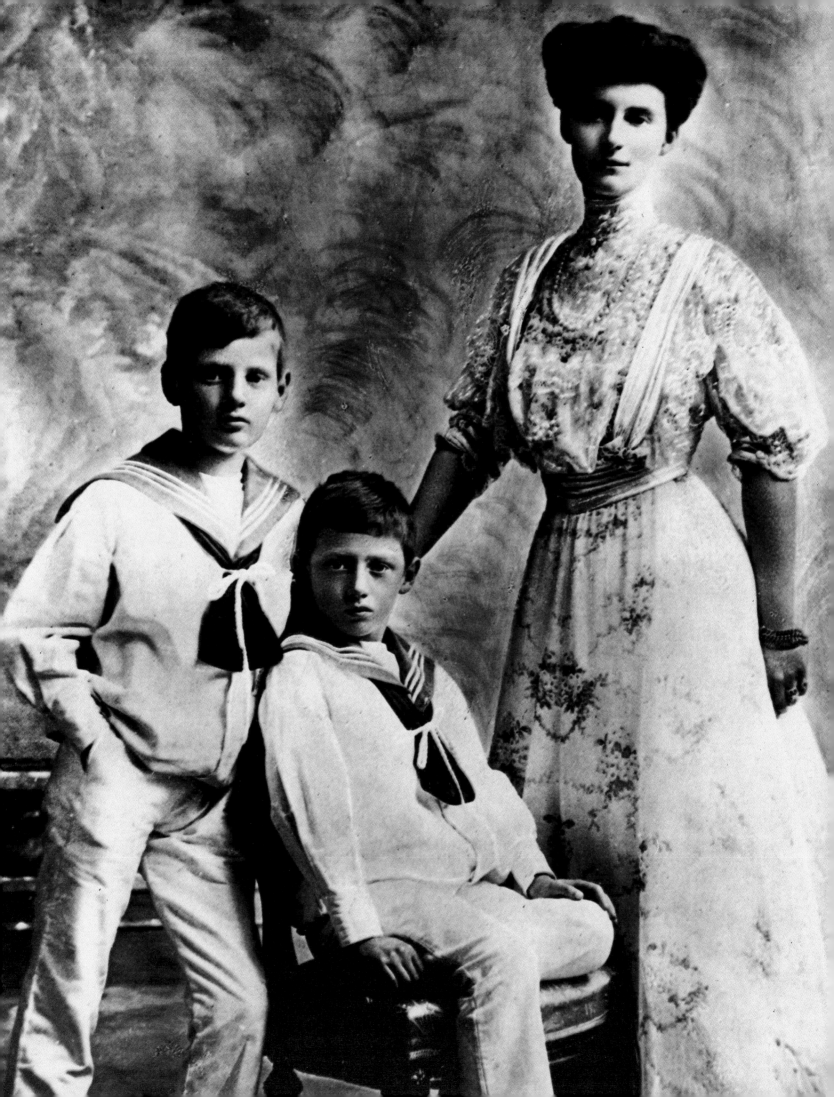

Norway

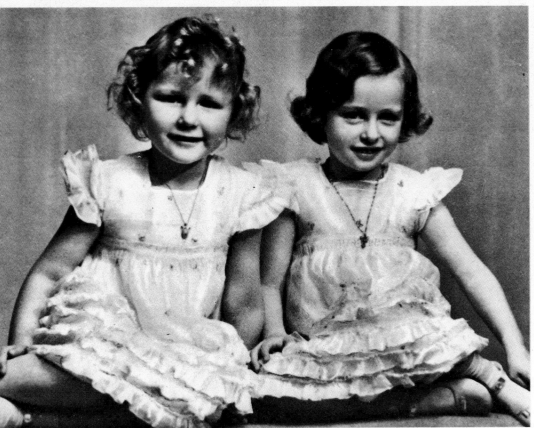

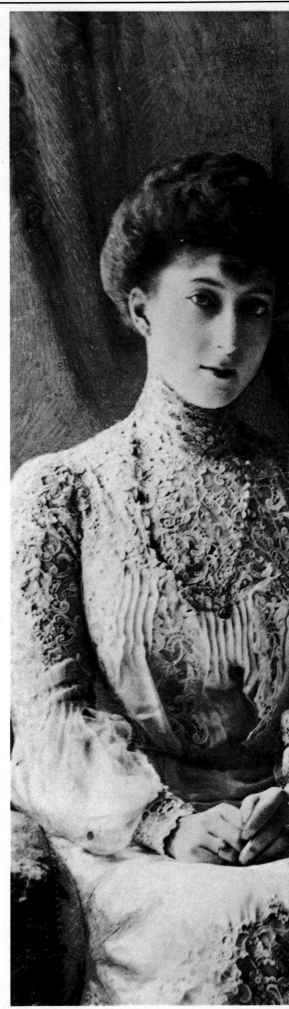

Right. A photograph of King Haakon VII, Queen Maud and Crown Prince Olav; taken in about 1905.

King Haakon VII (1872-1957) became the first King of the newly independent Norway in 1905. He was born Prince Carl of Denmark, the second son of King Frederick VIII and Queen Louise, a daughter of King Carl XV of Sweden. One of his aunts was Queen Alexandra, a sister of King Frederick VIII and consort of King Edward VII of England.

In 1896 he had married Princess Maud of Wales (1869-1938), the youngest daughter of King Edward VII and Queen Alexandra, and thus his first cousin.

Their only child was born in 1903. Originally Prince Alexander of Denmark, he acquired the style Crown-Prince Olav of Norway in 1905. In 1929 he married his first cousin Princess Martha of Sweden (1901-1954), second daughter of King Frederick VIII's sister Princess Ingeborg (1878-1958) and her Swedish husband Prince Charles (1861-1951), a brother of King Gustav V of Sweden. Their children are Princess Ragnhild (b. 1930), Princess Astrid (b. 1934) and Prince Harald (b. 1937).

Crown-Prince Olav succeeded his father on the latter's death in 1957 and became King Olav V. His son is now Crown-Prince Harald.

Opposite page, above right. A photograph of Queen Maud and her son, Crown Prince Olav, dated 1908.

Opposite page, lower right. Crown Prince Olav and his wife, Crown Princess Martha, c 1935.

Above. Princess Ragnhild and Princess Astrid of Norway, the only two daughters of King Olav V.

Princess Ragnhild is the elder daughter, born in 1930. In 1953 she married Erling Svend Lorentzen by whom she has three children, Haakon, Ingeborg and Ragnhild.

Princess Astrid was born in 1932. In 1961 she married Johann Fernher, and has five children.

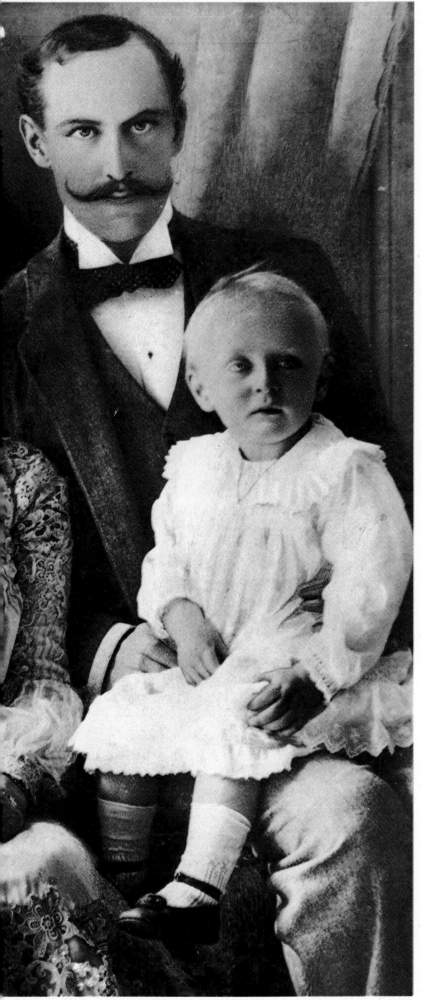

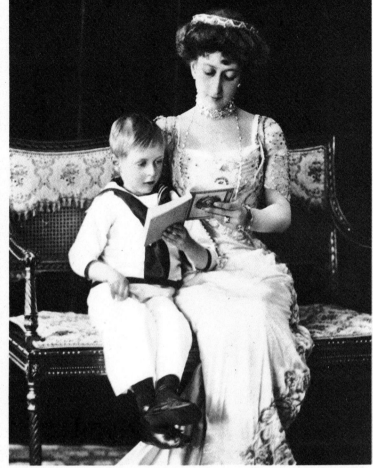

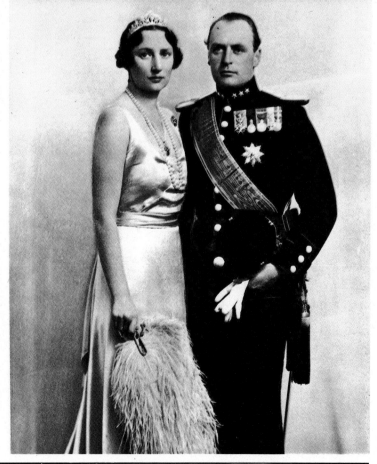

Sweden

Below. Queen Victoria of Sweden, who was born in 1862, was a Princess of the German Grand Duchy of Baden. Her father had, in 1856, become reigning Grand Duke of Baden as Frederick I (1826-1907); whilst her mother, Grand Duchess Louise (1838-1923), was the only daughter of King William I of Prussia. Queen Victoria of Sweden was thus a first cousin of Kaiser Wilhelm II of Germany.

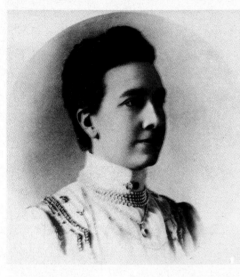

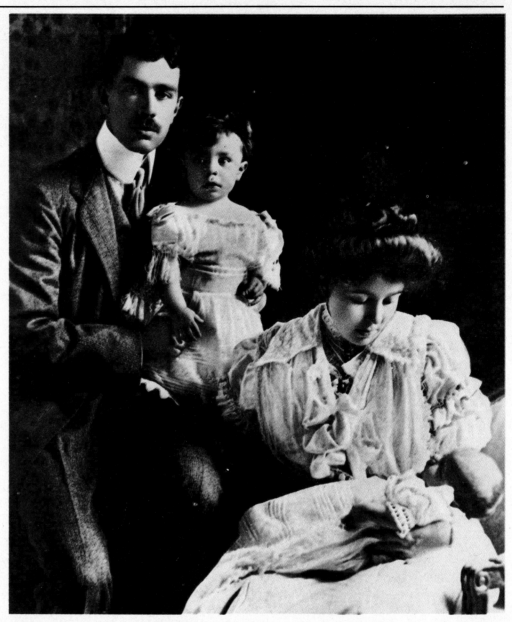

In 1881, she married King (then Crown Prince) Gustav V of Sweden, and became Queen Consort when her husband succeeded his father King Oscar II in 1907. She had three children. The eldest became King Gustav VI; the second child, Prince William (1884-1965), married Grand Duchess Marie Pavlovna of Russia (1890-1958), a niece of Tsar Alexander III; and the third child, Prince Eric, died unmarried in 1918 at the age of 29.

Queen Victoria of Sweden died in 1930, predeceasing her husband by 20 years. The present King of Sweden, Carl XVI (b. 1946) is her great-grandson.

This photograph was taken in about 1898.

Above, right. A photograph taken in 1907 of Crown Prince Gustav, Crown Princess Margaret, Prince Gustav, and Prince Sigvard.

Crown Prince Gustav (1882-1973), the eldest son of King Gustav V of Sweden and Queen Victoria, married Princess Margaret of Connaught in 1905 and had five children by her. After her death in 1920, he married Lady Louise Mountbatten (1889-1965), daughter of the 1st Marquess of Milford Haven, but their only child was stillborn in 1925. In 1950 his father died and he succeeded as King Gustav VI, and when he died in 1973 his grandson succeeded him as King Carl XVI.

Crown Princess Margaret (1882-1920) (also photographed, *right,* c 1905) was the elder daughter of Queen Victoria's third son Arthur, Duke of Connaught.

Prince Gustav, their eldest child, was born in 1906 and married Princess Sybilla of Saxe-Coburg-Gotha (1908-1973) in 1932: she was a daughter of Queen Victoria's grandson, Prince Charles Edward of Albany (1884-1954), the brother of Princess Alice of Athlone. Prince Gustav had five children – Princess Margarethe (b. 1934), Princess Birgitta (b. 1937) who, in 1961, married Prince Johann-Georg of Hohenzollern-Sigmaringen (b. 1932), Princess Desiree (b. 1938), Princess Christina (b. 1943), and Prince Carl Gustav (b. 1946). Prince Gustav having died in 1947, Prince Carl Gustav became the heir to the throne and succeeded when his grandfather, King Gustav VI, died in 1973. In 1976 he married Silvia Sommerlath by whom he has a daughter, Princess Victoria, born in 1977, and a son, Prince Carl-Philip, born in 1979.

Prince Sigvard (b. 1907), the second of five children of Crown Princess Margaret and Crown Prince Gustav, renounced his rights of succession in 1934, on his first marriage to Erika Patzek, whom he divorced in 1943. Later in 1943 he married Sonia Robbert, by whom he had a son, Michael (b. 1944) Count of Wisborg. His third wife is Marianne Lindberg.

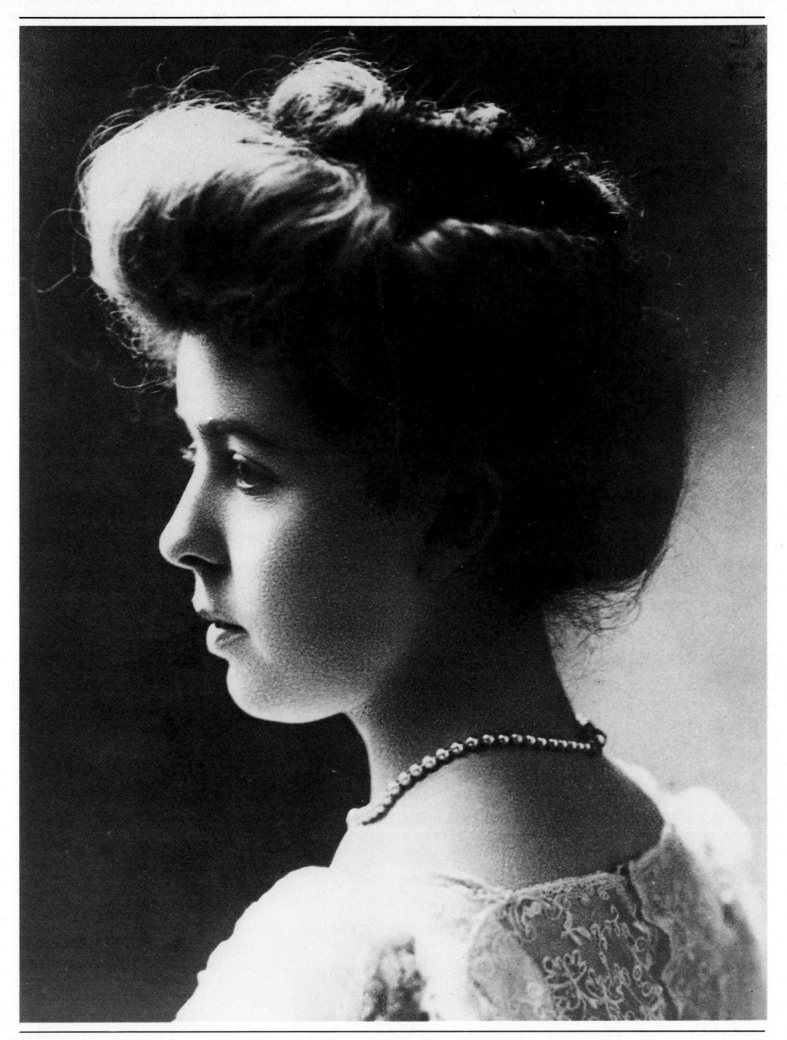

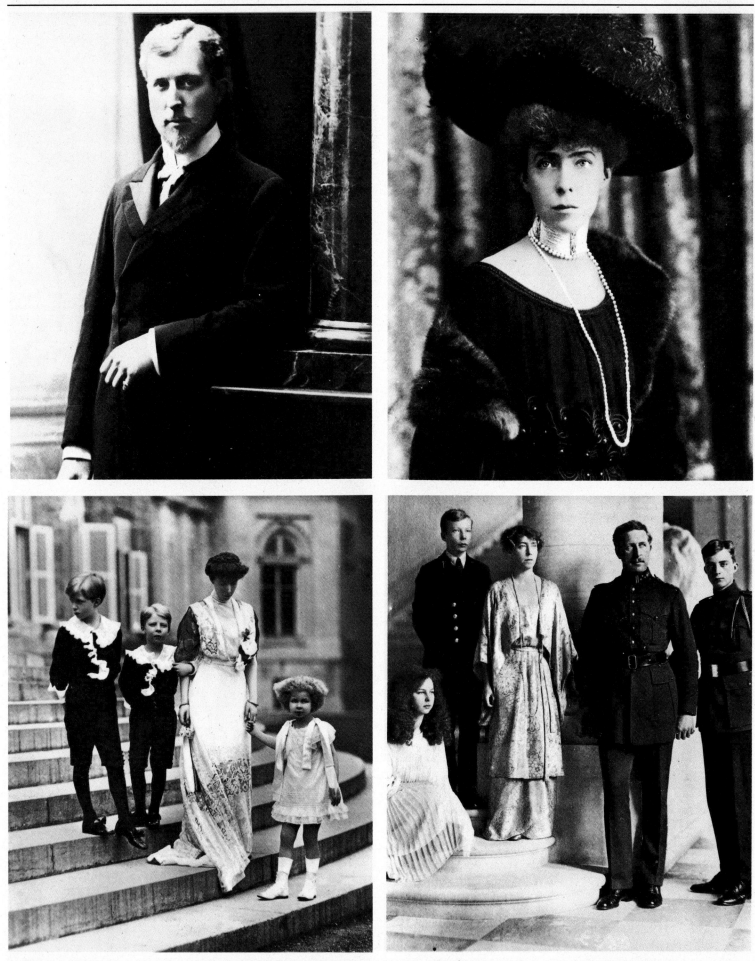

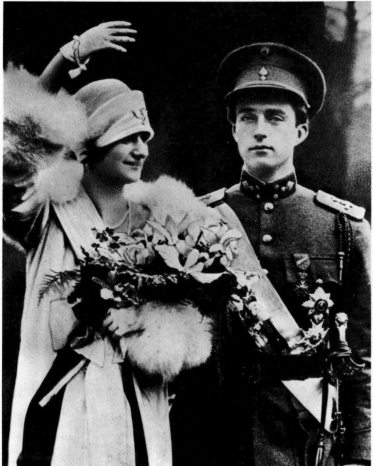

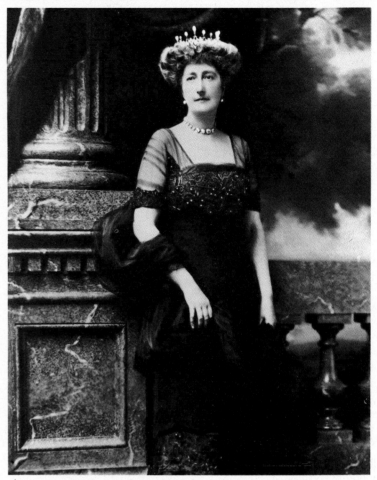

King Albert I of Belgium, *opposite page, top left,* was the third King of the Saxe-Coburg dynasty to rule that country. He was born in 1875, a grandson of the first Coburg King, Leopold I (1790-1865) – an uncle of Queen Victoria – and nephew of the second, Leopold II (1835-1909). His father was Prince Phillippe, Count of Flanders (1837-1905): his mother, Princess Marie of Hohenzollern-Sigmaringen (1845-1912) was the sister of King Carol I of Roumania (1839-1914).

King Albert succeeded to the throne in 1909 and died in 1934. This photograph of him was taken in about 1900, when he was Prince Albert of Flanders, and second in line of succession, after his father, to the Belgian throne.

Opposite page, top right. In 1900 King Albert I married Duchess Elisabeth of the ducal branch of the Bavarian house of Wittelsbach. Born in 1876, she was the younger daughter of reigning Duke Karl Theodor (1839-1909) and his second wife Duchess Marie Jose (1857-1943) formerly Infanta of Portugal and daughter of Prince Miguel, Duke of Braganza, who was at one time King of Portugal.

King Albert I and Queen Elisabeth of the Belgians had three children – two sons and a daughter.

The elder of the two sons is Prince Leopold (b. 1901) who succeeded his father as King Leopold III in 1934 and abdicated in 1950 in favour of his elder son, Prince Baudouin (b. 1930).

The second son, Prince Charles, was born in 1903 and has never married. He stood Regent for King Baudouin for a short period after King Leopold III's abdication in 1950.

King Albert I's only daughter is Princess Marie-Jose (b. 1906) who married Prince Umberto of Italy (b. 1904), and became, briefly in 1946, Queen of Italy before she and her husband were exiled. She has four children.

The photographs, *opposite page, lower left and right,* show the Royal Family in 1911 (at the palace at Laeken) and in 1918.

Above, left. The eldest son of King Albert I and Queen Elisabeth married Princess Astrid of Sweden (1905-1935). She was a niece of King Gustav V of Sweden (1858-1950) and sister to Princess Martha of Sweden (1901-1954) who became Crown-Princess of Norway on her marriage to Prince (now King) Olav.

Prince Leopold succeeded to the throne as King Leopold III on the death of his father in 1934 in a mountaineering accident. Queen Astrid was killed the following year in a car crash from which King Leopold escaped without substantial injury.

The couple had two sons and a daughter; the eldest son is the present King Baudouin (b. 1930) who, when his father abdicated in 1950, succeeded under the Regency of Prince Charles until he came of age in 1951. The second son, Prince Albert (b. 1934) is married to Princess Paola of Calabria and has three children, the eldest of whom, Prince Phillippe was born in 1960. The daughter is Princess Josephine-Charlotte (b. 1927) who is the present Grand Duchess of Luxemburg, consort of Grand Duke Jean.

This photograph was taken in about 1927.

Princess Clementine (1872-1955), *above, right,* was the youngest of four children of King Leopold II of Belgium (1835-1909) and Queen Maria-Henrietta (1836-1902), formerly Archduchess of Austria.

In 1910 she married the head of the house of Bonaparte, Prince Victor Napoleon (1862-1926), grandson of Jerome, King of Westphalia, who was a brother of the great Napoleon I.

This photograph was taken in about 1910.

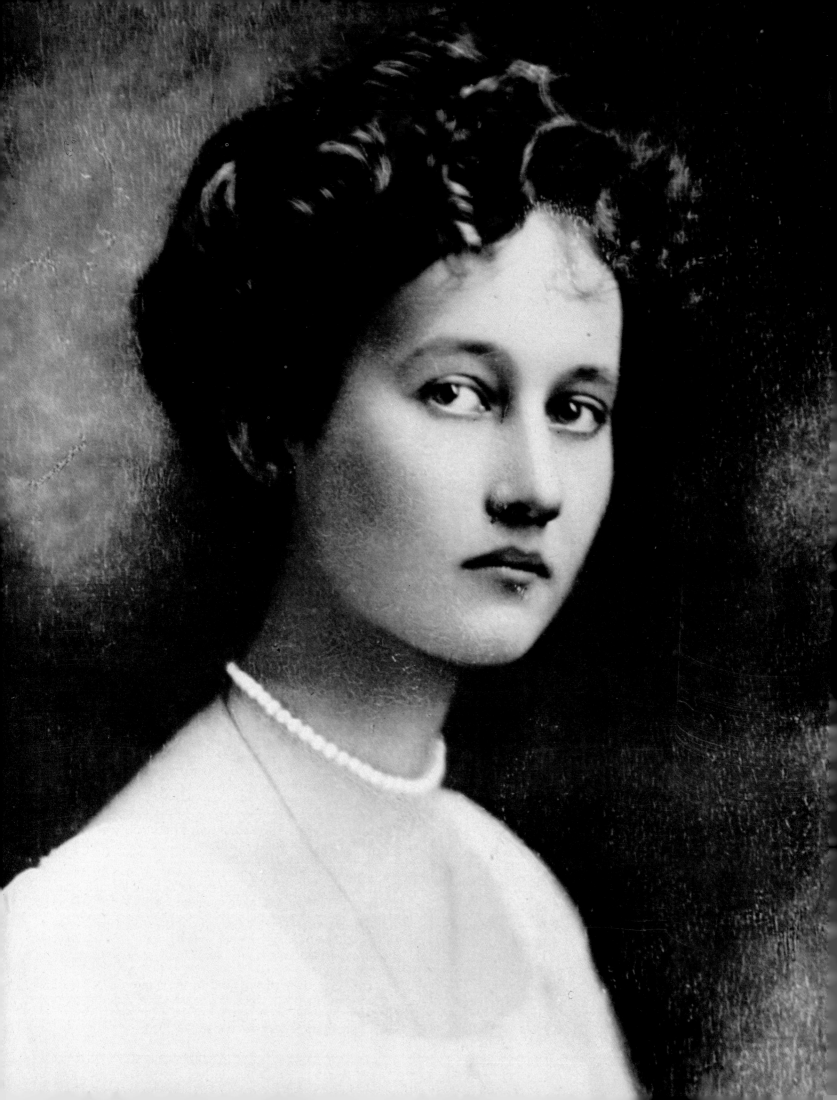

Luxemburg/Baden

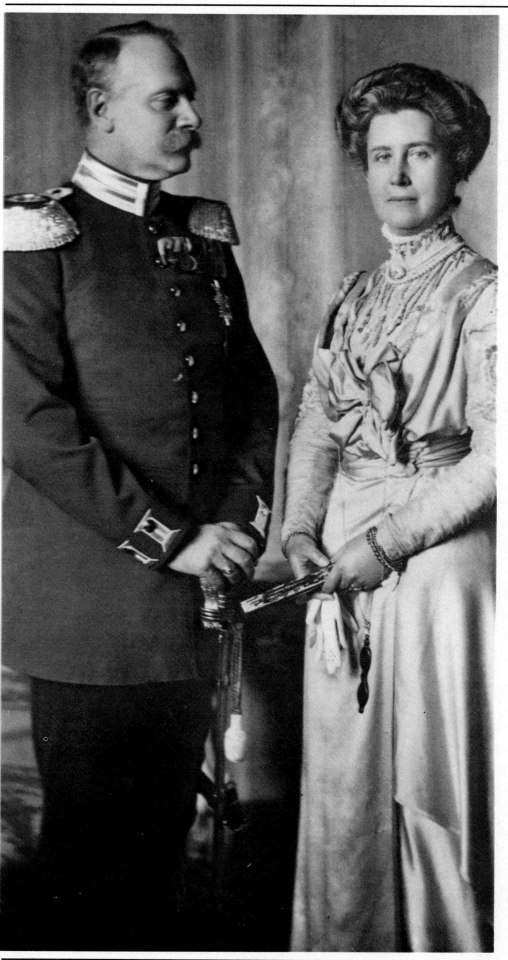

Grand Duchess Marie-Adelaide (photographed, *opposite page, left,* c 1912) was born in 1894, the eldest of the six daughters of the reigning Grand Duke William (1852-1912) and his wife, formerly the Infanta Maria Anna (1861-1942) of Portugal (the Royal House of Braganza).

In 1912 she succeeded to the throne on the death of her father. She did not marry. In 1919 she abdicated in favour of her eldest sister, Princess Charlotte (b. 1896) who herself abdicated in 1964 in favour of the present Grand Duke Jean. Grand Duchess Marie-Adelaide died in 1924.

Left. Frederick II of Baden (1857-1928) was the only son of Frederick I (1826-1907) and Princess Louise of Prussia (1838-1923). His mother was sister to Emperor Frederick III of Prussia and thus aunt to Kaiser Wilhelm II. His sister, Victoria, (1862-1930) became Queen of Sweden, wife of King Gustav V.

In 1885 Frederick II married Princess Hilda of Nassau (1864-1952), the sister of the reigning Grand Duke Adolphe of Luxemburg (1817-1905) and thus great-great-aunt to the present Grand Duke Jean (b. 1921). Frederick II succeeded to the Grand-Dukedom of Baden in 1907.

The couple had no children, and when Frederick II abdicated in 1918, he ceded the title of Grand Duke, to become Margrave of Baden. On his death in 1928 his cousin Prince Maximilien (1867-1929) succeeded him. He in turn was succeeded by his son Prince Berthold (1906-1963) who married Princess Theodora of Greece (1906-1969) one of the four sisters of Prince Philip, Duke of Edinburgh.

Portugal

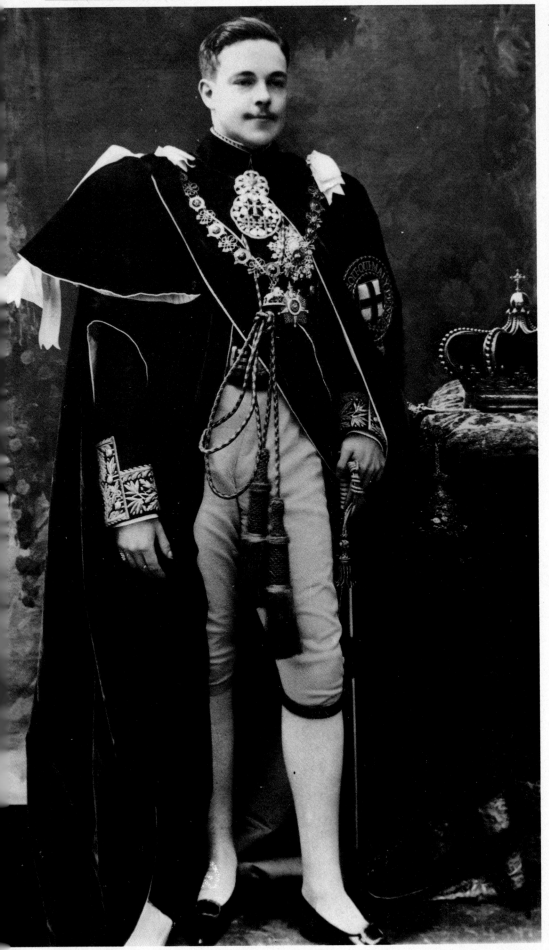

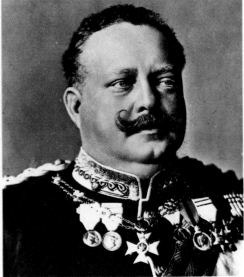

Carlos I of Portugal (*above,* c 1903) was born in 1863, the elder son of King Luis (1838-1889) and Queen Maria-Pia (1847-1911) formerly Princess of Savoy, a daughter of King Emmanuel II of Italy (1820-1878).

He succeeded to the throne in 1889, having married in 1886 Princess Amelie of Bourbon Orleans. She was born in 1865, the eldest child of Prince Louis-Phillippe, Count of Paris (1838-1894) who, being the senior grandson of the last King (Louis-Phillippe) of the French, was the claimant to the French throne. Her mother, Princess Maria-Isabella (1848-1919) was an infanta of Spain through the Spanish branch of the Bourbon-Orleans dynasty.

They had two children: Prince Luis-Felipe was born in 1887, and Prince Manoel in 1889. In 1908 King Carlos I and Prince Luis-Felipe were assassinated together, and the Crown devolved upon Prince Manoel who succeeded as King Manoel II.

Left. King Manoel II, whose reign lasted only until 1910 – when he was overthrown and Portugal was declared a Republic.

In 1913, he married Princess Augustine (b. 1890) (photographed, *opposite page, right,* in 1913) daughter of Prince Wilhelm of Hohenzollern-Sigmaringen (brother of King Ferdinand of Roumania) and of Princess Maria of Bourbon-Sicilies.

There were no children of this marriage, which ended with the death of ex-King Manoel II in 1932.

The photograph was taken in 1909, the year in which he was made Knight of the Garter by King Edward VII of England; he is wearing the robes of this Order in the picture.

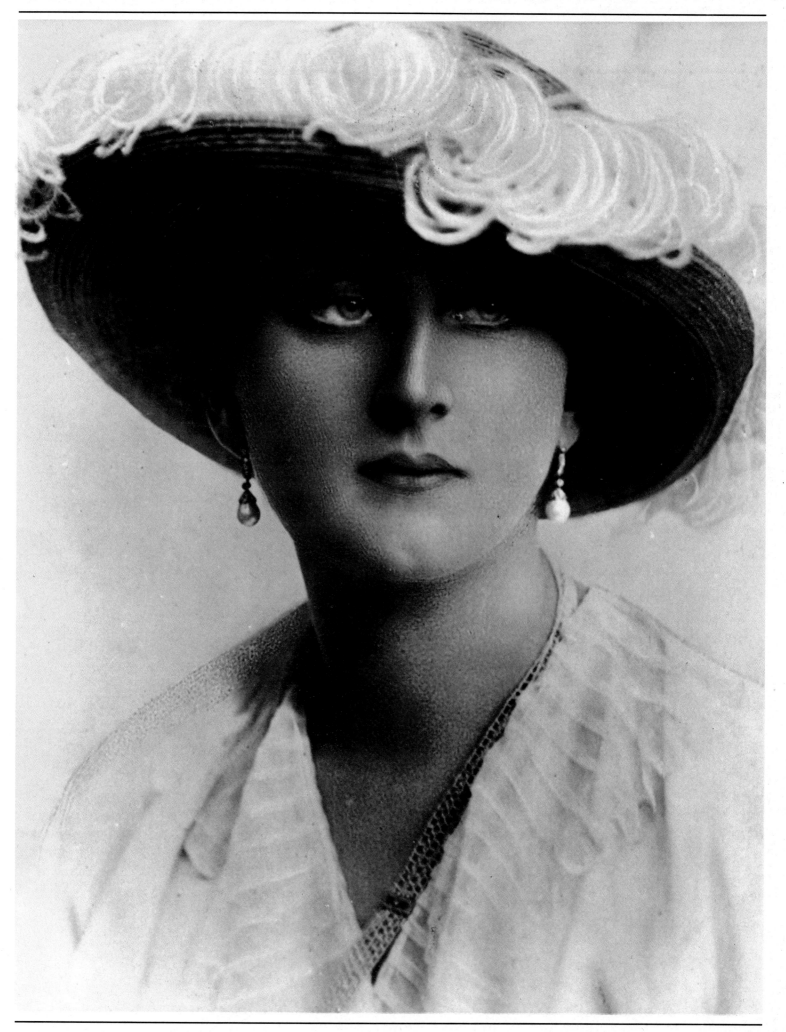

Spain

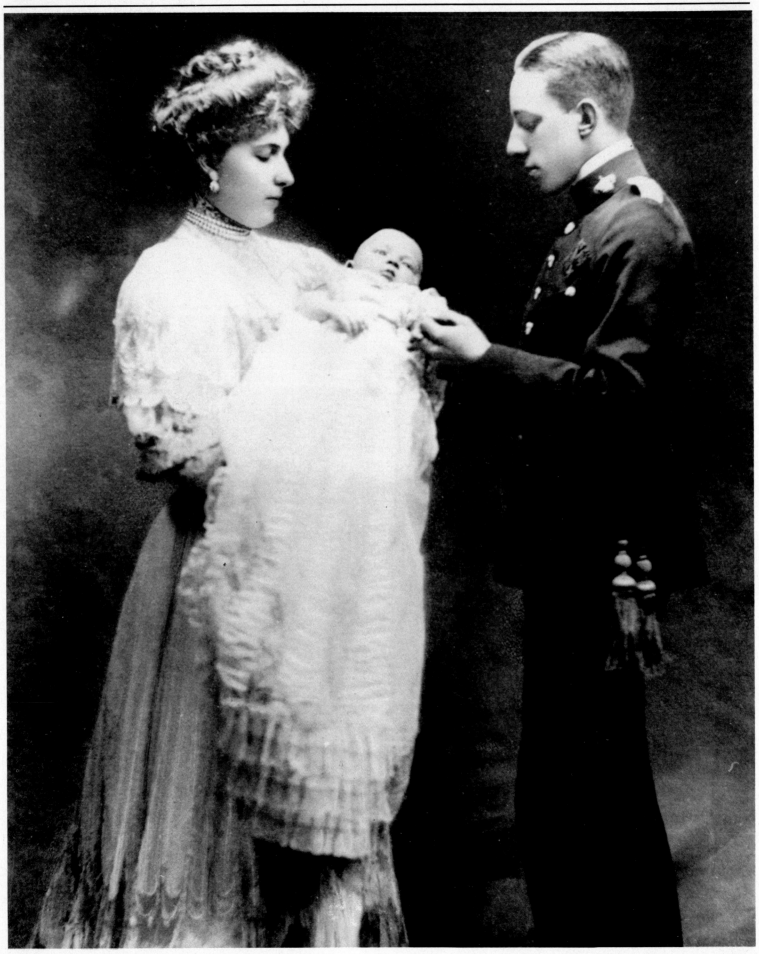

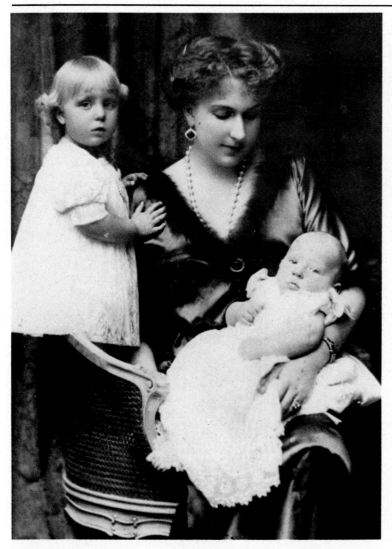

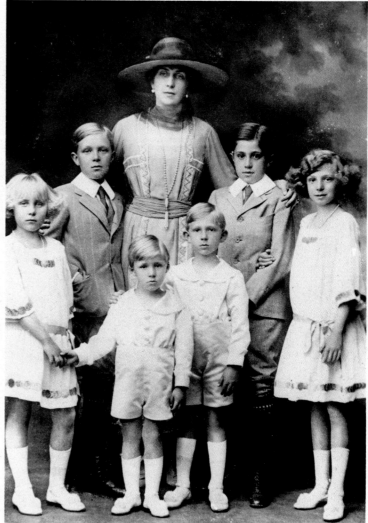

Opposite page, left. King Alfonso XIII of Spain, with his Queen, Victoria-Eugenie, and their eldest son, Prince Alfonso, photographed in 1907.

King Alfonso XIII (1886-1941) was the third child and only son of King Alfonso XII of Spain (1857-1885) and Queen Maria Christina (1858-1929) formerly an Archduchess of Austria and a distant cousin of Emperor Franz-Josef I of Austria. His mother ruled as Regent from his birth until 1902, when Alfonso XIII reigned in his own name until the republic was declared in 1931.

Queen Victoria-Eugenie whom he married in 1906, was a granddaughter of Queen Victoria. She was born in 1887, the only daughter of Princess Beatrice of England (1857-1944) and Prince Henry of Battenberg (1858-1896). She was the last but two of Queen Victoria's forty grandchildren to die – in 1969.

Above, left. Queen Victoria-Eugenie with Princess Maria-Christina and Prince Juan, two of her younger children, in 1913.

Above, right. Queen Victoria-Eugenie with her six children:

Prince Alfonso, Prince of the Asturias (second from left); born in 1907 and renounced his rights of succession in 1933 in anticipation of his marriage to Edelmira Sampredo-Ocejo y Robato. Divorced in 1937, he married that year Marta Rocafort y Altazarra. This second marriage ended in divorce in 1938, the year in which Prince Alfonso was killed in a car accident.

Prince Jaime, Duke of Segovia (second from right); born in 1908, he also renounced his rights of succession in 1933, being a deaf mute. In 1935 he married Emmanuelle de Dampierre (b. 1913), daughter of the Duke of San Lorenzo; they had two sons. In 1947 this marriage was terminated, and Prince Jaime married in 1949 Mlle. Charlotte Tiedemann (b. 1919). There were no children of this marriage, and Prince Jaime died in 1975.

Princess Beatriz (far right); born in 1909, she married Prince Alessandro Torlonia (b. 1911) in 1935. Princess Beatriz has four children.

Princess Maria Christina (far left); born in 1911, she married in 1940 Enrico, Count Marone (1895-1968). She also has four children.

Prince Juan, Count of Barcelona (third from right); he was born in 1913 and married Princess Maria (b. 1915) a daughter of Prince Charles of Bourbon-Sicilies. Of their four children, the second, Prince Juan Carlos (b. 1938) married Princess Sophie (b. 1938) daughter of King Paul I of Greece and sister of ex-King Constantine II of Greece, in 1962, and eventually became King when the monarchy was restored in Spain in 1975.

Prince Gonzalo (third from left) was born in 1914, and died unmarried in 1934, a victim of haemophilia.

The photograph was taken in about 1920.

Italy

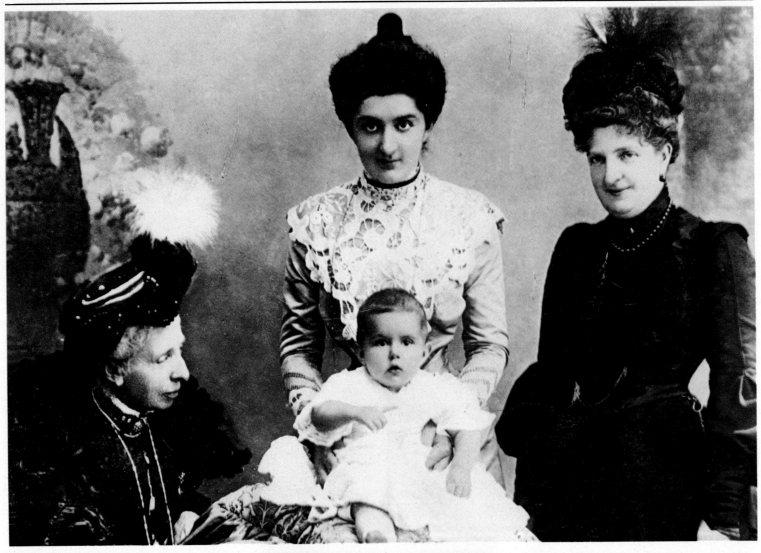

Above. Four generations of the Royal House of Italy. They are, (left to right): The Duchess of Genoa, Queen Elena, Prince Umberto and Dowager Queen Margharita.

The Duchess of Genoa (1830-1912) was formerly Princess Elizabeth of Saxony, a sister of King George of Saxony (1832-1904). In 1850 she married Prince Ferdinand, Duke of Genoa (1822-1855), the brother of King Victor Emmanuel II of Italy (1820-1878), and had two children.

Queen Margharita (1851-1926) was the elder of those two children. She married in 1868 her first cousin, Prince Umberto (1844-1900) son and heir of King Victor Emmanuel II. He succeeded his father in 1878 and was assassinated in 1900.

Queen Elena was a daughter of King Nicholas of Montenegro. She was born in 1873, and in 1896 married the elder son of King Umberto I and Queen Margharita, Prince Victor Emmanuel (1869-1947). He succeeded as King Victor Emmanuel III in 1900 and abdicated in 1946. Queen Elena died in 1952.

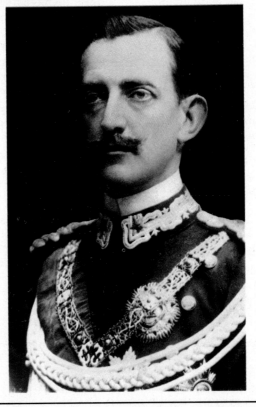

Prince Umberto was their only son, although there were also four daughters. Born in 1904, he married Princess Maria-Jose (b. 1906) daughter of King Albert I of Belgium, in 1930, and has four children. He became King Umberto II briefly in 1946, on his father's abdication, but was dethroned and exiled in the same year. He now lives in exile in Portugal.

This photograph was taken in 1905.

Left. Prince Emmanuel (1869-1931) was the eldest of three sons of Prince Amadeus of Savoy (1845-1890) and his first wife Princess Marie Victoria, formerly Princess dal Pozzo della Cisterna (1847-1876). Prince Amadeus, who was elected King of Spain for a short period between 1870 and 1873, was the only brother of King Umberto I of Italy (1844-1900); thus Prince Emmanuel was first cousin to King Victor Emmanuel III.

In 1895, he married Princess Helene of Orleans (1871-1951) a daughter of the one-time claimant to the French throne, Prince Louis-Phillippe (1838-1894), a great-granddaughter of the last King of

Italy

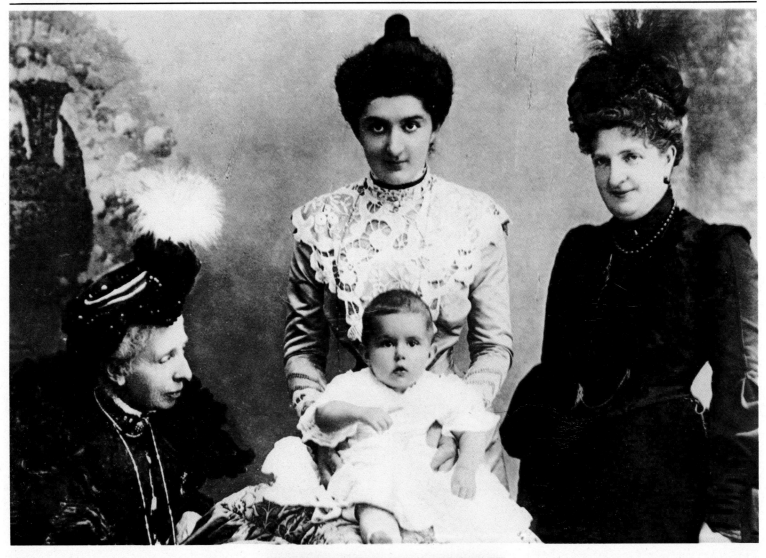

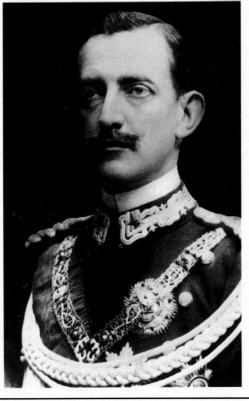

Above. Four generations of the Royal House of Italy. They are, (left to right): The Duchess of Genoa, Queen Elena, Prince Umberto and Dowager Queen Margharita.

The Duchess of Genoa (1830-1912) was formerly Princess Elizabeth of Saxony, a sister of King George of Saxony (1832-1904). In 1850 she married Prince Ferdinand, Duke of Genoa (1822-1855), the brother of King Victor Emmanuel II of Italy (1820-1878), and had two children.

Queen Margharita (1851-1926) was the elder of those two children. She married in 1868 her first cousin, Prince Umberto (1844-1900) son and heir of King Victor Emmanuel II. He succeeded his father in 1878 and was assassinated in 1900.

Queen Elena was a daughter of King Nicholas of Montenegro. She was born in 1873, and in 1896 married the elder son of King Umberto I and Queen Margharita, Prince Victor Emmanuel (1869-1947). He succeeded as King Victor Emmanuel III in 1900 and abdicated in 1946. Queen Elena died in 1952.

Prince Umberto was their only son, although there were also four daughters. Born in 1904, he married Princess Maria-Jose (b. 1906) daughter of King Albert I of Belgium, in 1930, and has four children. He became King Umberto II briefly in 1946, on his father's abdication, but was dethroned and exiled in the same year. He now lives in exile in Portugal.

This photograph was taken in 1905.

Left. Prince Emmanuel (1869-1931) was the eldest of three sons of Prince Amadeus of Savoy (1845-1890) and his first wife Princess Marie Victoria, formerly Princess dal Pozzo della Cisterna (1847-1876). Prince Amadeus, who was elected King of Spain for a short period between 1870 and 1873, was the only brother of King Umberto I of Italy (1844-1900); thus Prince Emmanuel was first cousin to King Victor Emmanuel III.

In 1895, he married Princess Helene of Orleans (1871-1951) a daughter of the one-time claimant to the French throne, Prince Louis-Phillippe (1838-1894), a great-granddaughter of the last King of

Spain

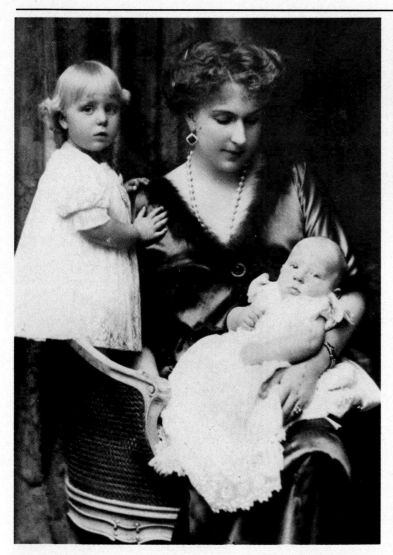

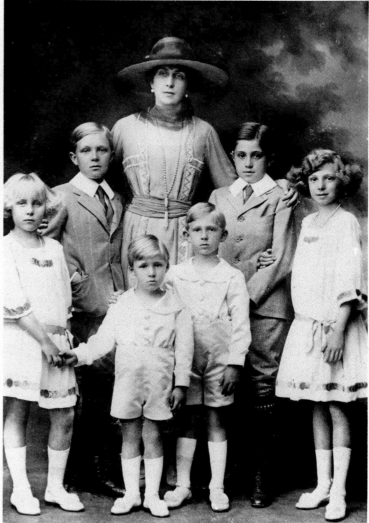

Opposite page, left. King Alfonso XIII of Spain, with his Queen, Victoria-Eugenie, and their eldest son, Prince Alfonso, photographed in 1907.

King Alfonso XIII (1886-1941) was the third child and only son of King Alfonso XII of Spain (1857-1885) and Queen Maria Christina (1858-1929) formerly an Archduchess of Austria and a distant cousin of Emperor Franz-Josef I of Austria. His mother ruled as Regent from his birth until 1902, when Alfonso XIII reigned in his own name until the republic was declared in 1931.

Queen Victoria-Eugenie whom he married in 1906, was a granddaughter of Queen Victoria. She was born in 1887, the only daughter of Princess Beatrice of England (1857-1944) and Prince Henry of Battenberg (1858-1896). She was the last but two of Queen Victoria's forty grandchildren to die – in 1969.

Above, left. Queen Victoria-Eugenie with Princess Maria-Christina and Prince Juan, two of her younger children, in 1913.

Above, right. Queen Victoria-Eugenie with her six children:

Prince Alfonso, Prince of the Asturias (second from left); born in 1907 and renounced his rights of succession in 1933 in anticipation of his marriage to Edelmira Sampredo-Ocejo y Robato. Divorced in 1937, he married that year Marta Rocafort y Altazarra. This second marriage ended in divorce in 1938, the year in which Prince Alfonso was killed in a car accident.

Prince Jaime, Duke of Segovia (second from right); born in 1908, he also renounced his rights of succession in 1933, being a deaf mute. In 1935 he married Emmanuelle de Dampierre (b. 1913), daughter of the Duke of San Lorenzo; they had two sons. In 1947 this marriage was terminated, and Prince Jaime married in 1949 Mlle. Charlotte Tiedemann (b. 1919). There were no children of this marriage, and Prince Jaime died in 1975.

Princess Beatriz (far right); born in 1909, she married Prince Alessandro Torlonia (b. 1911) in 1935. Princess Beatriz has four children.

Princess Maria Christina (far left); born in 1911, she married in 1940 Enrico, Count Marone (1895-1968). She also has four children.

Prince Juan, Count of Barcelona (third from right); he was born in 1913 and married Princess Maria (b. 1915) a daughter of Prince Charles of Bourbon-Sicilies. Of their four children, the second, Prince Juan Carlos (b. 1938) married Princess Sophie (b. 1938) daughter of King Paul I of Greece and sister of ex-King Constantine II of Greece, in 1962, and eventually became King when the monarchy was restored in Spain in 1975.

Prince Gonzalo (third from left) was born in 1914, and died unmarried in 1934, a victim of haemophilia.

The photograph was taken in about 1920.

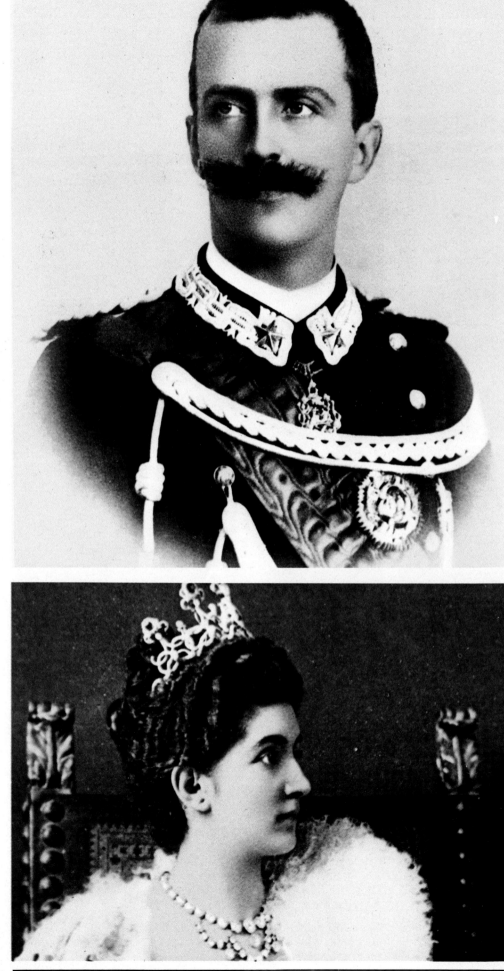

the French, King Louis-Phillippe (1773-1850), and sister of Queen Amelie of Portugal (1865-1951). They had two children: Prince Amadeus (1898-1942) who married Princess Anne of Orleans (b. 1906) – a first cousin once removed of Princess Helene – and who died in a Kenyan P.O.W. camp during the last War; and Prince Aimone (1900-1948) who, in 1939, married Princess Irene (1904-1974), a daughter of King Constantine I of Greece.

Above, left. Prince Victor Emmanuel, (1869-1947), the only son of King Umberto I of Italy and Queen Margharita, became King Victor Emmanuel III in 1900.

Victor Emmanuel married Princess Elena one of the many daughters of King Nicholas I of Montenegro, and they had five children. The only son is the present ex-King Umberto II who married Princess Marie-Jose of Belgium. Of their four daughters, Princess Yolande (b. 1901) married the Italian Count di Bergolo; Princess Mafalda (1902-1944) married Landgrave Philip of Hesse (b. 1896), a grandson of Emperor Frederick III of Germany, and died in Buchenwald concentration camp; Princess Giovanna (b. 1907) married Tsar Boris III of Bulgaria (1894-1943); and Princess Maria married Prince Louis (1899-1967) one of the nineteen children of Robert Duc de Bourbon-Parma (1848-1907) and brother to both Empress Zita of Austria (b. 1892) and to Grand Duke Felix (1893-1970), husband of Grand Duchess Charlotte of Luxemburg (b. 1896).

King Victor Emmanuel III was forced to abdicate in 1946, following Italy's defeat and his own support of Mussolini during the war. He was succeeded by his son, Umberto II, but the monarchy in Italy was abolished in the same year.

This photograph was taken in 1896.

Lower, left. Prince Victor Emmanuel's wife, Elena, then Princess of Naples, photographed in 1896.

In 1900, she became Queen of Italy when her husband succeeded his murdered father, as King Victor Emmanuel III. In 1946, the dethroned King and Queen lived in Egypt. When, in 1947, her husband died, ex-Queen Elena lived in Montpellier where she died of cancer in 1952.

France

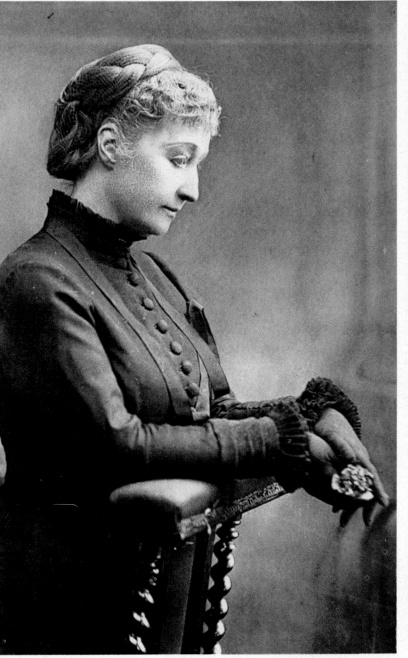

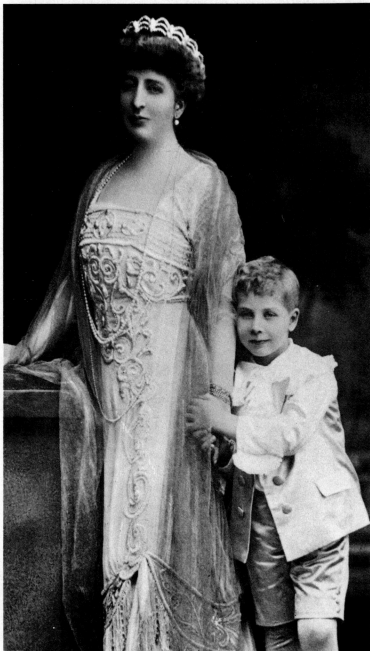

The Empress Eugenie (*above left,* photographed in about 1880) was formerly Marie-Eugenie de Guzman y de Portocarrero, Countess de Teba, and Marchioness de Moya. She was born in Grenada in 1826, the daughter of the Spanish Count Montijo, Duke of Peneranda and his Scottish wife Marie Manuela Kirkpatrick.

In 1853 she married the Emperor Napoleon III (1808-1873) by whom she had only one child, Prince Louis Napoleon (1856-1879), Prince Imperial, who was killed fighting on the British side in the Zulu war of 1879.

Napoleon III was dethroned following defeat in the Franco-Prussian war of 1870-1 and the family came to England, where the ex-Emperor died in 1873. Ex-Empress Eugenie died at the home of her nephew the Duke of Alba, in Castile, Spain, in 1920.

Above right. The Duchesse de Vendôme and her son, Prince Charles, photographed in 1912. The Duchesse was born Princess Henriette of Belgium in 1870. She was the eldest of three daughters of the Prince Phillippe, Count of Flanders (1837-1905)

and his wife, formerly Princess Marie of Hohenzollern-Sigmaringen (1845-1912) sister of Carol I, the first King of Roumania. She was thus sister to King Albert I of the Belgians (1875-1934). In 1896 she married Prince Emmanuel (1872-1931) of the French (Orleanist) line of the House of Bourbon: he was a great-grandson of King Louis-Phillippe (1773-1850) the last King of the French, and bore the titles of Duc de Vendôme et d'Alençon.

Of the couple's three children there was only one son, Prince Charles, who was born in 1905 and created Duc de Nemours. He married an American, Margaret Watson (b. 1899) in 1928. His sisters were Princess Marie-Louise (b. 1896) whose first husband was Prince Philip of Bourbon-Sicilies; Princess Sophie (1898-1928), unmarried, and Princess Genevieve (b. 1901) who married Antoine Marquis de Chaponay (1893-1956).

Opposite page, right. Princess Genevieve of Nemours and Alençon, photographed by Kenturah Collings – a London photographic firm – in about 1908.

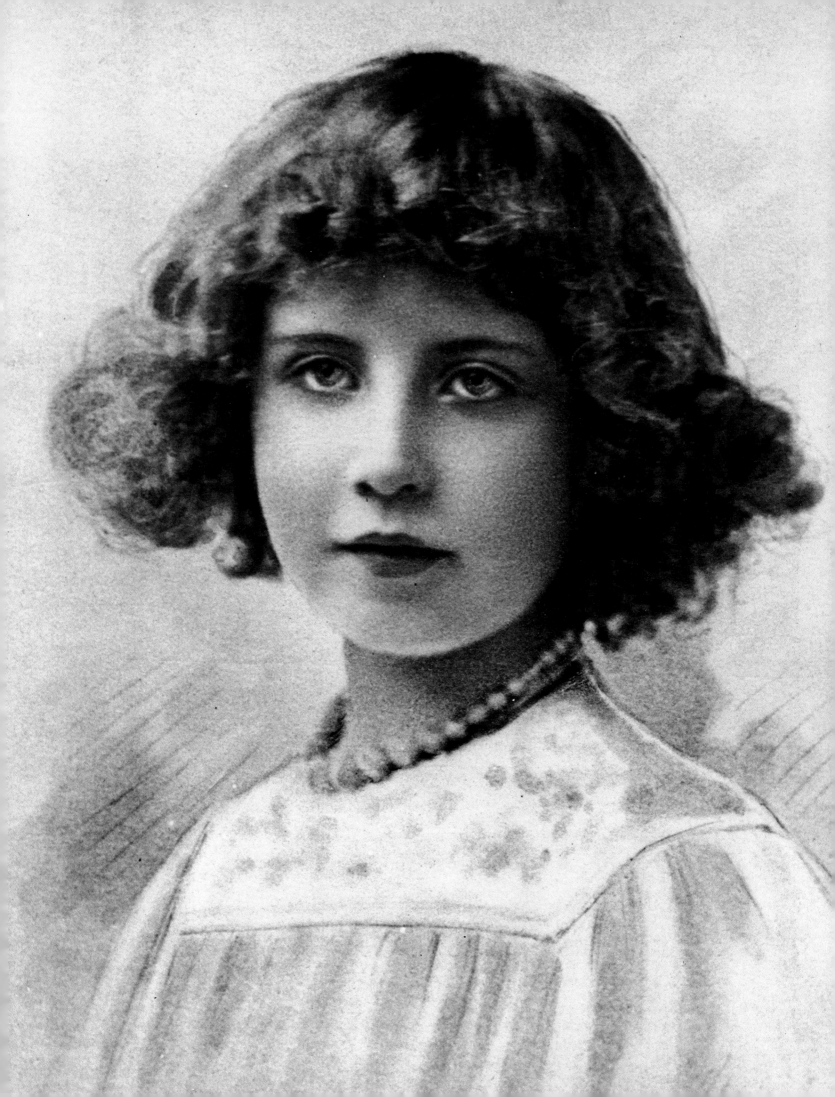

Austria

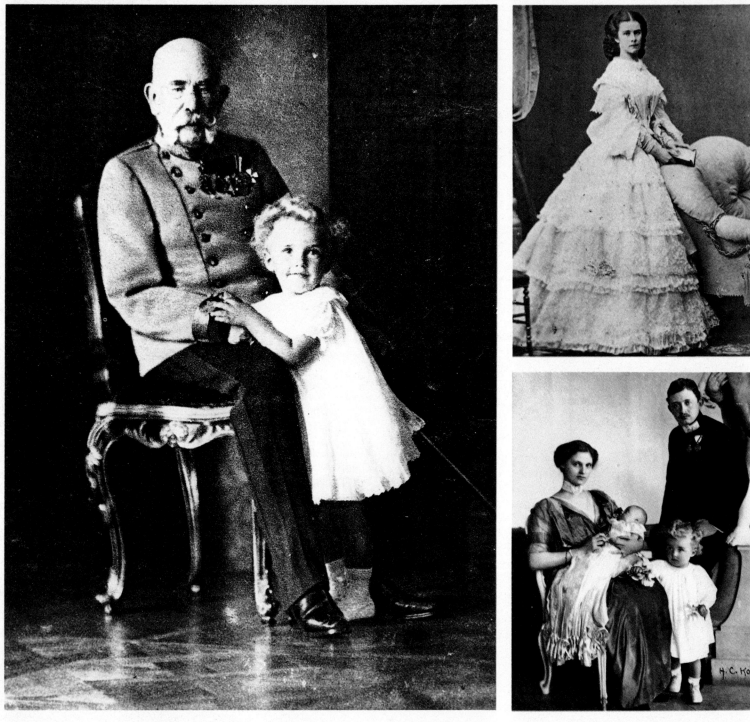

Above, left. The Austrian Emperor Franz-Josef I and his great-great nephew Archduke Franz-Josef-Otto; a photograph taken at the outbreak of the Great War.

The Emperor Franz-Josef I (1830-1916) became Emperor of Austria in 1848. By his marriage to Elizabeth, Duchess of Bavaria in 1854 he had a son and three daughters.

On the death by suicide of the son, Archduke Rudolf, who left only a daughter by his wife Princess Stephanie of Belgium (1864-1945), the succession passed to the Emperor's second brother Archduke Karl-Ludwig (1833-1896), the eldest brother Archduke Ferdinand having already died by firing squad as Emperor Maximilien of Mexico in 1867. On Karl-Ludwig's death his elder son, Archduke Franz-Ferdinand (1863-1914) became heir, but when he was assassinated at Sarajevo in 1914, the succession passed to the Archduke Karl (1887-1922), the son of Franz-Ferdinand's younger brother Archduke Otto (1865-1906). It was Karl who eventually succeeded Emperor Franz-Josef I in 1916.

His eldest son Archduke Franz-Josef-Otto (born 1912) succeeded Emperor Karl in exile in 1922 and in 1961 renounced his claim to the throne of the Austrian Empire. He married Princess Regina of Saxe-Meiningen (born 1925) in 1951, has four daughters and is a private citizen of Germany under the title of Dr. Otto von Hapsburg.

Above, top right. The Emperor Franz-Josef I's wife, the Empress Elizabeth, was born in 1837 in the junior (Grand Ducal) branch of the House of Wittelsbach, whose senior line ruled as Kings of Bavaria. She was the third of nine children of the Grand Duke Maximilien of Bavaria

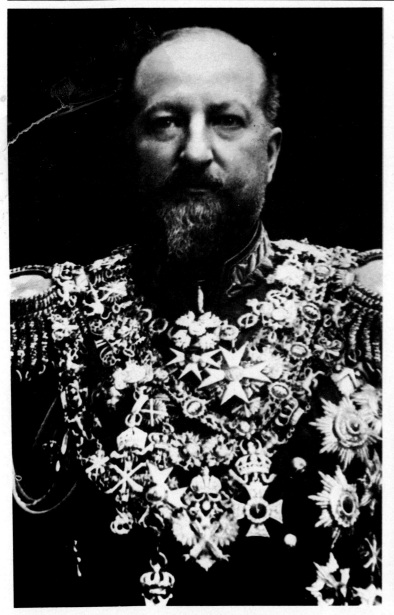

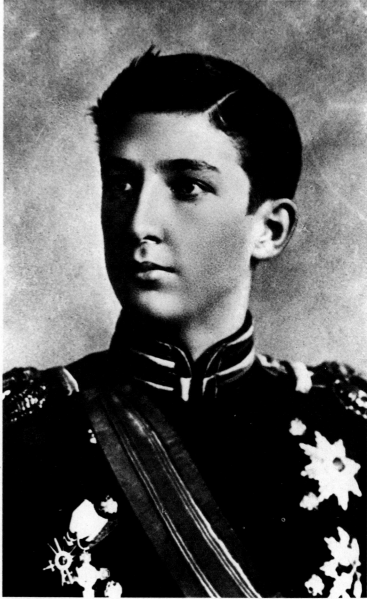

Above, left. Tsar Ferdinand (1861-1948) was born Prince Ferdinand of Saxe-Coburg-Gotha. He was the youngest of four children of Prince Augustus (1818-1881) and Princess Marie-Clementine (formerly of Orleans) of Saxe-Coburg-Gotha and was thus a great-nephew of King Leopold I of the Belgians and a first cousin once removed of both Queen Victoria of England and of her husband, Prince Albert of Saxe-Coburg-Gotha.

Like many members of his illustrious and reputable family, he was invited to become the reigning head of a foreign state – in this case Bulgaria, which had been created in 1879 following the Treaty of Berlin in 1878. He was elected to the Bulgarian throne as reigning Prince in 1887 and created himself Tsar in 1908.

In 1893 he married Princess Marie-Louise of Bourbon-Parma (1870-1899) by whom he had four children: Prince Boris, Prince Cyril (1895-1945) who was executed in the purge of 1945; and Princesses Eudoxia (b. 1898) and Nadjeda (1899-1958). The latter married Duke Albert Eugene of Wurttemberg (1895-1954).

Following the death of his Tsarina, Marie-Louise, in 1899, Ferdinand married in 1908 Eleonor, Princess Reuss (1860-1917). Tsar Ferdinand abdicated in favour of his eldest son Boris III in 1918. He lived for another thirty years and saw the Bulgarian monarchy abolished in 1946.

This photograph of him was taken in about 1908.
Above, right. Prince Boris, the eldest child of Tsar Ferdinand of Bulgaria, was born in 1894 and became Tsar Boris III on the abdication of his father in 1918.

He married in 1930 Princess Giovanna (b. 1907), daughter of King Victor-Emmanuel III of Italy (1869-1947). They had two children, Princess Marie-Louise (b. 1933) who, in 1957, married Prince Charles of Leiningen (b. 1928), brother of Prince Emich, 7th Prince of Leiningen and a descendant of Queen Victoria's stepfather; and Prince Simeon (b. 1937).

Boris III died in mysterious circumstances in 1943 while the Germans were in occupation of Bulgaria. His son succeeded him as Simeon II and is the present claimant to the throne.

This photograph of Crown Prince Boris was taken in 1912.

Roumania

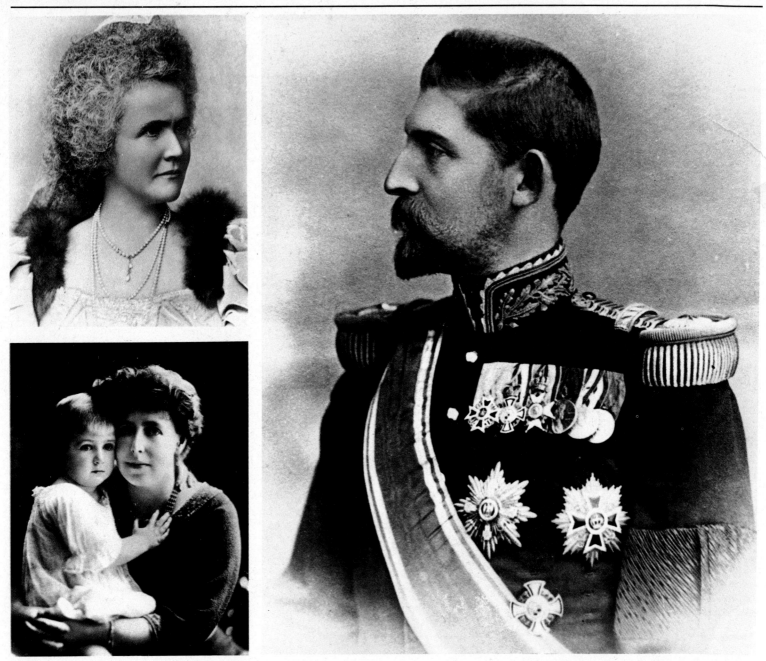

Above, top left. Queen Elisabeth (1843-1916) was formerly Princess Elisabeth of Wied, daughter of Hermann, the 4th Prince of Wied (1814-1864) and Princess Marie of Nassau (1825-1902).

In 1869 she married Prince Carl of Hohenzollern-Sigmaringen (1839-1914) who, in 1866, had been elected as first King of Roumania under the title King Carol I, and whose sister Princess Marie Louise (1845-1912) married Prince Phillippe Count of Flanders (1837-1905) and was mother of King Albert I of the Belgians (1875-1934).

Above, right. Crown Prince Ferdinand of Roumania (1865-1927), photographed in about 1898.

His father, Prince Leopold of Hohenzollern-Sigmaringen (1835-1905) was brother to King Carol I. His mother was Princess Antonia (1845-1913) who was the daughter of Prince Ferdinand of Saxe-Coburg-Gotha (later King Ferdinand II of Portugal) and also a second cousin to King Edward VII of England (Prince Ferdinand's father being brother both to Queen Victoria's mother and to the Prince Consort's father).

Crown Prince Ferdinand married, in 1893, Princess Marie (1875-1938), eldest daughter of Prince Alfred, Duke of Edinburgh and of Saxe-Coburg-Gotha, the second son of Queen Victoria. She was therefore his third cousin. Her mother was formerly Grand Duchess Marie (1853-1920), daughter of Alexander II, Tsar of Russia.

Of their six children, King Carol II (1893-1953), married Princess Helen (b. 1896), daughter of King Constantine I of Greece; Princess Elizabeth (1894-1956) married King George II of Greece (brother of Princess Helen); and Princess Marie (1900-1961) married King Alexander of Yugoslavia.

Crown Prince Ferdinand succeeded King Carol I in 1914 and died in 1927.

Above, lower left, Crown Princess Marie with her youngest daughter, Princess Ileana, (b. 1909).

Opposite page, right. Crown Princess Marie with the two eldest of her three daughters – Princess Elizabeth (left) and Princess Marie.

Austria

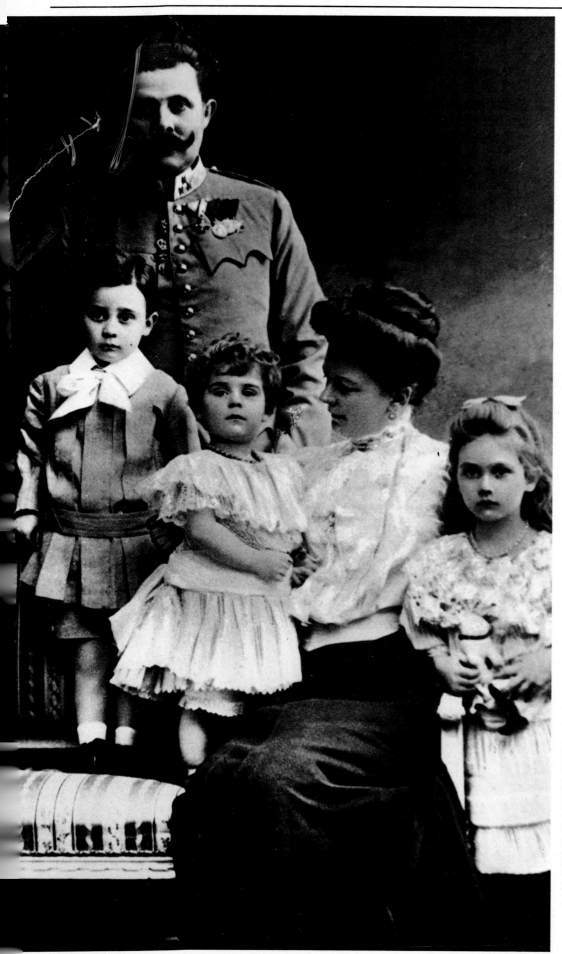

(1808-1888) and of his wife Princess Louisa (1808-1892) who was the second youngest daughter of King Maximilien I Josef of Bavaria, and sister-in-law of King William I of Wurttemberg, King Frederick William IV of Prussia, King John of Saxony, and King Frederick Augustus II of Saxony.

Her own prestigious marriage occurred when in 1854 she became the wife of Emperor Franz Josef I of Austria, the grandson of her mother's brother-in-law. She had four children by him: their only son, Crown-Prince Rudolf (1858-1889) married Princess Stephanie (1864-1945), a daughter of King Leopold II of Belgium, but committed suicide at Mayerling with his mistress. Of the Imperial couple's three daughters, Archduchess Gisela (1856-1932) married one of Empress Elizabeth's distant cousins, Prince Leopold of Bavaria (1846-1930) whilst Archduchess Maria-Valeria (1868-1924) married her fourth cousin Prince Franz-Salvator (1866-1939) of the Tuscan branch of the Austrian Imperial family. A third daughter, Archduchess Sophie died in 1857, aged two years.

The Empress Elizabeth died in 1898, assassinated by an Italian anarchist in Geneva. This photograph of her was taken in about 1860.

Opposite page, lower right. The Archduke Karl; his wife Archduchess Zita; his eldest son, Archduke Franz-Josef-Otto; and his daughter, Archduchess Adelaide. A photograph taken in 1914.

Left. A photograph dated 1906, showing Archduke Franz-Ferdinand of Austria-Este and his family. (Left to right):

Prince Maximilien, Archduke Franz-Ferdinand, Prince Ernst, the Princess of Hohenberg, Princess Sophie.

Archduke Franz-Ferdinand (1863-1914) was a nephew of Emperor Franz-Josef I of Austria (1830-1916), and heir to the Imperial throne from the death of his father in 1896 until his own death in 1914. In 1900 he married a Polish Countess, Sophie Chotek Chotkowa-Wognin (1868-1914), but the union was morganatic and, being unable to take her husband's titles, she was given the title Princess of Hohenberg. Their three children were excluded from the line of succession and assumed titles similar to their mother. Both Archduke Franz-Ferdinand and his wife died in the notorious assassination at Sarajevo in 1914.

Hanover (Brunswick-Luneburg)

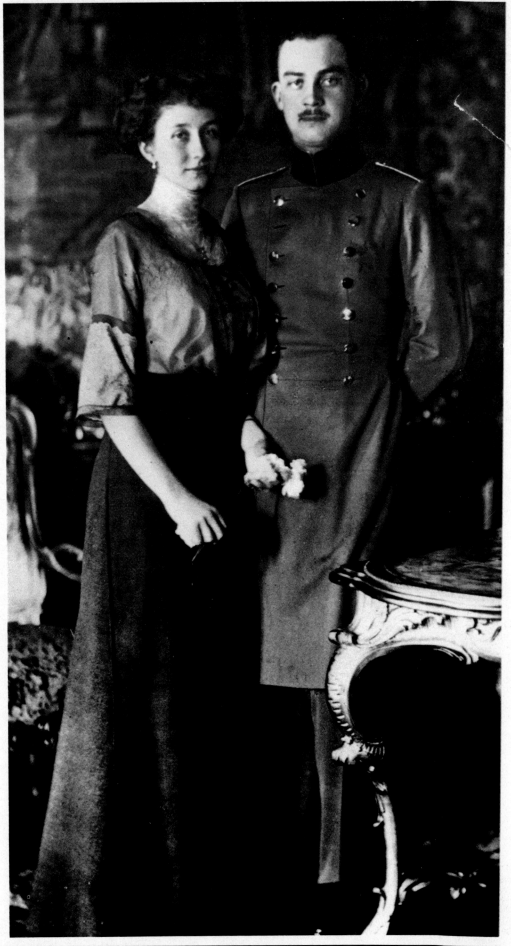

Right. Prince Ernst Augustus (1887-1953) was at the time of his marriage heir apparent to the former Kingdom of Hanover, which, until Queen Victoria became Queen of England in 1837 had been linked with Great Britain since the accession of George, Elector of Hanover as George I of England in 1714. By operation of the Salic Law, Queen Victoria could not succeed to the crown of Hanover, which then passed to the next in succession, Prince Ernest, Duke of Cumberland (1771-1851), the fifth son of King George III.

Prince Ernst Augustus was the great-grandson of the Duke of Cumberland. His father was Prince Ernst (1845-1923), and his mother was formerly Princess Thyra (1853-1933), youngest daughter of King Christian IX of Denmark, and sister of Queen Alexandra of England. Prince Ernst Augustus was thus well related to the British Royal Family even before his marriage to Princess Victoria Louise of Germany (1892-1980) in 1913.

Her connections with British royalty arose through her father, Kaiser Wilhelm II of Germany (1859-1941) whose mother, the Empress Frederick, was the eldest daughter of Queen Victoria.

Prince Ernst and Princess Victoria Louise had five children: Prince Ernst (b. 1914) who married Princess Ortrud (b. 1925) daughter of Prince Albert of Schleswig-Holstein-Sonderburg-Glucksburg, a cousin of King Frederick VIII of Denmark; Prince George (b. 1915), who became the second husband of Princess Sophie (b. 1914), widow of Prince Christopher of Hesse, and sister of Prince Philip Duke of Edinburgh; Princess Frederika (1917-1981) who, in 1938, married Prince (later King) Paul of Greece (1901-1964) and was the mother of ex-King Constantine II; Prince Christian (b. 1919) who married a commoner, Mireille Dutry; and Prince Guelf (b. 1923) who married Princess Sophie of Isemburg-Budingen.

This is an engagement photograph of the couple, taken on February 10th 1913.

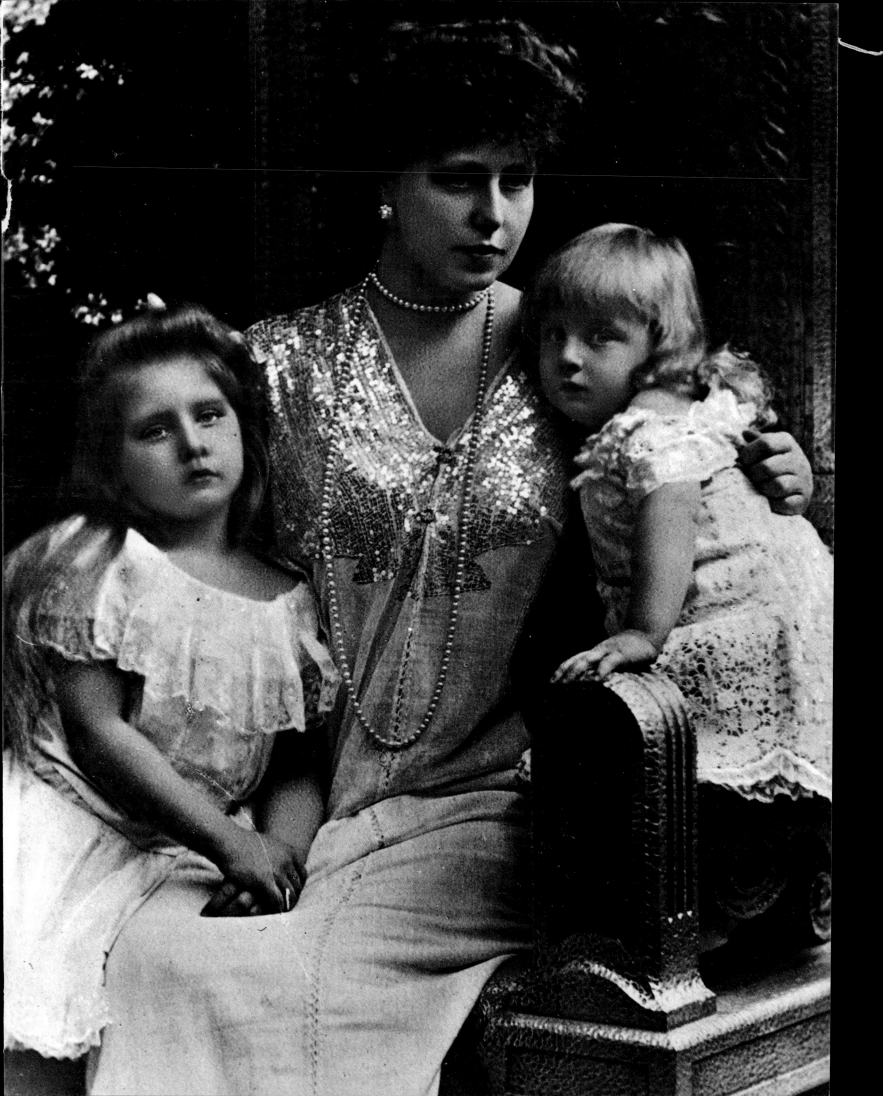

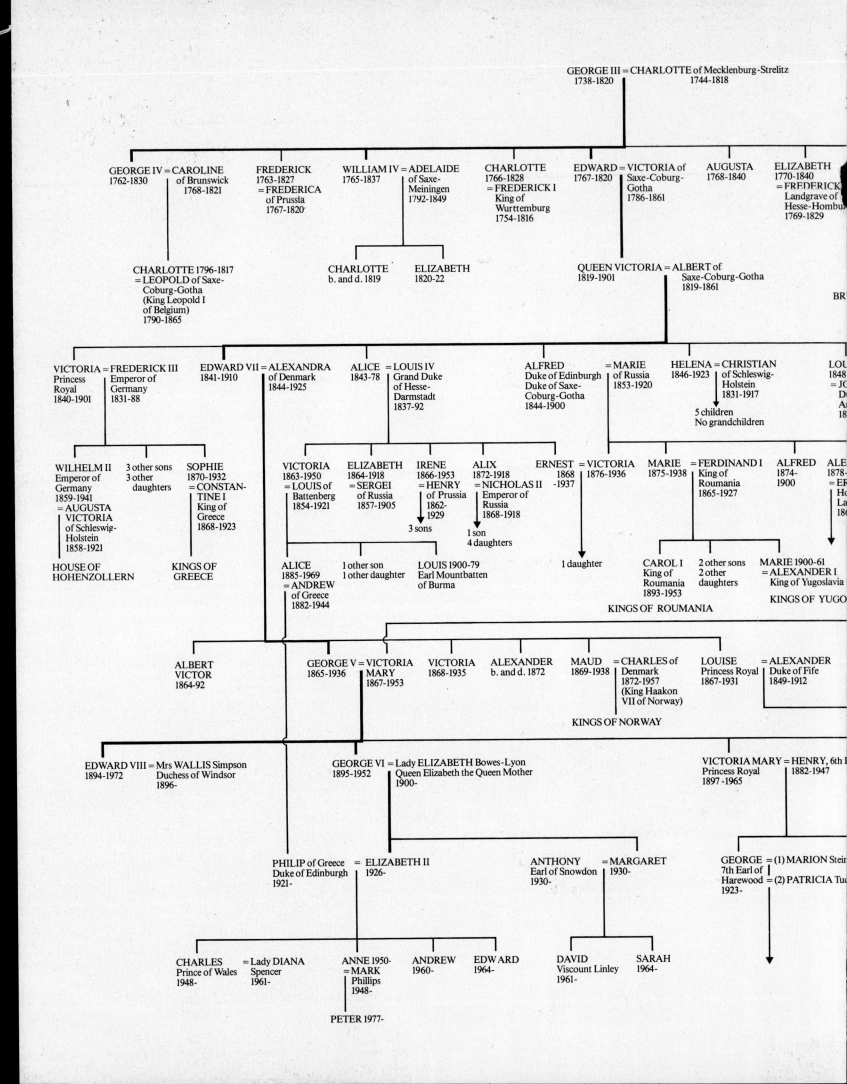

GEORGE III = CHARLOTTE of Mecklenburg-Strelitz
1738-1820   1744-1818

GEORGE IV = CAROLINE
1762-1830   of Brunswick
1768-1821

FREDERICK
1763-1827
= FREDERICA
of Prussia
1767-1820

WILLIAM IV = ADELAIDE
1765-1837   of Saxe-
Meiningen
1792-1849

CHARLOTTE
1766-1828
= FREDERICK I
King of
Wurttemburg
1754-1816

EDWARD = VICTORIA of
1767-1820   Saxe-Coburg-
Gotha
1786-1861

AUGUSTA
1768-1840

ELIZABETH
1770-1840
= FREDERICK
Landgrave of
Hesse-Homburg
1769-1829

CHARLOTTE 1796-1817
= LEOPOLD of Saxe-
Coburg-Gotha
(King Leopold I
of Belgium)
1790-1865

CHARLOTTE
b. and d. 1819

ELIZABETH
1820-22

QUEEN VICTORIA = ALBERT of
1819-1901   Saxe-Coburg-Gotha
1819-1861

BR

VICTORIA = FREDERICK III
Princess   Emperor of
Royal   Germany
1840-1901   1831-88

EDWARD VII = ALEXANDRA
1841-1910   of Denmark
1844-1925

ALICE = LOUIS IV
1843-78   Grand Duke
of Hesse-
Darmstadt
1837-92

ALFRED   = MARIE
Duke of Edinburgh   of Russia
Duke of Saxe-   1853-1920
Coburg-Gotha
1844-1900

HELENA = CHRISTIAN
1846-1923   of Schleswig-
Holstein
1831-1917

5 children
No grandchildren

LOU
1848
= JO
D
A
18

WILHELM II
Emperor of
Germany
1859-1941
= AUGUSTA
VICTORIA
of Schleswig-
Holstein
1858-1921

HOUSE OF
HOHENZOLLERN

3 other sons
3 other
daughters

SOPHIE
1870-1932
= CONSTAN-
TINE I
King of
Greece
1868-1923

KINGS OF
GREECE

VICTORIA
1863-1950
= LOUIS of
Battenberg
1854-1921

ELIZABETH
1864-1918
= SERGEI
of Russia
1857-1905

IRENE
1866-1953
= HENRY
of Prussia
1862-
1929

3 sons

ALIX
1872-1918
= NICHOLAS II
Emperor of
Russia
1868-1918

1 son
4 daughters

ERNEST = VICTORIA
1868   1876-1936
-1937

1 daughter

MARIE = FERDINAND I
1875-1938   King of
Roumania
1865-1927

CAROL I
King of
Roumania
1893-1953

2 other sons
2 other
daughters

ALFRED
1874-
1900

ALE
1878-
= ER
Ho
La
18

MARIE 1900-61
= ALEXANDER I
King of Yugoslavia

KINGS OF YUGO

ALICE
1885-1969
= ANDREW
of Greece
1882-1944

1 other son
1 other daughter

LOUIS 1900-79
Earl Mountbatten
of Burma

KINGS OF ROUMANIA

ALBERT
VICTOR
1864-92

GEORGE V = VICTORIA
1865-1936   MARY
1867-1953

VICTORIA
1868-1935

ALEXANDER
b. and d. 1872

MAUD = CHARLES of
1869-1938   Denmark
1872-1957
(King Haakon
VII of Norway)

LOUISE = ALEXANDER
Princess Royal   Duke of Fife
1867-1931   1849-1912

KINGS OF NORWAY

EDWARD VIII = Mrs WALLIS Simpson
1894-1972   Duchess of Windsor
1896-

GEORGE VI = Lady ELIZABETH Bowes-Lyon
1895-1952   Queen Elizabeth the Queen Mother
1900-

VICTORIA MARY = HENRY, 6th
Princess Royal   1882-1947
1897-1965

PHILIP of Greece = ELIZABETH II
Duke of Edinburgh   1926-
1921-

ANTHONY = MARGARET
Earl of Snowdon   1930-
1930-

GEORGE = (1) MARION Stein
7th Earl of
Harewood = (2) PATRICIA Tu
1923-

CHARLES = Lady DIANA
Prince of Wales   Spencer
1948-   1961-

ANNE 1950-
= MARK
Phillips
1948-

ANDREW
1960-

EDWARD
1964-

DAVID
Viscount Linley
1961-

SARAH
1964-

PETER 1977-